Kaplan Publishing are constantly finding new ways to make a difference to your studies and our exciting online resources really do different to students looking for ex

D1148171

This book comes with free EN-gage online resources so that you can study anytime, anywhere.

Having purchased this book, you have access to the following online study materials:

CONTENT	ACCA (including FFA,FAB,FMA)		AAT		FIA (excluding FFA,FAB,FMA)	
	Text	Kit	Text	Kit	Text	Kit
iPaper version of the book	✓	✓	✓	✓	✓	✓
Interactive electronic version of the book	✓					
Fixed tests / progress tests with instant answers	✓		✓			
Mock assessments online			✓	✓		
Material updates	✓	✓	✓	✓	✓	✓
Latest official ACCA exam questions		✓				
Extra question assistance using the signpost icon*		✓				
Timed questions with an online tutor debrief using the clock icon*		✓				
Interim assessment including questions and answers		✓			✓	
Technical articles	✓	✓			✓	✓

* Excludes F1, F2, F3, FFA, FAB, FMA

How to access your online resources

Kaplan Financial students will already have a Kaplan EN-gage account and these extra resources will be available to you online. You do not need to register again, as this process was completed when you enrolled. If you are having problems accessing online materials, please ask your course administrator.

If you are already a registered Kaplan EN-gage user go to www.EN-gage.co.uk and log in. Select the 'add a book' feature and enter the ISBN number of this book and the unique pass key at the bottom of this card. Then click 'finished' or 'add another book'. You may add as many books as you have purchased from this screen.

If you purchased through Kaplan Flexible Learning or via the Kaplan Publishing website you will automatically receive an e-mail invitation to Kaplan EN·gage online. Please register your details using this email to gain access to your content. If you do not receive the e-mail or book content, please contact Kaplan Flexible Learning.

If you are a new Kaplan EN-gage user register at www.EN-gage.co.uk and click on the link contained in the email we sent you to activate your account. Then select the 'add a book' feature, enter the ISBN number of this book and the unique pass key at the bottom of this card. Then click 'finished' or 'add another book'.

Your Code and Information

This code can only be used once for the registration of one book online. This registration and your online content will expire when the final sittings for the examinations covered by this book have taken place. Please allow one hour from the time you submit your book details for us to process your request.

Please scratch the film to access your EN-gage code.

Please be aware that this code is case-sensitive and you will need to include the dashes within the passcode, but not when entering the ISBN. For further technical support, please visit www.EN-gage.co.uk

KAPLAN

PUBLISHING

INTERNAL CONTROL AND ACCOUNTING SYSTEMS

Qualifications and Credit Framework

Level 4 Diploma in Accounting

British Library Cataloguing-in-Publication Data

A catalogue record for this book is available from the British Library.

Published by
Kaplan Publishing UK
Unit 2, The Business Centre
Molly Millars Lane
Wokingham
Berkshire
RG41 2QZ

ISBN 978-0-85732-606-5

The text in this material and any others made available by any Kaplan Group company does not amount to advice on a particular matter and should not be taken as such. No reliance should be placed on the content as the basis for any investment or other decision or in connection with any advice given to third parties. Please consult your appropriate professional adviser as necessary. Kaplan Publishing Limited and all other Kaplan group companies expressly disclaim all liability to any person in respect of any losses or other claims, whether direct, indirect, incidental, consequential or otherwise arising in relation to the use of such materials.

Printed and bound in Great Britain.

We are grateful to the AAT for their kind permission to reproduce the Practice Assessment. They are ©The Association of Accounting Technicians.

We are grateful to the Association of Accounting Technicians for permission to reproduce past assessment materials and example tasks based on the new syllabus. The solutions to past answers and similar activities in the style of the new syllabus have been prepared by Kaplan Publishing.

We are grateful to HM Revenue and Customs for the provision of tax forms, which are Crown Copyright and are reproduced here with kind permission from the Office of Public Sector Information.

KAPLAN PUBLISHING

CONTENTS

INTRODUCTION

HOW TO USE THESE MATERIALS

These Kaplan Publishing learning materials have been carefully designed to make your learning experience as easy as possible and to give you the best chance of success in your AAT assessments.

They contain a number of features to help you in the study process.

The sections on the Unit Guide, the Assessment and Study Skills should be read before you commence your studies.

They are designed to familiarise you with the nature and content of the assessment and to give you tips on how best to approach your studies.

STUDY TEXT

This study text has been specially prepared for the revised AAT qualification introduced in July 2010.

It is written in a practical and interactive style:

- key terms and concepts are clearly defined

- all topics are illustrated with practical examples with clearly worked solutions based on sample tasks provided by the AAT in the new examining style

- frequent practice activities throughout the chapters ensure that what you have learnt is regularly reinforced

ICONS

The study chapters include the following icons throughout.

They are designed to assist you in your studies by identifying key definitions and the points at which you can test yourself on the knowledge gained.

 Definition

These sections explain important areas of Knowledge which must be understood and reproduced in an assessment

 Example

The illustrative examples can be used to help develop an understanding of topics before attempting the activity exercises

 Activity

These are exercises which give the opportunity to assess your understanding of all the assessment areas.

UNIT GUIDE

Internal Control and Accounting Systems consists of two units.

Principles of Internal Control (Knowledge)

3 credits

Evaluating Accounting Systems (Skills)

4 credits

Purpose of the units

The AAT has stated that the general purpose of these units is to ensure that learners know and understand the role of accounting in an organisation, and why internal controls should be in place. They should be able to recognise systemic weaknesses where errors of fraud may occur. Learners should be able to evaluate an accounting system, or part of a system (either based on a real situation or a scenario), and be able to make recommendations for improvement. Learners may draw upon their knowledge and experience gained in completing other units within this qualification, or may wish to approach these units as a standalone objective.

Another purpose of these units is to ensure that learners are able to communicate clearly, both orally and in writing, at level 4 standards and in a manner appropriate to the workplace. This will be part of the assessment for these units.

Learning objectives

On completion of these units the learner will be able to:

- Understand the principles of internal control
- Make recommendations on how to implement or improve a system
- Evaluate the accounting systems within an organisation
- Explain where improvements could be made

Learning Outcomes and Assessment Criteria

The unit consists of five learning outcomes, three for Knowledge and two for Skills, which are further broken down into Assessment criteria. These are set out in the following table with Learning Outcomes in bold type and Assessment criteria listed underneath each Learning Outcome. Reference is also made to the relevant chapter within the text.

Knowledge

To perform this unit effectively you will need to know and understand the following:

		Chapter
1	**Demonstrate an understanding of the role of accounting within the organisation**	
1.1	Describe the purpose, structure and organisation of the accounting function and its relationship with other functions within the organisation	2, 3
1.2	Explain the various business purposes for which the following financial information is required	2
	• Income statement (profit and loss account)	
	• Forecast of cash flow (cash flow statement)	
	• Statement of financial position (balance sheet)	
1.3	Give an overview of the organisation's business and its critical external relationships with stakeholders	2
1.4	Explain how the accounting systems are affected by the organisational structure, systems, procedures, and business transactions	2, 3
1.5	Explain the effect on users of changes to accounting systems caused by	2, 4
	• External regulations	
	• Organisational policies and procedures	

KAPLAN PUBLISHING

Skills

To perform this unit effectively you will need to be able to do the following.

Chapter

1 Evaluate the accounting system and identify areas of improvement

1.1	Identify an organisation's accounting system requirements	8
1.2	Review record keeping systems to confirm whether they meet the organisation's requirements for financial information	8
1.3	Identify weaknesses in and the potential for improvements to, the accounting system and consider their impact on the operation of the organisation	8
1.4	Identify potential areas of fraud arising from lack of control within the accounting system and grade the risk	8
1.5	Review methods of operating for cost effectiveness, reliability and speed	8

2 Make recommendations to improve the accounting system

2.1	Make recommendations for changes to the accounting system in an easily understood format, with a clear rationale and an explanation of any assumptions made	8
2.2	Identify the effects that any recommended changes would have on the users of the system	8
2.3	Enable individuals who operate accounting systems to understand how to use the system to fulfil their responsibilities	8
2.4	Identify the implications of recommended changes in terms of time, financial costs, benefits, and operating procedures	8

KAPLAN PUBLISHING

Delivery guidance

The AAT have provided delivery guidance giving further details of the way in which the unit will be assessed.

Knowledge 1: Demonstrate an understanding of the role of accounting within an organisation

Learners should be able to identify the relationship between other internal departments and the accounting function, and clearly define the structure, purpose and organisation of the accounting function within the overall organisation.

They should know the reasons why financial reports are produced.

Learners should be able to give an overview of an organisation – identifying the important external relationships it holds. This may include – but is not restricted to – any of the following: customers, suppliers, shareholders, banks, trade organisations, government departments/organisations.

They will know that different organisations have different accounting needs depending on the size of the organisation and the type of business it conducts.

Learners must recognise the effect that change has on the users of the system; and that change may be necessary to comply with statutory or organisational reasons.

Knowledge 2: Understand the importance and use of internal control systems

Learners must be able to understand and apply external regulations that will influence the organisation's accounting practices (e.g. accounting standards)

Learners should be aware of the common types of fraud, how these can be caused, and the impact that fraud has upon an organisation. They should be able to identify ways of detecting fraud and the types of internal controls that could be established to prevent these instances occurring. They should be aware of a range of internal controls that an organisation could use to ensure they meet both organisational and statutory requirements.

Knowledge 3: Understand the importance and use of internal control systems

The accounting system and the internal control system should be reviewed and evaluated for areas where there is a potential for errors and also and possible areas of fraud. Areas where there is a potential for fraud should be highlighted and the risk of this should be graded. Learners should understand the relationship between the accounting system and the internal control mechanisms. They should be aware of the ways that staff can achieve the necessary skills and knowledge (through appropriate training) to ensure they can use the accounting systems effectively. This could be provided by internal or external courses, and the use of manuals or other written guidance and help menus in computer software. Learners should be able to identify the benefits of different accounting systems/software packages to a specific organisation.

Skills 1: Evaluate the accounting system and identify areas for improvement

The learner needs the skills to be able to decide on what an organisation requires from its accounting systems. These requirements will differ depending on the nature and size of the organisation. They will then need to review the accounting systems to ensure they meet these requirements. This can be achieved by identifying the strengths and weaknesses of the accounting system (not the organisation). This should include a review of the working methods used within the accounting system to ensure that the optimum results are being achieved especially in terms of cost effectiveness, reliability and speed.

Learners need to identify weaknesses and then to review them and explain their impact upon the organisation. This should be considered in terms of time, money and reputation (i.e. loss of revenue, time wasting, customer expectations not being met). Areas where fraud may occur should be noted. Potential areas of fraud can include anything that poses a threat of loss to an organisation. This loss may include, but not restricted to, inventory based or time based frauds. Examples include fictitious employees or fictitious creditors being paid; over-ordering and theft of stock; or employees who overstate the time they have worked. Risk of fraud can be graded as low, medium or high – or given numerical grades of 1-5 where the more serious the risk is given a higher grade.

Skills 2: Make recommendations to improve the accounting system

Learners will need the ability to be able to make clear and sensible recommendations to improve the weaknesses identified in the evaluation of the accounting systems. For every weakness identified there must be at least one recommendation made for improvement.

The impact of the recommendations upon the staff in the accounting function should also be considered, and systems put into place to ensure that staff have the necessary skills and knowledge through appropriate training to ensure they can use the accounting systems effectively. This training could be provided by internal or external courses, and could also include the use of manuals or other written guidance and help menus in computer software.

The benefits of the proposed recommendations must be reviewed, and measured against the costs involved. Whilst it may not be possible to identify all benefits in terms of cost, as some may be qualitative, it is essential that all costs are at least identified, and quantified wherever possible in terms of monetary value. For example, if the recommendation includes staff training for three days, the cost of the employees time must be taken into account as well as the cost of training, as this is a lost opportunity cost. It is much better to make an approximation of difficult to measure costs than to just ignore them altogether.

THE ASSESSMENT

The format of the assessment

The assessment will take the form of a formal report

It will be written by the learner and assessed locally by the training provider

The 3,500 – 4,000 word report can be based on the workplace or an AAT on-line case study. The report must cover all the assessment criteria for both Principles of Internal Control and Evaluating Accounting Systems.

The report should be

- Written in the third person

- Spelling and grammar should be of a suitable level for a business report

- Word processed

The content of the report should:

- Cover the review of the current accounting systems, focussing on record keeping systems, principles of internal control, current methods of fraud protection, and working methods and training.

- Include an analysis of the above, identifying weaknesses or areas where improvement could be made and making recommendations to improve the accounting system and a cost benefit analysis.

The assessment material will normally be delivered online and assessed locally. The local assessor (training provider) will be required to ensure that all assessment criteria are covered. Learners will be required to demonstrate competence across the assessment criteria for this learning and assessment area.

STUDY SKILLS

Preparing to study

Devise a study plan

Determine which times of the week you will study.

Split these times into sessions of at least one hour for study of new material. Any shorter periods could be used for revision or practice.

Put the times you plan to study onto a study plan for the weeks from now until the assessment and set yourself targets for each period of study – in your sessions make sure you cover the whole course, activities and the associated questions in the workbook at the back of the manual.

If you are studying more than one unit at a time, try to vary your subjects as this can help to keep you interested and see subjects as part of wider knowledge.

When working through your course, compare your progress with your plan and, if necessary, re-plan your work (perhaps including extra sessions) or, if you are ahead, do some extra revision / practice questions.

Effective studying

Active reading

You are not expected to learn the text by rote, rather, you must understand what you are reading and be able to use it to pass the assessment and develop good practice.

A good technique is to use SQ3Rs – Survey, Question, Read, Recall, Review:

1   **Survey the chapter**

    Look at the headings and read the introduction, knowledge, skills and content, so as to get an overview of what the chapter deals with.

2   **Question**

    Whilst undertaking the survey ask yourself the questions you hope the chapter will answer for you.

3   Read

Read through the chapter thoroughly working through the activities and, at the end, making sure that you can meet the learning objectives highlighted on the first page.

4   Recall

At the end of each section and at the end of the chapter, try to recall the main ideas of the section / chapter without referring to the text. This is best done after short break of a couple of minutes after the reading stage.

5   Review

Check that your recall notes are correct.

You may also find it helpful to re-read the chapter to try and see the topic(s) it deals with as a whole.

Note taking

Taking notes is a useful way of learning, but do not simply copy out the text.

The notes must:

- be in your own words
- be concise
- cover the key points
- well organised
- be modified as you study further chapters in this text or in related ones.

Trying to summarise a chapter without referring to the text can be a useful way of determining which areas you know and which you don't.

Three ways of taking notes

1   Summarise the key points of a chapter

2   Make linear notes

A list of headings, subdivided with sub-headings listing the key points.

If you use linear notes, you can use different colours to highlight key points and keep topic areas together.

Use plenty of space to make your notes easy to use.

KAPLAN PUBLISHING

3   Try a diagrammatic form

The most common of which is a mind map.

To make a mind map, put the main heading in the centre of the paper and put a circle around it.]

Draw lines radiating from this to the main sub-headings which again have circles around them.

Continue the process from the sub-headings to sub-sub-headings.

Highlighting and underlining

You may find it useful to underline or highlight key points in your study text – but do be selective.

You may also wish to make notes in the margins.

Further reading

In addition to this text, you should also read the "Student section" of the "Accounting Technician" magazine every month to keep abreast of any guidance from the examiners.

Report writing

1

Introduction

Internal Control and Accounting Systems (ICAS) – is assessed by means of a project plus assessor questioning and employer testimony. The project takes the form of a report to management that analyses the internal controls and management accounting system. The report should identify how both might be enhanced to improve their effectiveness.

It is therefore essential that you know precisely how to arrange such a report and present it to management. This is a valuable skill to have, as no doubt you will be writing many more reports throughout your career.

1 Assessment

1.1 Introduction

It is easy to think that the final level of your AAT qualifications consists only of computer based tests. However, there is a project to be undertaken which is equally important to any of the other assessments you do and you must therefore give this as much attention as your studying and revision for any of the other units.

This guide has been designed for any student as an aid to writing and presenting your report and completing this unit successfully. It is not meant to be followed slavishly or to be prescriptive but as a rough outline and guide to what the AAT is looking for in a proving competence in this unit.

1.2 Nature of the project

The project takes the form of a report to management that analyses the internal control and management accounting system. It should identify how both might be enhanced to improve their effectiveness. In producing this report students will need to prove competence in the co-ordination of work activities and the identification and grading of fraud in that system. Students must be able to identify weaknesses and make recommendations for improvement. All changes made must be monitored and reviewed for their effectiveness.

The total length of the project (excluding appendices) should not exceed 4000 words. An appropriate manager should attest to the originality, authenticity and quality of the project report. The project should be based on an actual management accounting system, or part-system, within the student's workplace in the present or recent past.

There are three ways of approaching the project depending on your own circumstances.

1   You actually manage an accounting function – therefore you can use your own real work experiences to prove your ability to meet the competencies of the accounting standards.

2   You work in the accounting environment – therefore you will have to observe, talk to managers and critically analyse their performance to make recommendations that prove that you understand and could meet the required level of competence if given the opportunity.

3   You are not employed or not in relevant employment – your Approved Assessment Centre (AAC) will be able to advise, for instance they may have contacts with employers in your area who would be willing to help. Other ideas include accounting systems experienced:

- in recent employment (in the last two years)

- in a period of work placement

- in a voluntary organisation, club or charity – some students have deliberately joined or helped an organisation in order to collect evidence for their project

- in a college department (e.g. a canteen or library).

You might also like to contact your local AAT branch (again your AAC should be able to do this on your behalf, especially if a number of students are not able to draw from their work experience) since other AAT members may be able to help.

Alternatively, you will have to use the AAT case study, which is a case study that should enable you to observe a scenario and critically analyse it and make recommendations that prove that you understand and could meet the required level of competence if given the opportunity. Whichever approach you use, the assessment is the same:

- 3500 – 4000 word report

- assessor interview/questioning

- employer testimony.

1.3   Skill building

The use of a formal written report to assess this unit is to ensure that you have gained a wider range of skills than those assessed by examination. These include:

- Planning skills – you will need to plan all aspects of the recommendations that you make, plan for any contingencies and plan for the consequences of any changes made.

- Analytical skills – the report in analytical in nature, not descriptive. You will need to be able to analyse a current situation in a clear non-judgemental manner.

- Research skills – the report and recommendations will need to be researched and evidence of that included in the appendices. Research tools used need to be listed in the methodology.

- Report writing skills – a skill you will need to use in your career.

- Communication skills – a necessary skill which often proves lacking at interview.

- Time management skills – management skills needed to ensure that all aspects of the report are completed on schedule.

1.4 The Approved Assessment Centre's role

The AAC should undertake the following steps:

- make an initial assessment of the project idea

- use one-to-one sessions to advise and support the student

- encourage workplace mentors to participate (testimony, etc) · ensure the project is the student's original work

- use formative assessments and action plans to guide the student

- undertake summative assessment against performance criteria, range statements and knowledge and understanding · sign off each performance criterion

- conduct a final assessment interview with documented questioning.

1.5 Your role

As an AAT student it is your responsibility to choose a topic or theme for your project that will generate high quality evidence. You will need this to prove to your assessor and verifier that you are competent against the standards.

To do this you will need to think about which of your activities are relevant and how you can use these to build a report, which will demonstrate your competence. It is important that you regard not just the writing of the report but the presentation of the final product as being an opportunity for you to develop.

It is your duty to reference the report against the accounting standards, performance criteria, range and underpinning knowledge. This is to ensure that you have covered every aspect and to easily guide the assessor and verifier through your report.

Remember, that with the aid of your assessor, it is your responsibility to:

- meet with the assessor at agreed times · identify your theme for the project

- draft the report

- map to the standards

- present the final report

- keep your assessor informed about your progress – stick to target dates and deadlines.

You should ensure that the project's format is such that it:

- covers all assessment criteria
- covers the objectives set out in the Terms of Reference of the project, is well laid out, easy to read and includes an executive summary
- uses report form style with appropriate language
- shows clear progression from one idea to the next
- cross-refers the main text to any appendices
- uses diagrams and flowcharts appropriately
- starts each section on a fresh page.

You should ensure that the project's content is such that:

- issues and objectives are clearly identified
- the current situation is clearly analysed
- recommendations are subjected to cost-benefit analysis
- key data is included, and superfluous detail is omitted
- the methodology is fully described
- a strategic approach is taken
- the project focuses on company needs, not personal feelings.

1.6 Workplace mentor

It is almost essential that you receive support and guidance from your employer as well as your assessor throughout every stage of your project. It is after all, your employer who will stand to benefit from this free consultancy work that you are doing. They will also have a greater understanding about your chosen topic than your assessor can have.

It is therefore strongly recommended that you arrange for someone to be a workplace mentor. Your mentor does not have to be your boss but should be someone who can help you through your project, providing both technical and motivational support. You should ensure that your mentor is involved in your work from the outset and understands the standards and timescales you are working to. They may be able to offer guidance on suitable ideas for the project by identifying current problems either in your workplace or that of clients. They may also help with the planning of work and 'opening doors' to introduce you to key staff. It may be helpful to find someone who has recently written a report themselves, perhaps as part of their own studies.

1.7   Assessment plan

It is vital that you plan and schedule your work to ensure you complete your project within the allotted timescale. An assessment plan, agreed with your assessor at the beginning of your studies, should help you achieve this.

Task stage	Proposed date	Actual date
1. Identify theme		
2. Find workplace mentor		
3. Prepare project outline		
4. Complete research		
5. Complete first draft		
6. Assessment interview		
7. Prepare final report		
8. Assessment interview		

Declaration

I confirm I have agreed the proposed dates as listed and I will endeavour to meet these targets.

Learner name ....

Learner signature ....

Assessor signature .... Date ....

2   How to produce the project

2.1   Introduction

This introduction contains detailed and practical guidance on how to produce your project, and should be read very carefully before you start.

The steps involved in producing the project can be summarised practically as follows.

1.	Initial planning	• Think of a suitable topic.
		• Address the performance criteria.
		• Check suitability with your manager at work. Perform initial research. Submit a proposal to the assessor.
2.	Project proposal and preliminary assessment	• The assessor considers the suitability of the project proposal.
3.	Research	• Set up a research file.
		• Make notes from the Text, producing answers to guidance checklists at the end of each chapter.
4.	Write up, using Chapter 1 of the Text	• The project should be 3,500–4,000 words excluding Appendices.
		• Report writing and presentation skills will be important.
5.	Assessment process	
6.	Complete the project checklist	

Each of these steps is covered in detail below.

2.2 Initial planning

An interesting topic

Choosing the topic is a very important part of the project. Get this right and you are halfway there – get it wrong and you can waste many hours trying to write a report on something where you have very little evidence. The final decision is yours in negotiation with your assessor. There are various ways to choose your topic.

- Identify a weakness in a system in your own area or work.

- Ask your college for a list of topics that have led to successful projects.

- Think about your department and ask 'what would I do differently to make the process or system better?' Are there areas that you think could be improved?

- Ask your line manager and other colleagues for ideas about something which could be improved at work.

- Look at a similar report at work (it need not be on accounting). Although the project has to be your own original work, you will be able to get an idea of how your final report will look, the writing style and what each section contains.

- Ask your centre for a list of past project topics

- Analyse the various work functions e.g. payroll, purchase ledger, capital expenditure, reconciliation, petty cash, control systems etc – are they well managed? Is there a weakness in the chain that could be improved? Are there any gaps?

Before looking at possible topics, it is important to remember that the best project for you will be the one that interests you and which is relevant to your workplace. A selection of possible topics is listed on the following page.

Possible projects

- Issues relating to staff management and motivation in a purchases ledger department.

- Relationship between treasury department and accounts department, including appraisal of internal procedures. Problems relating to work allocation, communication and decision-making within the group finance function.

- Issues arising from a change of ownership of a business and the effect upon staff roles.

- Problems arising from complex sales pricing and invoicing and their effects upon staff efficiency.

- Internal controls over purchases invoice recording and the impact on staff. Review of work allocation in a payroll department, including motivation issues. Review of training needs within a small company accounts department, with reference to payroll.

- Relationships of a credit department with its internal and external customers.

This list is to start you thinking!

Projects should cover one limited section of the accounting system and one limited aspect of that section, such as contract accounting. Many students choose to return to areas of competence covered at the previous stages, such as payroll or fixed asset accounting. The list of sample topics is by no means comprehensive, but it may give you a starting point for considering an idea of your own.

Students have completed projects in very diverse areas. The project does not have to be based exclusively on an accounting system, although there must be some element of 'management information' which links into the accounting system - for example, time recording in an accounting and audit practice.

Key considerations

It is important that your project is of sufficiently limited scope to be written up in approximately 3,500 words. Although this recommended length is only a guideline, projects should not exceed 4,000 words. Many students encounter problems when they try to cover too much within the project. While it is difficult to generalise, it will, for example, be adequate to look at the payroll section of the accounts department rather than the whole department.

Projects should be based on a real system in a real organisation. The organisation will normally be your current employer or job placement or a voluntary organisation. If you have any problems finding a suitable live system you can use a case study but please contact your Approved Assessment Centre for more details.

Real life issues

The best project for you will be based on something which interests you and which has your line manager's full support. You need to consider the real life issues currently facing your department or organisation. It is advisable to discuss your proposed topic with your line manager because you will normally have to interview other staff (possibly from other departments) as part of the research phase and there may be sensitive issues of which you are unaware. In addition, your line manager may be able to assist you with the project or may suggest an alternative topic that would be of real value to the organisation.

Your own work

The project must be your own unaided, original piece of work. In carrying out the project, however, you will inevitably speak to other system users who will undoubtedly give you information or ideas, and it is acceptable to include these in your project as long as you write them up in your own words. Where you wish to base your project on an existing piece of work already carried out within the organisation, you must make this clear.

2.3 Project proposal and preliminary assessment

When you have decided on a topic, you should submit a project proposal to your assessor. This enables the assessor to make a preliminary assessment of the suitability of the topic before you start any time-consuming research.

The proposal should cover no more than one side of A4 paper and should address some of the following points:

(a) Identify precisely the section of your work upon which you will base your project.

(b) What is the role of this section?

(c) What is the current organisational structure?

(d) Who are the customers, both internal and external?

(e) How is quality measured?

(f) Give a brief outline of current issues or problems.

(g) Will you be able to research the area with the approval of your manager, with the support of others and without breaching any confidentiality requirements?

(h) What problems are you likely to face?

(i) How will you overcome them?

(j) How are you preventing fraud in the accounting system?

The project proposal is then assessed. The assessor will comment on the suitability of the topic and the scope of your proposal. Also, if there are areas for improvement, the assessor will highlight them at this stage. Make sure your assessor approves before you carry on.

2.4 Research

Practical research

Your project aim is to review the current systems and perhaps make recommendations for improvements. First of all, therefore, you must spend some considerable time researching and documenting the current system. Most people spend considerably more time researching the project than they do writing it up.

It is only once you have gained a thorough understanding that you can consider making recommendations. It is very important that you speak to all users of the system, in particular those who would be affected by your proposed changes. You must limit the amount of disruption to other users that your research might cause.

If you have a number of questions to ask, think and write these all out in advance and arrange a mutually convenient time to discuss them. Give an estimate of how long the interview is likely to last.

You may prefer to draft a questionnaire which other users could complete before the interview takes place.

Research file

Document all your research carefully and store it in a separate file with any notes you make from the text.

2.5 Use of the Text, and writing up

It is at the research stage that this Text will be most useful. It contains all the relevant theory to enable any student to achieve competence for the ICAS project. However, not all parts will be applicable to all projects because there are many possible areas that any one project may cover. Therefore, a suggested approach to using the Text is to read the relevant chapters carefully and produce answers to the checklist tasks at the end of each chapter.

Once you have completed the research, you should have a file full of diagrams, notes and ideas. Now you have to turn this into a report to management. Before attempting to write anything, you should re-review the Standards and your original project plan. This will remind you of your objective (to prove your competence) and the aim of your project.

You should now review the contents of your research file and start to draft out the contents of the project, in rough only. At this stage you should decide which material you will include in the project and which is not required.

Once you have a set of notes showing the outline structure of the project, you can start to write it out properly.

Although you are not required to submit a word-processed project, it will be easier for you to make revisions and considerably easier for the assessor to review if it is typed.

This chapter contains detailed guidance on report writing skills.

2.6 Assessment process

Finally, let us look at the assessment process for projects.

Your project will be reviewed by the assessor and assessed against the standards. In most cases, the assessment process will also involve a short interview. At the interview you may be asked questions, such as 'What effect will the changes have on the company?' or 'What alternative solutions to the problem did you consider?'

There are two possible outcomes of the process. You will be assessed as either competent or not yet competent. In the case of the latter, you will receive feedback as to where improvements need to be made within your accounting portfolio and invited to re-submit it at a later date.

(**Note:** Grades are not awarded for projects.)

To help you complete your project, let us look at the sorts of factors, which the assessor will consider when assessing your project. Before submitting your project, you should review it critically, asking yourself the same questions:

- Is the project structured as a report to management with all the relevant sections?

- Does it contain clear background information on the purpose, function and organisational structure of the section?

- Can the reader easily identify the issues being discussed?

- Does the project focus on 'internal controls'?

- Are all conclusions and recommendations supported by the contents of the report, including any appendices as required?

- Is the report written and presented in an appropriate style to be presented to management?

You should include a signed statement from your manager, which confirms that this is your own unaided work. Comments on the validity of your conclusion will make the assessment process more efficient.

2.7 Complete the project checklist

You should have received the checklist below from the AAT. It is a good idea to look at it now closely, and complete it as you proceed through the project process.

Candidate name:	
Summative Assessor:	
Formative Assessor/ Advisor:	
Internal Verifier:	

Project checklist – Student use

		Yes/No	Dates	Report ref
1.	Have you discussed your initial project idea with your assessor and has this been approved?			N/A
2.	Have you met regularly with your assessor to discuss progress?			N/A
3.	Have you enclosed workplace testimony (where applicable) with your completed project?			
4.	Has your employer (where applicable) authenticated your project in writing?			
5.	Does the project report cover all assessment criteria?		N/A	N/A
6.	Is it well laid out and easy to read?		N/A	N/A
7.	Is there clear progression from one idea to the next?		N/A	N/A
8.	Have you cross-referenced the main text to the appendices?		N/A	N/A
9.	Have you used diagrams and charts appropriately?		N/A	N/A
10.	Have you started each section on a fresh page?		N/A	N/A
11.	Have you identified issues and objectives clearly?		N/A	N/A
12.	Have you clearly analysed the current situation?		N/A	
13.	Have you justified recommendations by cost/benefit analysis?		N/A	
14.	Have you included key data, omitting superfluous information?		N/A	N/A

15.	Have you described the project methodology?		N/A	N/A
16.	Have you taken a strategic approach?		N/A	N/A
17.	Have you considered company needs, not personal feelings?		N/A	N/A

3 Reports – effective business communiction

3.1 Introduction

A report is a clearly structured document that presents information about an investigation that you have undertaken. The clear structure allows specific parts of that information to be easily located by the reader. Reports range from verbal explanations through to many-paged complex documents. In this chapter, the basic skills of writing a report are considered. These can then be applied to any situation and specifically to your management report.

The purpose of a report is to convey information to particular readers or to answer a question. Its objective is communication, not the display of how much knowledge the writer possesses. Therefore, only relevant information must be included. The writer must constantly bear in mind the needs of the readers.

The reason for writing the report may be to:

- **Inform** – by simply gathering the information and incorporating it into a report.

- **Analyse** – by analysing the information and presenting that analysis in a report.

- **Evaluate** – by evaluating the information so that the reader can make a decision as a direct result of reading the report.

- **Recommend** – the report writer might be charged with the task of making a recommendation for a future course of action.

- **Describe** – the writer might have been asked to investigate how a specific job of work was progressing and to produce a report noting his or her observations.

3.2 Types of report

A report can take on a variety of different forms:

- **Formal or informal reports** – a report to the board of a company analysing the potential profitability for a new product might be in the form of a large formal document incorporating large amounts of detail such as marketing information and competitor product detail. However, a report to a manager explaining how an employee dealt with a problem customer yesterday may well be a simple memorandum on a single sheet of paper.

- **Routine and special reports** – routine reports may be produced on a regular basis, for example, weekly sales reports and annual labour turnover and, because they are often statistical in nature, may require diagrammatic, tabulated or graphical data. Other reports may be one-off or special reports and commissioned on an ad-hoc basis, for example, the effect of computerisation or the level of employee wage rates.

- **Reports for an individual or a group** – the report might be commissioned by an individual such as the sales manager (effectiveness of advertising report) or requested by the board of directors (balance sheet and profit and loss accounts).

- **Internal or external** – most reports are for use within the organisation but there may be situations where a report for an outside organisation is required.

- **Confidential** – these are usually of a more formal nature, following a formal layout and must be clearly labelled as confidential.

 Activity 1

From the following examples of reports decide whether they would be classed as general reports or reports addressed to either the manager of the production department or the marketing and sales department managers.

- Financial reports (e.g. Balance sheets and profit and loss accounts)
- Idle time reports
- Machine downtime reports
- Advertising reports (e.g. costs, effectiveness)
- Shift reports (e.g. units produced, materials used, hours worked)
- Sales order reports

- Material usage reports
- Maintenance reports
- Customer complaints reports
- Cash reports (ranging from daily to monthly) · Rejection/scrap reports

3.3 Aim of the report

To make a report effective, it is obviously important that the aim of the report is clearly understood by the report writer. One way of ensuring that the aim is clear is to set out the following statement and then complete it: 'As the result of reading this report, the reader will...'

'... agree to authorise the project.'

'... take the necessary action.'

'... make a decision.'

3.4 Checklist for planning

Like any piece of written work, it is essential that any report is properly planned. When planning a report the following points should be considered:

- Who commissioned the report and who is to use the report? It may be that there are a number of different users of the report with different needs, levels of knowledge and levels of understanding.
- What information does the user of the report require?
- What background information does the user of the report already have?
- What type of report would best suit the subject matter and the user?
- What is required in the report: information only or judgement, opinions and recommendations?
- What is the time scale of the report?
- What is the cost budget for preparation of the report?
- What is the format to be used i.e. should there be appendices, graphs, diagrams, etc?
- What detailed points will need to be made in the body of the report?
- Is the report confidential?

3.5 Principles of report writing

Once the outline of a report has been sketched in the planning stage, the report will need to be written in detail. When writing any type of report it is worth bearing in mind a few style points:

Layout of the report – information is not only conveyed by the contents but also by its design and presentation. The overall impression is important. Good layout impresses readers. Bad layout makes reports difficult to read.

- Make sure there is plenty of space between the various parts of the report.

- Write on **one side of the paper only** and leave a good margin.

- The different sections of the report usually begin on a **new page**, though the sub-sections of the main body of the report will generally follow on from each other.

- The report needs **headings** that are used as signposts for the reader to find his way about easily. Headings are very necessary for referring to the report later or finding particular points quickly. A lack of headings will frustrate the reader and make it very difficult to use the report for purposes of reference.

Visual aids – include graphs, diagrams, charts, etc where relevant. They should have their main points explained in the text, have an explanatory heading and be labelled with source and date. They should be positioned as near as possible to the part of the text to which they refer. Visual aids should add to, simplify, explain or illustrate the text, not merely repeat it. If the reader has to refer to a visual aid at several different points throughout the text, arrange for the aid to be on a foldout sheet so that it can be kept open while reading the relevant pages. If there are many illustrations, they are sometimes numbered and a list included after the table of contents.

Size of the report – diagrammatic, tabulated or graphical illustrations might make the data clearer and emphasise key facts and figures but will obviously add to the bulk of the report. Care should be taken not to waste managers' time by making a report overly long.

Logic of argument – the report should be clearly structured into sections under relevant headings so that the main topic of the report is clearly set out, developed and explained, and the subsequent conclusions fully supported.

Writing style – there are different styles of writing used in different circumstances. 'C U 2nite at 8 at pub' is acceptable when texting friends or 'We are having a fab time, booze cheap, hotel out of this world and fantastic scenery' may be just right for a postcard home your sister but a formal business report should follow certain guidelines.

- Write in third person e.g. 'it should now be clear that' instead of 'you will be able to see that' (do not use I, me, or we).

- Use standard English and grammar ('is not' not 'isn't', 'for example' not 'e.g.' 'thriving' not 'buzzing').

- Avoid abbreviations (if used they should be written in full the first time and the abbreviation shown in brackets).

- Start a new page for every part of the report.

- Number the sections and paragraphs.

Simple reports in memo, letter or report format concerning day-to-day problems tend to be from and to people who address each other informally. The writing style tends to be more personal, using I, you and we.

Language – a report should communicate as quickly, as easily and as precisely as language will permit. There are a number of points to note:

- avoid abbreviations, slang, jargon, acronyms, foreign phrases and colloquialisms (a Scot may use 'wee' in speech but should use 'little' in writing)

- prefer the active to the passive voice (more important for informal reports) e.g. 'a receipt was issued by the shopkeeper' (passive) should be written 'the shopkeeper issued a receipt'

- shorter sentences can improve clarity

- use words economically e.g. 'in short supply' can be replaced by 'scarce'

- avoid clichés ('explore any avenue'), ambiguity (For sale – bull dog. Eats anything. Very fond of children) and split infinitives (I want to fully understand you)

- choose the right word – some words are simpler than others. Plan, growth, limit and objective are easier than blueprint, escalation, ceiling and target

- replace longer words with shorter. Can you think of short words for perception, initiate and utilise? It might be easier to use view, start or use.

Objectivity – Even if the report is to inform rather than to reach any conclusions it is important that it appears to be written from an objective point of view i.e. is unbiased and impartial. Any emotive or loaded wording should be avoided at all costs.

Activity 2

Our language is cluttered with phrases that are best replaced by shorter expressions. Try to replace the following with one word.

- In the near future
- Along the lines of
- In short supply
- At this moment in time
- Prior to
- In very few cases
- With regard to / in connection with
- A number of

4 Structure of the report

4.1 The sections in a report

Structure is very important – the report will be used for reference, so readers need to be able to find their way about the report quickly and easily.

Reports usually contain the sections listed below, though there are slight variations and sometimes slight differences of heading.

- Title page
- Table of contents
- Terms of reference
- Executive summary
- Methodology
- Introduction
- Analysis of current system
- Recommendations
- Appendices
- Manager's authenticity
- Referencing document

Title page – should give a good idea of what the report is about and have an expressed purpose, without being too long. It should be along the lines of the following

'An investigation into…..'

'A review of……'

'Recommendations for the improvement of…….'

'An analysis of……'

'Improvements to the system of……'

It should also show the following:

(a)   date of issue

(b)   circulation list (person or persons receiving the report), if appropriate

(c)   name of author(s) and membership number

(d)   author's position and department

(e)   name and address of organisation.

At this stage it would be worth stating clearly if the report is to be treated as confidential.

Contents page – many reports will be quite extensive and will include not only the main report but also appendices. This page should contain a list of headings and sub-headings, tables/figures, appendices, etc, and their corresponding page numbers. Remember to start every section on a new page

Terms of reference – this shows what the reasons behind the report are. As there are two reasons why you are writing this, these must both be stated. An example is:

'This project has been prepared to cover the requirements of the Internal Control and Accounting Systems unit, of the Level 4 Stage for the Association of Accounting Technicians….'

'The report looks at ……(what the report is about expressed in one sentence.) For example,…'the need to make improvements to the management of the petty cash system for ABC Limited'.

Executive Summary – can also be called management summary or report summary. The major uses of this are to:

• help readers decide whether to read the whole report

• enable readers to see the key points

• focus attention on the aim of the report.

It gives the reader a general overview/summary of the whole report without them having to read the entire document. It should be able to stand alone as a separate document if required. This section usually includes:

- the background to the report

- the purpose of the report, i.e. an explanation of why the report was required

- the scope and limits of the investigation including brief details of the general procedure, i.e. what was investigated, and how the investigation was conducted

- the important findings or results of the investigation, and the conclusions which you drew from the results, i.e. an explanation of what outcomes the investigation provided

- recommendations for action, if required, i.e. suggestions for what future action needs to be taken.

Write the summary after the report is finished. As a rough guide, it should be about 10% of the length of the report and should only contain material included in the main report.

Methodology – this is how you have planned and prepared the report, it is often called procedures. This should give an overview of the research methods you have used in producing the report.

- You may have designed and used a questionnaire for colleagues or clients.

- You may have monitored a system over a period of time.

- You may have used the Internet or books (do not list them here use that in the appendices)

Acknowledgements can be made here to people who have helped you in the preparation of the report.

Introduction – this should be a BRIEF outline of the organisation or the section of the organisation that the report is based on. Give background factual information sufficient to 'set the scene', familiarise the reader with the context and prepare him for what is to follow. (You may also be required to give terms of reference.) Whilst it is important to set the context do not waste words on this area. It should be the ONLY part of the report that is descriptive. There is no need to go into detailed explanations of job roles, processes or systems. Remember this is a report for management and they will already have a good understanding of how their company works. Organisational charts should not be included here – they belong in the appendices. If you need to add any more detail this should also be in the appendices, but only if referred to in the main text of the report.

Analysis of current system – this is where the main body of the report starts. It is an analysis and evaluation of the current systems not a description. Here you describe what you found out from your investigation, and analyse what those findings mean. Each section and sub-section should have informative headings. The sections include:

- A fuller statement of the problem.

- How it was investigated and what was discovered – there is usually a paragraph that explains or identifies the methods of investigation or research used. When other sources of information have been used in writing the report, they can be acknowledged here.

- The results or findings.

- An analysis, discussion and interpretation of the results.

A section may comprise one or more paragraphs, consisting of a main point, reasons and factual evidence. It needs to identify the strengths and weaknesses of the accounting system in question, and the impact of these on the organisation. The areas to consider are those highlighted in the performance criteria and range, for example, contingency planning, training and areas of possible fraud.

You may find the following suggestions helpful in writing this part of the report:

- Adapt you preliminary plan if necessary to organise your ideas under headings and sub-headings.

- Be clear about what points you want to make to report your findings. Put what you consider to be the most important points first, followed by those of lesser importance. Support each of these points with relevant evidence, elaboration or explanation.

- Add any diagrams (e.g. graphs, tables, figures, etc) to support and present your material visually. Each diagram must have a title, and be numbered consecutively.

Conclusions – the purpose of the conclusion is to restate in a shortened form the most significant points from your investigation and analysis and to make a general statement about the significance of these. This prepares the reader for any recommendations you go on to make. Note that no new information should be included in this section.

Recommendations – the purpose of the recommendations section is to make suggestions about the action(s) or future direction(s) that should be taken as a result of your conclusions. These should be written in order of priority. Any recommendations made should be prepared for in the main body, along with consideration of their viability, economics, practicality, etc. Within this area you need to do some type of a cost-benefit analysis.

Try to make this both quantifiable and qualitative. For example £x, will be saved by using this method and the clients will also receive a better, faster and more time efficient service.

Note that in some reports, the recommendations are presented as part of the conclusion. This allows any recommended action to follow directly on from the conclusion that it leads from.

Appendices – are used to present detailed information (numerical, graphical or tabular) that supports the arguments, findings or conclusions of the report and which is of interest but either too technical or too peripheral for most readers of the report. They may also include documentation (letters) or computer programs for facts presented in the report. The contents of the appendices will be referred to in the main body of the report. Do not include charts, etc that you require readers to refer to in order to follow the main text; their place is usually in the main text. Appendices should be numbered, given informative headings and structured so that the reader can understand them. Only include those appendices which are relevant to the text and are mentioned and referenced in the text, or are part of the research methods, for example a questionnaire.

Acknowledgements – can be at the beginning or at the end if it is felt appropriate to thank people.

References – include here a bibliography of any text books, articles and web sites that you have consulted. When referring to information from these books, etc in the body of the report, the source must be acknowledged there too by means of a referencing system.

The list of references needs the following details:

Books: Author, title, publisher, edition (unless first), place of publication, date, chapter and page number if relevant

Journals: Author, title, journal, volume, number, date and page number if relevant

Manager's authenticity – this serves a few purposes. It helps to add value to the report if the manager states that the recommendations have been acted upon. It allows the assessor to see that someone in the organisation has read the report and can vouch for its authenticity. The testimony can also prove that all matters of a confidential nature have been taken into account when the report was written. It can prove that it is all your own work and that you are not using other people's work from your organisation.

Referencing document – all assessment criteria must be covered and the report MUST be referenced to the standards in some way. You can reference it in the margins, or in the contents and/or cross reference it against a grid.

4.2   Citing sources in the text

Make sure you have factual evidence to support your points and that the reader can discover the source and date of this evidence. If your source is a book or journal, it is usual to use a referencing system in the main text, which refers the reader to a section of references or a bibliography at the end of the report. There are several ways of doing this. One way is to number the references as they appear in the text and then list them in the Bibliography or References in the order in which they appear in the report.

It is important to use a range of sources and to be aware of any potential for bias or for unreliability in the source.

Your text must be basically your points and ideas, with factual evidence to support these points, which need to be obtained by research of some kind. If the source is a written one, then either the appropriate information can be paraphrased (put into your own words) or it can be quoted, using quotation marks, though quotations must be used sparingly. In both cases, the source of the information must be acknowledged. The main body of a report should never consist of a long series of quotations or paraphrases with little or no text of your own.

Quotations and paraphrases must be introduced, seen by the reader to be relevant and smoothly integrated into your text and not stick out like sore thumbs!

5   Writing the report

5.1   Introduction

Write the **first draft** in **double spacing**, so that corrections can be made if necessary. If possible, try to leave a day or two between the first and second drafts

Paragraphs should be more than one sentence long and each should revolve round a common theme or sub-topic. Paragraphs usually consist of a key sentence making a point, with examples or evidence in support of the point made.

Sections should consist of one or more paragraphs, dealing with different aspects of the same sub-topic, if necessary divided into sub-sections each with an appropriate heading. All headings should appear in the table of contents.

5.2 Style

(a) Use relatively short sentences and paragraphs, although not too short. There should be more variation of length. Sentences should not average more than 20 words. The sentence is the 'unit of thought' and should not attempt to convey more than one main idea. Paragraphs should be more than one sentence long.

(b) Use the active voice of the verb, in preference to the passive, unless you have particular reasons for not doing so.

(c) Avoid using too many long, abstract words, particularly if you find yourself influenced by referring to books that may phrase themselves in this fashion. Make sure your readers are familiar with any technical terms you use. If you are using a lot of technical terms, then the surrounding language should be relatively uncomplicated. Similarly, if the concept to be expressed is complicated, the language in which it is expressed should not be too complex or the reader will have his work cut out!

Difficulty of concept + Difficulty of language = Confusion

5.3 Checking the project

- **Material**

  Does the report contain all that should be included?

  Has unnecessary padding been eliminated? The project should be between 3,500 – 4,000 words, so cut down if necessary.

- **Design**

  Is it well planned?

  Are the sections in the right order?

  Are the paragraphs in logical sequence?

  Is it attractively set out?

- **Language**

  Are the words well chosen, precise and appropriate?

  Is their meaning clear?

  Is the report easy to read and understand?

6 Writing a report – example

6.1 Introduction

In this section the process of writing a report will be considered step-by-step using an example. The information required for the report will be given and then each of the main elements of the report will be produced.

6.2 Example information

Given below is a five-year summary of the financial results of a division of your organisation. You are required to write a report explaining, analysing and highlighting these results. The report is to the Employee Representatives Committee of that division and should make particular reference to the part played by wages costs over the period.

Information is also supplied showing the organisation's overall summarised profit and loss account for 2005.

Five-year summary – Division

	2005	2004	2003	2002	2001
	£000	£000	£000	£000	£000
Turnover	1,000	1,200	900	750	700
Production materials	440	500	400	350	300
Wages	310	300	220	170	150
Selling costs	100	100	80	70	60
Administrative costs	40	50	46	44	20
Profit	110	250	154	116	170

2005 Summarised profit and loss account - Organisation

	£000
Turnover	9,400
Production materials	4,500
Wages	2,000
Selling costs	700
Administrative costs	600
Profit	1,600

6.3 Steps to report writing

Step 1 – Produce the heading

Headings – the first step is to show the addressee of the report, its date, who it is from and its title.

REPORT	
To:	Employee Representatives Committee
From:	Accounts Clerk
Date:	12 January 2006
Subject:	Divisional financial performance 2001 to 2005

Step 2 – Analysis of figures and explanations

Main body of the report – this will appear after the synopsis but the synopsis cannot be written until after the main body of the report.

To write the report it will often be necessary to further analyse the data given and prepare tabulations. Such analysis and tabulations will be presented in an appendix to the report.

> **Explanation of figures in appendix**
>
> **Purpose of report** – this report has been commissioned to provide analysis and explanation of the division's profits from 2000 to 2004 for the division's Employee Representatives Committee.
>
> **Information** – the explanation and analysis provided in the report is based upon summarised profit and loss information for the five years from 2001 to 2005 together with the overall organisation's results for the year 2005. This information has been summarised and tabulated in Appendix 1 to this report.
>
> **Annual turnover** – over the last five years annual turnover has increased from £700,000 to £1,000,000, an increase of 43% over the period. There was however a peak of £1,200,000 in 2004 but this fell to £1,000,000 in 2005.
>
> **Annual profit** – the annual profit has however decreased over the period both in absolute terms and as a percentage of annual turnover. The 2005 profit of £110,000 is only 11% as a percentage of turnover. This compares particularly unfavourably to a 21% profit in 2004 and 24% in 2001.

Annual costs – the percentage of turnover represented by each of the major cost classifications is given in Appendix 1. This illustrates the areas of cost that have altered significantly during the five-year period. Most of the costs have remained reasonably constant as a percentage of turnover over the period with the exception of the wages cost that has risen significantly.

Wages costs – these costs, as a percentage of turnover, have increased from 21% in 2001 to 31% in 2005. The increase was fairly steady from 2001 to 2004 but then jumped from 25% in 2004 to 31% in 2005. This increase seems to have played a major part in the reduced profit percentage over the period discussed above.

Divisional and organisation wage costs – the final table in Appendix 1 compares the costs classifications for the division and the organisation as a whole for 2005 in terms of their percentage of turnover. This shows that all of the cost categories for the division, with the exception of wages, have been reasonably in line with the overall organisational cost. However whereas wages for the organisation as a whole totalled 21% of turnover (2,000 ÷ 9,400 × 100%) in 2005, for the division the relevant percentage was 31%.

APPENDIX 1

Five-year summary – division – costs as a percentage of turnover.

	2005 %	2004 %	2003 %	2002 %	2001 %
Production materials	44	42	45	47	43
Wages	31	25	24	23	21
Selling costs	10	8	9	9	9
Administrative costs	4	4	5	6	3

Five-year summary – division – profit as a percentage of turnover

Profit £000	110	250	154	116	170
	11%	21%	17%	15%	24%

KAPLAN PUBLISHING

2005 – division and organisation – costs and profits as a percentage of turnover

	Division		Organisation	
	£000	%	£000	%
Turnover	1,000	100	9,400	100
Production materials	440	44	4,500	48
Wages	310	31	2,000	21
Selling costs	100	10	700	8
Administrative costs	40	4	600	6
Profit	110	11	1,600	17

Step 3 – Write the report conclusion

The conclusion of this explanatory report is that the divisional profits have significantly decreased over the last five years and that this is largely due to a disproportionate increase in wages costs.

Step 4 – Write a report summary

This report has summarised, in Appendix 1, the profit and loss account information for the division for the years 2001 to 2005. This has shown a significant decrease in divisional profit over the period and the figures indicate that a major cause of this loss of profitability is a disproportionate rise in the level of wage costs. The wage costs for the division, as a percentage of turnover, were also compared to those of the organisation as a whole and again the wage costs for the division seem to be disproportionately high.

Step 5

Prepare any necessary graphs or diagrams – at this stage it is necessary to consider whether there are any alternative ways in which the information in the report might be usefully presented, for example by using graphs or other types of diagrams.

In this instance it might be interesting to plot a graph, for example, showing total turnover, wage costs and profit for each of the five years for the division. Another useful diagram might be a pie chart illustrating the differing proportions of cost classifications in the division and organisation as a whole. This information would be shown in Appendix 2.

6.4 The final report

The final step is to put all of the elements of the report together as one package. This might also include a contents page to show the contents of the report.

> **REPORT**
>
> To: Employee Representatives Committee
>
> From: Accounts Clerk
>
> Date: 12 January 2006
>
> Subject: Divisional financial performance 2001 to 2005
>
>   Contents page
>
>   Synopsis
>
>   Report
>
>   Summary
>
>   Appendix 1
>
>   Appendix 2

SYNOPSIS

This report has summarised, in Appendix 1, the profit and loss account information for the division for the years 2001 to 2005. This has shown a significant decrease in divisional profit over the period and the figures indicate that a major cause of this loss of profitability is a disproportionate rise in the level of wage costs. The wage costs for the division, as a percentage of turnover, were also compared to those of the organisation as a whole and again the wage costs for the division seem to be disproportionately high.

REPORT

Purpose of report

This report has been commissioned to provide analysis and explanation of the division's profits from 2001 to 2005 for the division's Employee Representatives Committee.

(1) **Information**

The explanation and analysis provided in the report is based upon summarised profit and loss information for the five years from 2001 to 2005 together with the overall organisation's results for the year 2005. This information has been summarised and tabulated in Appendix 1 to this report.

(2) **Annual turnover**

Over the last five years annual turnover has increased from £700,000 to £1,000,000, an increase of 43% over the period. There was however a peak of £1,200,000 in 2004 but this fell to £1,000,000 in 2005.

(3) **Annual profit**

The annual profit has however decreased over the period both in absolute terms and as a percentage of annual turnover. The 2005 profit of £110,000 is only 11% as a percentage of turnover. This compares particularly unfavourably to a 21% profit in 2004 and 24% in 2001.

(4) **Annual costs**

The percentage of turnover represented by each of the major cost classifications is given in Appendix 1.This illustrates the areas of cost that have altered significantly during the five-year period. Most of the costs have remained reasonably constant as a percentage of turnover over the period with the exception of the wages cost that has risen significantly.

(5) **Wages costs**

The wages costs, as a percentage of turnover, have increased from 21% in 2001 to 31% in 2005.The increase was fairly steady from 2001 to 2004 but then jumped from 25% in 2004 to 31% in 2005. This increase seems to have played a major part in the reduced profit percentage over the period discussed above.

(6) **Divisional and organisation wage costs**

The final table in Appendix 1 compares the costs classifications for the division and the organisation as a whole for 2005 in terms of their percentage of turnover. This shows that all of the cost categories for the division, with the exception of wages, have been reasonably in line with the overall organisational cost. However whereas wages for the organisation as a whole totalled 21% of turnover (2,000 ÷ 9,400 × 100%) in 2005,for the division the relevant percentage was 31%.

APPENDIX 1

Five-year summary – division – costs as a percentage of turnover

	2005	2004	2003	2002	2001
	%	%	%	%	%
Turnover	100	100	100	100	100
Production materials	44	42	45	47	43
Wages	31	25	24	23	21
Selling costs	10	8	9	9	9
Administrative costs	4	4	5	6	3

Five-year summary – division – profit as a percentage of turnover

Profit £000	110	250	154	116	170
11%		21%	17%	15%	24%

2005 – division and organisation – costs and profits as a percentage of turnover

	Division		Organisation	
	£000	%	£000	%
Turnover	1,000	100	9,400	100
Production materials	440	44	4,500	48
Wages	310	31	2,000	21
Selling costs	100	10	700	8
Administrative costs	40	4	600	6
Profit	110	11	1,600	17

APPENDIX 2

At this point appropriate graphs and charts would be included.

 Activity 3

You are an accounts clerk in a division of a manufacturing organisation that makes and sells three products. The marketing department has commissioned some market research indicating the mix of sales that could be achieved by changing the selling prices and/or quality of the products.

There are two scenarios that have been proposed:

- to increase the price and quality (therefore also cost) of product C. This, however, will mean a drop in sales quantity

- to cut the price but not the quality of product B in order to increase the number of units sold.

In both scenarios, product A will remain the same.

The results of this market research are summarised below.

You are required to prepare a report for the marketing manager summarising the financial implications of the findings of the market research.

MARKET RESEARCH FINDINGS

	Selling per unit (£)	Cost per unit (£)	Number of units sold
Current year (2006) sales and costs			
Product A	20	15	10,000
Product B	50	34	2,000
Product C	5	3	40,000
Proposal 1 – Estimated sales 2007			
Product A	20	15	10,000
Product B	50	34	2,000
Product C	8	5	30,000

Proposal 1 – Estimated sales 2008			
Product A	20	15	12,000
Product B	50	34	3,000
Product C	8	5	32,000

Proposal 2 – Estimated sales 2007			
Product A	20	15	10,000
Product B	44	34	4,000
Product C	5	3	40,000

Proposal 2 – Estimated sales 2008			
Product A	20	15	12,000
Product B	44	34	6,000
Product C	5	3	44,000

7 Checklist of tasks

- Read and then carefully follow the steps laid out in this chapter in order to write your final report.

- Check that the report only contains material relevant to its purpose. Avoid the temptation to cram too much into the report, which readers will find unhelpful.

8 Summary

Once you have overcome the main difficulties of choosing your topic and collecting the facts, preparing the report should be easy. Many people do not find it at all easy to 'get going' on writing up their project, but if you follow our ideas on structure you should find it easier. You don't have to start at the beginning – starting with the main body is often the best way, going back later to the summary and the introduction.

Good luck!

Answers to chapter activities

 Activity 1

Production reports – addressed to the manager of the production function responsible:

- idle time reports
- machine downtime reports
- shift reports
- material usage reports
- maintenance reports
- rejection/scrap reports.

Marketing and sales reports – addressed to the managers of marketing and sales:

- advertising reports
- sales order reports
- customer complaints reports.

General reports:

- financial reports
- cash reports.

 Activity 2

- In the near future – soon
- Along the lines of – like
- In short supply – scarce
- At this moment in time – now
- Prior to – before
- In very few cases – seldom
- With regard to / in connection with – about
- A number of – several

Activity 3

Step 1

Prepare the headings for the report.

Step 2

Write the main body of the report.

Step 3

Write the conclusion to the report.

Step 4

Write the synopsis to the report.

Step 5

Prepare any graphs or diagrams that might help to illustrate the data.

Step 6

Put the entire report together in its correct order, possibly with a contents page.

REPORT

To: Marketing Manager

From: Accounts Clerk

Date: 24 January 2006

Subject: Market research into sales price and mix

Contents page

Synopsis

Report

Conclusion and recommendations

Appendix 1

SYNOPSIS

This report summarises the financial effects of the two alternative marketing proposals regarding selling price and cost per unit of each of the three products. The estimated profit to be achieved under each of the proposals is shown in Appendix I. Each of the proposals shows an estimated profit in 2007 and 2008 that is greater than the current 2006 profit. The effect of each proposal on the number of units of each product sold is indicated in Appendix 2.

There are however a number of limitations to the market research information that makes a full analysis impossible to perform.

REPORT

1   **Purpose of the report**

This report has been commissioned by the marketing manager in order to assess the financial implications of the market research that has been undertaken. The market research concerned the selling price, cost and number of units of each of our products estimated to be sold in 2007 and 2008 under two possible alternative proposals.

2   **Information**

The information provided by the market research indicates the estimated selling price, cost per unit and number of units to be sold of each of the three products in 2007 and 2008. These estimates are given for two independent proposals as follows:

Proposal 1 – to increase the price and quality (therefore also cost) of product C. This however will mean a drop in sales quantity.

Proposal 2 – to cut the price but not the quality of product B in order to increase the number of units sold.

The information provided also gives the current year (2006) details for the selling price, cost per unit and number of units sold. This is before any alternative marketing strategies are considered.

1   **Annual profit**

In Appendix 1 the market research has been tabulated to show the estimated profit for 2007 and 2008 under each of the two proposals. The actual profit for 2006 has also been shown.

2   **Effect on profit**

The overall effect on the profit for 2007 and 2008 under both proposals is that there will be an increase over the current 2006 profit figure. Proposal 1 gives a marginally higher profit in 2007 and Proposal 2 a marginally higher profit in 2008.

3   **Effect on market share**

The effect on changes in market share for each product beyond 2008 cannot be established from the information given. However it would appear that if Proposal 1 were adopted there would be a dramatic decrease in the number of Product C units sold in 2007 followed by a small increase in 2008.

If Proposal 2 were chosen then the figures would indicate a remarkable strengthening of demand for Product B in both 2007 and 2008. However there is no indication whether this increase in sales could be sustained.

An illustration of the effect on the unit sales is given in Appendix 2.

4   Limitations of the information

As well as the limitations mentioned above regarding unit sales beyond 2008 there is one further limitation of the market research that should be highlighted at this stage.

There would appear to be no information available regarding the unit sales for 2007 and 2008 if neither proposal were adopted. In order to fully assess the proposals suggested it would be necessary to compare the profits under each proposal to the profits that could be achieved if the current situation were to remain.

CONCLUSION

From the information given in the market research there would appear to be little difference in the financial effects of the two proposals. Both proposals show an increase in profit over 2006 although there is no way to show the 2007 and 2008 profit level if neither of the proposals were adopted.

APPENDIX 1

Current year (2006) profit	£
Product A (£20 – £15) × 10,000 units	50,000
Product B (£50 – £34) × 2,000 units	32,000
Product C (£5 – £3) × 40,000 units	80,000
	———
	162,000
	———

Proposal 1 – Estimated Profit		2007	2008
		£	£
Product A	(£20 – £15) × 10,000 units	50,000	
	(£20 – £15) × 12,000 units		60,000
Product B	(£50 – £34) × 2,000 units	32,000	
	(£50 – £34) × 3,000 units		48,000
Product C	(£8 – £5) × 30,000 units	90,000	
	(£8 – £5) × 32,000 units		96,000
		———	———
		172,000	204,000
		———	———

Proposal 2 – Estimated Profit

Product A	(£20 – £15) × 10,000 units	50,000	
	(£20 – £15) × 12,000 units		60,000
Product B	(£44 – £34) × 4,000 units	40,000	
	(£44 – £34) × 6,000 units		60,000
Product C	(£5 – £3) × 40,000 units	80,000	
	(£5 – £3) × 44,000 units		88,000
		170,000	208,000

APPENDIX 2

At this point appropriate graphs and charts would be included.

The purposes and uses of accounting statements

2

Introduction

For your project it is vital that you have an understanding of the financial statement and their relevance to the organisation. Much of the information in this chapter will be familiar to you from your Unit 11 studies.

KNOWLEDGE

1.1 Describe the purpose, structure and organisation of the accounting function and its relationship with other functions in the organisation.

1.2 Explain the various business purposes for which the following financial information is required.

- Income statement
- Forecast cash flow
- Statement of financial position.

1.3 Give an overview of the organisation's business and its critical external relationships with stakeholders.

1.4 Explain how the accounting systems are affected by the organisational structure, systems, procedures and business transactions.

1.5 Explain the effect on users of changes to accounting systems caused by:

- External regulations
- Organisational policies and procedures.

2.1 Identify the external regulations that affect accounting practice.

CONTENTS

1 Introduction

2 The purpose of financial statements

3 The legal framework

4 Accounting standards

5 User groups

1 Introduction

The accounting function in a organisation fulfills a number of important roles least of which is the supply of information for a variety of uses and users and here we shall consider these aspects of that purpose.

2 The purpose of financial statements

2.1 Introduction

The main purpose of financial statements is to provide information to a wide range of users.

The statement of financial position provides information on the financial position of a business (its assets and liabilities at a point in time).

The income statement provides information on the performance of a business (the profit or loss which results from trading over a period of time).

The statement of other comprehensive income shows income and expenses that are not recognised in profit or loss. The statement of changes in equity provides information about how the equity of the company has changed over the period.

The statement of cash flow provides information on the financial adaptability of a business (the movement of cash into and out of the business over a period of time).

2.2 Stewardship

Financial statements also show the results of the stewardship of an organisation. Stewardship is the accountability of management for the resources entrusted to it by the owners or the Government. This applies to the financial statements of limited companies as well as to central and local government and the National Health Service.

2.3 Needs of users

All users of financial statements need information on financial position, performance and financial adaptability. However, many different groups of people may use financial statements and each group will need particular information. Users of financial statements may include investors, management, employees, customers, suppliers, lenders, the government and the public. Investors need to be able to assess the ability of a business to pay dividends and manage resources. Management need information with which to assess performance, take decisions, plan, and control the business. Lenders, such as banks, are interested in the ability of the business to pay interest and repay loans. HM Revenue and Customs uses financial statements as the basis for tax assessments.

2.4 Legal requirements

The law requires limited companies to prepare financial statements annually. These financial statements must be filed with the Registrar of Companies and are then available to all interested parties. Most businesses, whether incorporated or not, are required to produce financial statements for submission to HM Revenue and Customs.

In the UK, the form and content of limited company accounts is laid down within the Companies Acts. The preparation of limited company accounts is also subject to regulations issued by the Accounting Standards Board if the company is still following UK standards or the International Accounting Standards Board if the company has adopted International standards.

3 The legal framework

3.1 Introduction

The financial statements of limited companies must usually be prepared within the legal framework relevant to that company. In the case of UK companies, the Companies Act 1985 (CA85) contains guidance and rules on:

- Formats for the financial statements

- Fundamental accounting principles

- Valuation rules.

The Companies Act has been amended to take account of the companies who have adopted International Financial Reporting Standards (IFRSs). It allows companies to use the format of accounts set out in IAS 1 *Presentation of Financial Statements* if they have adopted IFRS or continue to use the format in the CA85 if they have not.

3.2 Fundamental accounting principles

The CA85 embodies five accounting principles: · going concern

- consistency
- prudence
- accruals
- separate valuation.

In previous years going concern, consistency, prudence and accruals were known as the 'four fundamental concepts' and were to be considered in preparing accounts. In recent times, only going concern and accruals are seen as being key accounting concepts. These two are discussed in the next chapter.

Prudence is less important now as excessive prudence in accounting can cause financial statements to misrepresent the true picture. Consider a company that makes large non specific provisions. This would misrepresent the true results for the period as the profit should have been higher had the provisions not been made.

Consistency in terms of accounting means to use the same method and policies year on year. This would not necessarily be relevant if a business changed its key operations and needed to change its method of accounting to reflect this.

4 Accounting standards

4.1 IFRSs and IASs

Accounting standards give guidance in specific areas of accounting. The DFS syllabus follows International standards which consist of the following:

- *International Financial Reporting Standards (IFRSs)*

    These are issued by the International Accounting Standards Board. Many countries have used IFRSs for some years. Back in 2002, the Council of Ministers of the European Union (EU) decided that any company which is listed on a European Stock Exchange must prepare their consolidated accounts in line with IFRSs with effect from 1 January 2005.

- *International Accounting Standards (IASs)*

  IASs were created by a body known as the International Accounting Standards Committee (IASC) the predecessor of the IASB. When the IASB was formed it adopted the standards of the IASC which were called IASs. In recent times, the IASB has introduced many new standards so several IASs have now been superseded.

4.2 The structure of the IASC

The structure of the International Accounting Standards Committee Foundation (IASCF) and its subsidiary bodies is shown below:

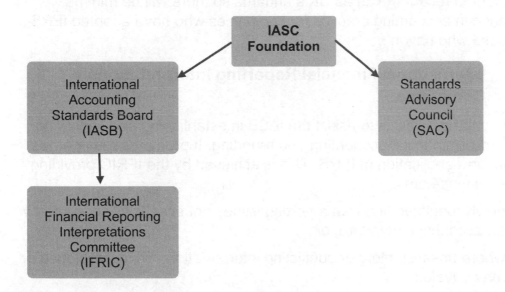

4.3 The International Accounting Standards Committee Foundation (IASCF)

The IASCF is an independent not-for profit foundation based in the US. The Trustees of the Foundation appoint the members of the International Accounting Standards Board, Standards Advisory Council and International Financial Reporting Interpretations Committee.

4.4 The International Accounting Standards Board

The IASB has sole responsibility for the setting of international accounting standards. The members of the IASB are independent experts in accounting.

The IASB's objectives are:

(a) to develop a single set of high quality, global accounting standards that require transparent and comparable information in general purpose financial statements;

(b)   to promote the use and rigorous application of those standards; and

(c)   to work actively with national standard setters to bring about convergence of national accounting standards and IFRSs.

IFRSs set out the recognition, measurement, presentation and disclosure requirements of transactions and events that are important in accounting. They apply to all general purpose financial statements and any limitation in scope of the standard is stated within the standard.

The IASB cooperates with other accounting standard setters with the aim of achieving harmony of accounting practice throughout the world. This has been the case in the UK as the Accounting Standards Board (ASB) has adopted recent IFRSs as UK standards so there will be minimal difference in accounting practice for companies who have adopted IFRS and those who haven't.

4.5   International Financial Reporting Interpretations Committee

The aim of the IFRIC is to assist the IASB in establishing and improving standards of financial accounting and reporting. It promotes the rigorous and uniform application of IFRS. This is achieved by the IFRIC providing timely guidance on:

1   newly identified financial reporting issues not specifically covered by an accounting standard; or

2   where unsatisfactory or conflicting interpretations have developed or may develop.

The guidelines the IFRIC publishes are called IFRIC Interpretations. If a company complies with IFRSs, then it is automatically presumed that this includes the IFRIC Interpretations as well as the relevant standards. Previously IFRIC Interpretations were called SICs and many of these are still relevant.

4.6   Standards Advisory Council

The SAC advises the IASB and sometimes the Trustees of the IASCF. The objectives of the SAC are:

1   to give advice to the IASB on priorities in the IASB's work

2   to inform the IASB of the implications of proposed standards for users and preparers of financial statements

3   to give other advice to the IASB or the Trustees.

4.7 The standard setting process

There are a number of steps in the process of developing and issuing a new accounting standard by the IASB. These are detailed below:

(a) The staff are asked to identify and review all the issues associated with the topic and to consider the application of the IASB Framework to the issues;

(b) Study of national accounting requirements and practice and an exchange of views about the issues with national standard-setters;

(c) Consulting the SAC about the advisability of adding the topic to the IASB agenda;

(d) Formation of an advisory group to give advice to the IASB on the project;

(e) Publishing for public comment a discussion document;

(f) Publishing for public comment an exposure draft approved by at least eight members of the IASB, including any dissenting opinions held by IASB members;

(g) Publishing within an exposure draft a basis for conclusions;

(h) Consideration of all comments received within the comment period on the discussion documents and exposure drafts;

(i) Consideration of whether to hold a public hearing and to conduct field tests and, if necessary, holding such hearings and conducting such tests;

(j) Approval of a standard by at least eight members of the IASB and inclusion in the published standard of any dissenting opinions; and

(k) Publishing within a standard a basis for conclusions, explaining, among other things the steps in the IASB due process and how the IASB dealt with public comments on the exposure draft.

Test your knowledge

1 What are the four statements that would be seen in a set of financial statements?

2 What is meant by the term 'stewardship'?

5 User groups

5.1 The purpose of accounting

The purpose of accounting is to provide information to users of financial statements. Legally, company financial statements are drawn up for the benefit of the shareholders, so that they can assess the performance of their Board of Directors. However, in practice many other groups will use these financial statements, and these groups will all have different needs. These groups, and their needs, are described below.

5.2 Management

Management will be interested in an analysis of revenues and expenses that will provide information that is useful when plans are formulated and decisions made. Once the budget for a business is complete, the accountant can produce figures for what actually happens as the budget period unfolds, so that they can be compared with the budget. Management will also need to know the cost consequences of a particular course of action to aid their decision making.

5.3 Shareholders and potential shareholders

This group includes the investing public at large and the stockbrokers and commentators who advise them. The shareholders should be informed of the manner in which management has used their funds that have been invested in the business. This is a matter of reporting on past events. However, both shareholders and potential shareholders are also interested in the future performance of the business and use past figures as a guide to the future if they have to vote on proposals or decide whether to sell their shares.

Financial analysts advising investors such as insurance companies, pension funds, unit trusts and investment trusts are among the most sophisticated users of accounting information, and the company contemplating a takeover bid is yet another type of potential shareholder.

5.4 Employees and their trade union representatives

These use accounting information to assess the potential performance of the business. This information is relevant to the employee, who wishes to discover whether the company can offer him safe employment and promotion through growth over a period of years, and also to the trade unionist, who uses past profits and potential profits in his calculations and claims for higher wages or better conditions. The viability of different divisions of a company is of interest to this group.

5.5 Lenders

This group includes some who have financed the business over a long period by lending money which is to be repaid at the end of a number of years, as well as short-term payables such as a bank which allows a company to overdraw its bank account for a number of months, and suppliers of raw materials, which permit a company to buy goods from them and pay in, say, four to twelve weeks' time.

Lenders are interested in the security of their loan, so they will look at an accounting statement to ensure that the company will be able to repay on the due date and meet the interest requirements before that date. The amount of cash available and the value of assets, which form a security for the debt, are of importance to this group. Credit rating agencies are interested in accounts for similar reasons.

5.6 Government agencies

These use accounting information, either when collecting statistical information to reveal trends within the economy as a whole or, in the case of the Inland Revenue, to assess the profit on which the company's tax liability is to be computed.

5.7 The business contact group

Customers of a business may use accounting data to assess the viability of a company if a long-term contract is soon to be placed. Competitors will also use the accounts for purposes of comparison.

5.8 The public

From time to time other groups not included above may have an interest in the company e.g. members of a local community where the company operates, environmental pressure groups, and so on.

6 Summary

This chapter considered the purpose of financial statements and the end user and its effect upon the organisation. It demonstrates the role of accounting within the organisation

Answers to 'test your knowledge' questions

Test your knowledge

1   Statement of financial position, income statement, statement of changes in equity and statement of cash flow.

2   Stewardship is the accountability of management for the resources entrusted to it by the owners or the Government.

KAPLAN PUBLISHING

The organisation

3

Introduction

Organisations are groups of people working towards a common objective or set of objectives. We are surrounded by organisations of all kinds – big and small, formal and informal. When an organisation has grown too big for control by a single individual it needs a clearly defined structure with specified lines of authority and responsibility if it is to run efficiently. This chapter considers the various types of structure and the factors influencing the choice of structure and the role of accounting in the organisation.

KNOWLEDGE	CONTENTS
1.1 Describe the purpose, structure and organisation of the accounting function and its relationship with other functions within the organisation.	1 Organisations
	2 Objectives
	3 Structure
	4 The grouping of activities within organisations
1.4 Explain how the accounting systems are affected by the organisational structure, systems, procedures and business transactions.	5 The accounting/ finance function
	6 Organisation review
	7 Checklist of tasks

1 Organisations

Definition

'Organisations are social arrangements for the controlled performance of collective goals'.

The key aspects of this definition are:

- *Collective goals* – organisations are defined primarily by their goals. A school has the main goal of educating pupils and will be organised differently from a company where the main objectives are to make profits and pay dividends to shareholders.

- *Social arrangements* – someone working on his own does not constitute an organisation. Organisations have structure to enable people to work together towards common goals.

- *Controlled performance* – organisations have systems or procedures to ensure goals are achieved.

The word 'organisation' has two distinct meanings.

- It is used to refer to the entity as a whole. Thus, it might refer to any type of business: public or private, nationalised industries, and central and local government.

- All these concerns may be referred to as organisations in the overall sense of being undertakings formed, designed and structured with the intention of ultimately attaining certain goals and objectives. The word can thus be used to refer to the undertaking as a whole.

- Alternatively, the word may refer to the structure of the business i.e. the way its owners or management have designed the processes, flows and arrangements deemed necessary to aid the organisation as a whole in achieving its overall objectives.

The business entity's structure will be designed to ensure effective co-ordination of all its procedures, systems and functions, and also of its communication links (themselves a pre-requisite to effective co-ordination).

1.1   Classifying organisations

Classifications that highlight similarities and differences among organisations can be based on any of the following:

Level of activity – there are three levels of activity:

- Primary – organisations involved in the first stages of production e.g. quarrying, mining and agriculture.

- Secondary – this second stage of production is manufacturing. This includes capital or investment goods e.g. plant and machinery, durable consumer goods such as cars and non-durable goods such as food.

- Tertiary – organisations providing services e.g. education, banking and catering.

Sector – simply describes the organisation as being in the public sector (controlled by government and providing services for the public, the community and the nation) or in the private sector. Private enterprises include:

- sole traders

- partnerships and limited partnerships

- private limited companies

- public limited companies

- holding companies – which are themselves private or public limited companies.

Legal structure – depending on how it is legally constituted an organisation may have a legal existence separate from that of its owners and/or its members. This is not the case for sole traders or partnerships where unlimited liability means that the individual or partner is personally liable to the full extent of his or her private assets for the debts of the business. Neither can provide a type of investment that allows for a share of the ownership to be readily marketable. This shortcoming is removed by the formation of a limited company.

The separate legal personality of the company and the limited liability of its shareholders are two important characteristics that distinguish companies from sole traders and partnerships. A corporation (i.e. a company) is a distinct artificial 'person' created in order to separate legal responsibility for the affairs of a business from the personal affairs of the individuals who own or operate the business.

Since a corporation exists only to establish legal responsibilities, it can only be created, operated and dissolved in accordance with the legal rules governing it (e.g. the Companies Acts in the UK).

Consequently, the business debts and liabilities are those of the company and not those of its members (shareholders). In other words, if the assets owned by the business are not sufficient to pay off the debts incurred by the business, the owners cannot be compelled to make up the deficit from their private resources. The point is that the business debts are not the owners' responsibility. They 'belong' to the company, which is regarded as a separate person in its own right.

Size – the concept of size is problematic. It can be viewed in terms of: ·
numbers employed

- volume of output
- volume of sales
- assets employed
- profits earned
- net worth in real terms.

Technology – is the machinery or equipment, along with the associated technique, which is used for carrying out certain tasks. Some organisations e.g. mobile telephone manufacturers, have a high technology usage compared to others e.g. a window cleaning company.

Activity – organisations can be categorised according to the work they do, for example:

- Agriculture, forestry and fishing
- Mining and quarrying
- Manufacturing industries
- Construction
- Gas, water and electricity
- Transport and distribution
- Distributive trades
- Insurance, banking and finance
- Professional and scientific services
- Miscellaneous services
- Public administration.

Social aspects – historically, it was expected that, no matter who managed an organisation, they had economic responsibilities to operate an efficient and profitable organisation. More recently, however, the trend is to emphasise the social, ecological and ethical responsibilities.

This involves considering:

- relations with customers and suppliers
- attitudes to employees
- attitudes to both the local and world communities
- attitudes to the environment
- the type and quality of product and/or service.

Needs of the members – organisations can be classified according to the particular needs of their members:

- **Government organisations** that satisfy the need for order and continuity – national and local government.

- **Protective organisations** that protect persons from harm – the armed forces, the police, fire and ambulance services.

- **Economic organisations** that provide goods and services in return for some form of payment - sole traders, partnerships, companies and public corporations.

- **Social service organisations** that stand ready to help persons without requiring payment for the service offered – schools, hospitals, parks, etc.

- **Social organisations** that serve the social needs for contact with others – sporting clubs for activities such as golf, cricket, etc.

- **Voluntary organisations** that satisfy social and welfare needs. However, there are differences between these type of organisation e.g. the anti-smoking body ASH advances a cause, and trade unions and employer associations are primarily concerned to advance the material interests of their members.

 Activity 1

Write a short informal report for a colleague, Mr Horn, classifying the organisation you work for.

1.2 Common factors in organisations

Despite the differences among various organisations, there are many common factors, including:

- people
- objectives
- structure
- management.

It is the interaction of people in order to achieve objectives, which forms the basis of an organisation. Some form of structure is needed by which people's interactions and efforts are channelled and co-ordinated and some process of management by which the activities of the organisation, and the efforts of its members, are directed and controlled towards the pursuit of objectives.

The actual effectiveness of the organisation will be dependent upon the quality of its people, its objectives and structure, and the resources available to it.

1.3 Establishing an organisation

The stages outlined below are expressed in general terms:

(a) determining the aims, goals and objectives of the organisation as a whole

(b) determining the policies and procedures necessary to attain the aims, goals and objectives of the organisation as a whole

(c) determining responsibility for each policy and procedure area and the subsequent allocation via the establishment of functional areas

(d) allocating responsibilities within each functional area to individuals and groups of individuals

(e) establishing formal relationships between functions and between individuals within those functional areas

(f) recognising the fact that, whilst formal relationships exist, there are informal relationships also.

Organisations exist because they are more efficient at fulfilling needs than individuals attempting to cater for all their requirements in isolation and without assistance from others. The primary reason for this can be attributed to the ability that organisations have of being able to employ the techniques of specialisation and the division of labour.

2 Objectives

2.1 The importance of objectives

Objectives are defined as the important ends towards which the organisational and individual activities are directed. Without clear objectives, managing is haphazard. As well as acting as targets or standards that orientate the activities of an organisation, objectives can also be used as standards by which the performance of the organisation as a whole can be measured. Target setting motivates staff and enables the organisation to control its performance.

The terms 'objectives', 'aims' and 'goals' in everyday language tend to be used interchangeably. The aim of an organisation is sometimes outlined in its mission statement, which could be called the topmost statement in a hierarchy of organisational objectives.

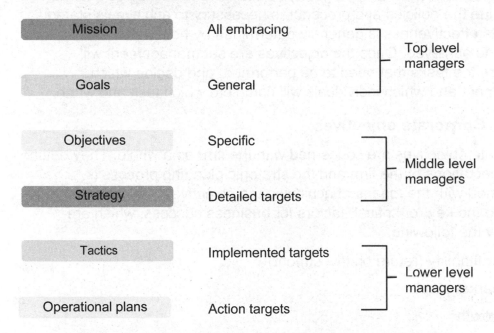

Mission	All embracing	Top level managers
Goals	General	
Objectives	Specific	Middle level managers
Strategy	Detailed targets	
Tactics	Implemented targets	Lower level managers
Operational plans	Action targets	

- The mission statement describes the basic purpose of an organisation, i.e. what it is trying to achieve. The statement can be quite lengthy or short and punchy. Federal Express Corporation's US operation has a short, but powerful mission statement 'Absolutely, Positively Overnight!' Everyone in the company knows what the statement means. Almost nothing more has to be said to ensure that every action of every person is aimed at total customer satisfaction.

- Goals are derived from the mission. They are long run, open-ended attributes or ends a person or organisation seeks and are sufficient for the satisfaction of the organisation's mission.

- Objectives are time-assigned targets derived from the goals. An organisation's goals are the intentions behind its decisions or actions, and objectives are goals expressed in a form in which they can be measured. Strategies – relate to broad areas of an enterprise's operations and can be used as a framework for more detailed tactical planning and action.

- Tactics – are actions carried out to put into effect the details of a strategic decision – tactics can therefore be seen as the detailed implementation of a strategy. In addition, same tactical decisions will be made in response to changing circumstances.

- Actions, programmes and rules - are the operational practices that will translate the intention of the tactics into action by individuals and are therefore detailed, short term and subject to immediate control.

If your organisation has a mission statement, you will find it in the latest Report and Accounts or other similar documentation.

An organisation will establish goals, objectives and strategies and then determine the policies and procedures necessary to achieve its stated aims. Its effectiveness is generally determined by how well the objectives are being achieved. Once the objectives are set management will structure the tasks that need to be performed, and decide which department and which individuals will complete which task and when.

2.2 Corporate objectives

Corporate objectives are concerned with the firm as a whole. They outline the expectations of the firm and the strategic planning process is concerned with the means of achieving the objectives. Objectives should relate to the key (or critical) factors for business success, which are typically the following.

- profitability (return on investment)

- market share

- growth

- cash flow

- customer satisfaction

- the quality of the firm's products

- industrial relations

- added value.

Objectives should be explicit, quantifiable and capable of being achieved. The acronym **SMART** in relation to characteristics of good objectives is *very* useful.

- Specific – all objectives should be specific and deal with some manageable feature of the organisation or individual such as profit, return on capital or output e.g. 'improve performance' is too vague; 'improve profit after tax' is better.

- Measurable – they should have a quantifiable yardstick of attainment e.g. 'improve image' is difficult to verify compared to 'increase profit after tax by 5%'.

- Achievable – to avoid discouraging people with unattainable objectives e.g. 'improve profit after tax by 1000%' probably will be impossible to achieve. Relevant (or realistic) e.g. 'resurface car park' will not have the same impact as 'avoid liquidation'.

- Time bounded – means that there should be a deadline to complete the objective e.g. 'eliminate hospital waiting lists' – when? By the end of the year or the decade.

Some typical corporate objectives for various managers are now given:

Sales/Marketing manager

- Increase the turnover by X% in six months at a rate of a % per month.

- Increase our share of the market for Widgets from 15% to 20% in the next 18 months.

- Successfully introduce our new baby Widget and obtain sales of £10,000 per week after three months.

- Recruit and train effectively six new sales people.

Production manager

- Operate plant at maximum practical operating output.

- Reduce overall costs of manufacturing by 5% over a six-month period using the new equipment.

- Improve the performance of junior managers and supervisors by the use of in-plant training courses.

- Contain wage levels to the lowest possible increase but in any case no larger than X% in line with expected domestic inflation.

2.3 The profit objective

Profitability, as a financial objective, can be expressed as a return on capital employed (ROCE) or a return on investment (ROI), a return on shareholders' capital, earnings per share or another type of management ratio.

As well as making a profit, other objectives of a business organisation are generally to survive and to develop and grow. However, profit maximisation must be seen as the main objective of a company as it tries to satisfy the desire of shareholders for high dividends. If survival is the ultimate objective of the organisation, then this requires a steady and continuous profit. Development and growth is not itself a prime objective but a means of satisfying the shareholders' demand for an adequate return. It also requires profit to provide for future investments.

Unfortunately, the meaning of profit maximisation is not *very* clear – management must also consider the quality of the product/service, the operational costs and the environmental influences. If the expenditure on quality, after-sales service, R&D, sales promotion, management development, satisfaction of staff and their employment conditions is cut, this may increase profitability in the short term but it is likely to jeopardise future growth and development and may even put the survival of the organisation at risk.

2.4 Non-financial objectives

Unless they are discussing a not-for-profit organisation, some writers assume that an enterprise's primary objective is to make a profit and that all other objectives, e.g. sales growth, market share and social responsibility, are secondary and take a lower priority. That is not to say that the secondary objectives are not important or relevant to many firms, merely that, without the profits, firms do not survive. They view some of the secondary objectives more as ways of making a profit than as objectives in their own right, so that objectives to increase market share, extend geographical coverage or develop new products are linked to profitability. Some of the social objectives are promoted by managers for public relations reasons, with the hope of increased business and therefore increased profits.

2.5 Hierarchy of objectives

Organisations will have a whole range of objectives. Some are short-term in nature while others are longer term. Some may be the objectives of a small department whilst others may cover the whole organisation. The term objective may be used to denote any of the possibilities below, ranging from the broad aim to the specific individual objectives – the zenith to the lowest level in the hierarchy.

- The basic long-term objectives of the company as a whole, which might be exemplified by such aims as 'to remain a biscuit manufacturer' or 'to provide a productive and satisfying work environment for employees'. These are *very* often objectives without a time limit ('open' objectives) and expressed in qualitative rather than quantitative terms. Statements of this nature are also frequently designated strategies rather than objectives. But a basic <u>V</u> objective may be quantitative, for example, 'to increase shareholders' earnings by 5% per annum'.

- The more detailed objectives, which convert the basic objectives into general action plans capable of being interpreted in quantitative terms and given a limited time scale. These are the key result areas in which performance is essential for the success of the enterprise. They include profitability, market share, sales volume growth, research and development and production. Examples might be 'to increase our market share for product A to 20% within three years' or 'to market our new executive car during year 2'. Budget objectives that, within the framework of the basic and detailed long-term objectives, set targets for achievement within the budget period. Departmental action plans, which include objectives for short-term achievement by various functional managers.

- Individual objectives, which include performance and personal development objectives.

Managers at different levels in the organisational hierarchy are concerned with different kinds of objectives.

- The board of directors and top managers are *very* much involved in determining the purpose, mission and overall objectives of the organisation, as well as the more specific objectives in the key result areas.

- Middle level managers e.g. the production manager, are involved in setting key result area objectives, division objectives and department objectives.

- Lower level managers are concerned in setting the objectives of departments and units, as well as their subordinates.

 Example

At each higher level in the hierarchy the objectives are more relevant to a greater proportion of the organisation's activities so that the objectives at the top of the hierarchy are relevant to every aspect of the organisation. An example of a long-term objective is that of Avis:' We want to become the fastest growing company with the highest profit margin in the business of renting and leasing vehicles'.

One of the objectives Avis could set to achieve this could be: 'To increase our market share for family saloon rentals worldwide to 20% within three years'.

Activity 2

Describe the three components of the Avis objective identified above.

2.6 Personal objectives

The requirements are not too difficult to meet as far as organisational objectives are concerned but obvious problems of definition exist when the objectives of individuals are being considered. Most people have needs, abilities, skills, aspirations and preferences but their objectives may vary in changing circumstances.

People act in pursuit of particular goals or purposes. These goals influence:

- the person's perception – because messages that are not relevant to goals are filtered out

- the person's learning – because learning is a process of selecting and analysing experiences in order to take into account future actions so that goals and objectives may be met more effectively

- the person's actions – because people behave in a way that satisfies goals. This is the basis of motivation.

Often people's behaviour is difficult to reconcile with their declared objectives and the correct way to motivate them is difficult to find.

Whenever both the organisation and the individual perceive a positive gain in their relationship with each other, the relationship is likely to be successful. Personal objectives are all-important to the formation and maintenance of organisation. An understanding of individual needs and objectives enhances effective organisational management.

 Activity 3 (no feedback)

Establish your own hierarchy of objectives. You probably have a career mission, a means of getting there and, by the availability of this course, a means of measuring your progress towards the goal.

2.7 Types of objectives for individuals and teams

Individual objectives must be directed towards or 'dovetailed' with organisational goals. Each managerial job must be focused on the success of the business as a whole, not just one part of it, so that the results can be measured in terms of his or her contribution. People must know what their targets of performance are.

Work objectives – at team level, they relate to the purpose of the team and the contribution it is expected to make to the goals of the department and the organisation. At individual level, they are related specifically to the job. They clarify what the individual is expected to do and they enable the performance of the individual to be measured.

Standing aims and objectives include qualitative aims – issues such as promptness and courtesy when dealing with customer requests – and quantified targets e.g. for a sales team would be to ensure that all phone calls are picked up within three rings.

Output or improvement targets – have most of the features of SMART objectives. A sales person may be given a target of increasing the number of sales made in a particular district in a certain time. Many organisations have targets that involve reducing the number of defects in goods produced, or finding ways of working more efficiently.

Development goals – deal with how an individual can improve his or her own performance and skills. These goals are set at the appraisal interview and are part of the performance management system.

3 Structure

3.1 Introduction

The allocation of responsibilities, the grouping of functions, decision-making, co-ordination, control and reward are all fundamental requirements for the continued operation of an organisation. The quality of the organisation's structure will affect how well these requirements are met.

For the efficient running of an undertaking, which has grown too big for control by a single individual, key activities must be grouped. Roles, tasks and lines of authority and responsibility must be established and relationships and lines of communication must be specified.

An important feature of any organisation is the optimum number of people who report to any single individual. Attempts by managers to resolve this problem have produced various forms of organisation.

The type of structure chosen depends on the:

(a)   degree of specialisation within the organisation

(b)   number of levels of authority deemed desirable

(c)   amount of decentralisation permitted.

3.2　Specialisation and the division of labour

Specialisation is perhaps the oldest organisational device. It occurs when organisations or individual workers concentrate on a limited type of activity. They are thus able to build up a far greater level of skill and knowledge than they would if they attempted to become 'Jacks of all trades'.

The advantage of arranging production in this way lies in the fact that by concentrating on one type or aspect of production it is possible to become much more efficient. By concentrating its expertise into a limited range of activities, the organisation plans and arranges its production to achieve the most efficient use of resources. A key facet of specialisation involves what is called the 'division of labour', i.e. different tasks being assigned to different people. It is important to note, however, that the excessive use of labour specialisation techniques means that each worker may be restricted to a boring and repetitive job, which provides *very* little satisfaction.

3.3　Authority, responsibility and accountability

The term hierarchy refers to the number of levels and the distribution of authority, responsibility and accountability within the organisation. It is the structure of ranks so that at each level those receiving delegated authority are answerable to their immediate superiors for the functions under their control and for those performing them.

- **Authority:** if an organisation is to function as a co-operative system of individuals, some people must have authority or power over others. Authority and power flow downwards through the formal organisation.

- **Responsibility (for)**: the allocation of tasks to individuals and groups within the organisation. It means being held accountable for personal performance and achievement of the targets specified by the organisation's plans.

- **Accountability (to):** the need for individuals to explain and justify any failure to fulfil their responsibilities to their superiors in the hierarchy. It is the extent to which persons are answerable for their actions, the consequences of those actions and the measured effect on end results.

3.4 Delegation

Delegation is the act by which a person transfers part of their authority to a subordinate person. This creates a hierarchy or chain of command where authority flows downwards from the top management to each level of the organisation. This chain is illustrated below with the arrows down showing the delegation:

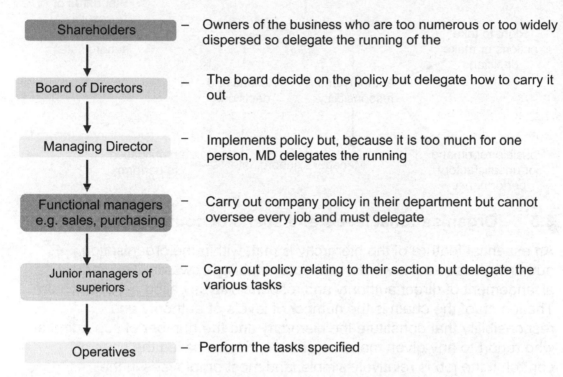

Shareholders	– Owners of the business who are too numerous or too widely dispersed so delegate the running of the
Board of Directors	– The board decide on the policy but delegate how to carry it out
Managing Director	– Implements policy but, because it is too much for one person, MD delegates the running
Functional managers e.g. sales, purchasing	– Carry out company policy in their department but cannot oversee every job and must delegate
Junior managers of superiors	– Carry out policy relating to their section but delegate the various tasks
Operatives	– Perform the tasks specified

The chain of delegation gives employees the means to resolve or refer any problems or queries regarding work activities to the appropriate person.

The basis of delegation is illustrated below showing how the subordinate is responsible to the manager for doing the job, the manager is responsible for seeing that the job gets done and the manager is accountable to the superior for the actions of subordinates.

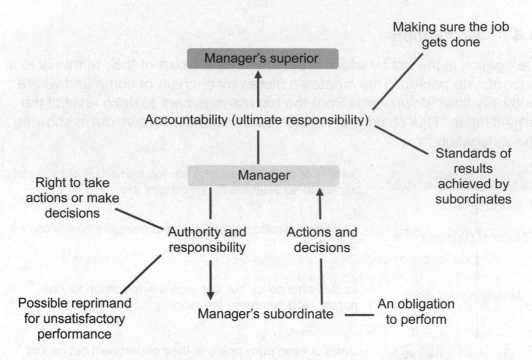

3.5 Organisational levels and spans of control

An essential feature of the hierarchy is that, within the organisation, authority passes downwards, and accountability upwards. The vertical arrangement of direct authority and responsibility is called a 'scalar chain'. The length of the chain is the number of levels of authority and responsibility that constitute the hierarchy and the number of subordinates who report to any given manager or supervisor is called the span of control. If the job is relatively simple, and most employees in the department are doing the same job, then large numbers can be controlled by one manager or supervisor quite easily. However, if the jobs are complex, fewer people can be supervised effectively. The vertical structure of an organisation can be either tall or flat, as in the figure below:

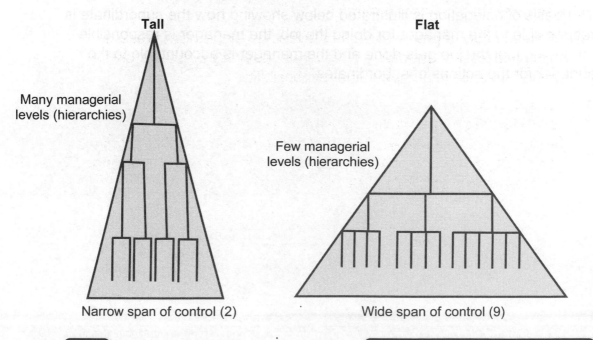

A 'tall' organisation is one that has a large number of levels in its management hierarchy – the National Health Service is normally quoted as an example.

On the other hand, a 'flat' organisation is one with only a few levels in the hierarchy, which implies a wide span of control.

There is no universally correct size for the span of control. It will depend on the nature of the work, the ability and training of subordinates and supervisors, the effectiveness of communications and the personality of the manager.

Advantages of a flat organisation

(a)   A wide span of control encourages delegation and therefore motivation through job enrichment.

(b)   There are usually lower management overhead costs.

(c)   Communications tend to be better as horizontal and lateral communication is encouraged.

(d)   Promotions are real and meaningful.

(e)   Fewer levels mean closer contact between top management and lower levels.

Disadvantages of a flat organisation

(a)   A wide span of control could lead to lack of sufficient executive time being spent with each person directly reporting to the boss.

(b)   Responsibilities between the levels are widely different and so promotion prospects are fewer and carry greater risk of failure than in a tall organisation where there may be an overlap of responsibilities between boss and subordinate.

Advantages of a tall organisation

(a)   A steady flow of promotion opportunities occurs and progression from one level to another is relatively smooth since there is only a minor increase in authority and responsibility.

(b)   Spans of control can be kept small hence increasing the opportunities for personal contact between manager and each subordinate. This can be important in such areas as research and marketing where the role of the boss is often to act as a sounding board in discussing subordinates' initiatives.

Disadvantages of a tall organisation

(a)   More expensive in terms of management overheads.

(b)   Real increases in power and responsibility between one level and another are minor and this creates overlapping of responsibility and artificial, meaningless differences of status (e.g. size of carpets, number of chairs in the room).

(c)   Messages, plans, etc pass through more levels and so multiply communication difficulties.

(d)   Planning and co-ordination become more difficult as more levels of management and more people become involved.

(e)   The number of levels between senior management and shop floor creates a remoteness which is detrimental to staff motivation and performance.

(f)   There is little scope for delegation, job enrichment or team building – status barriers and overlapping of responsibilities mitigate against such initiatives.

 Activity 4

What does the term hierarchy refer to?

3.6   Line and staff relationships

(a)   **Line relationships**

Line authority gives a superior a line of authority over a subordinate. It enables a manager to allocate work, direct and control subordinates and delegate authority. The people that are directly concerned with attaining the objectives of the organisation (e.g. production and sales managers) are called line managers.

(b)   **Staff relationships**

As organisations become larger and more complex, tasks such as recruiting staff, training them, keeping accounts and paying wages, providing technical support and so on cannot be performed by those who either manufacture the product or offer the service. Special individuals may be engaged to provide such expert advice. These are referred to as staff specialists and they exist to help make line activities more effective (e.g. personnel manager, financial controller, company secretary).

The nature of the staff relationship is advisory. Individuals may offer specialist advice to others on certain technical matters. The people concerned may assist a manager, appointed to assist with the workload of a superior. He or she has no authority of his own, but acts in the name of his superior and on his authority.

Unfortunately, this is an aspect of organisation and structure, which causes enormous friction. Line managers are thought of as 'first class citizens' and staff or functional managers are relegated in status to the second rank as expensive 'overheads' that do not contribute anything of worth to the organisation. Staff people are seen by line managers as assuming too much authority, taking credit for the better ideas, failing to keep line personnel informed and of seeing problems from a theoretical viewpoint. Staff personnel often feel that the line does not make proper use of staff, resists suggestions and advice and does not give staff the authority that would enable them to do their job effectively.

4 The grouping of activities within organisations

4.1 Organisation charts

The organisation chart describes the structure of the organisation in diagrammatic form. It is the skeleton upon which every other activity depends. More importantly, it is the framework that explains the communication pattern, process and the linking mechanisms between the roles. It illustrates to everyone who communicates with whom, how the control system works, who is in control, who has authority and above all, who is responsible. It explains how the organisation is co-ordinated and how individual departments relate. Formal structures are often based on specific tasks and it is how these tasks are allocated and the authority that they carry that is explained by the organisational structure.

Authority relationships can be traced by following the lines of an organisational chart downwards. Responsibility relationships can be traced by following those same lines upwards.

4.2 The different types of organisational structure

The structure of an organisation is concerned with the **grouping of the activities** carried on so that it can meet its objectives in the best possible way. It achieves this by assigning certain activities to various parts of the organisation and by providing for the necessary authority and co-ordination.

It must ensure that there is no **duplication of effort,** since apart from the additional costs involved, this might result in the organisation not being competitive within the market place, that is, not being able to sell its goods or services as cheaply as someone else.

Work can be divided, and activities linked together, in a variety of different ways. The main types of organisational structure are as follows.

- entrepreneurial structure

- functional structure

- product or service structure

- geographical or territorial structure

- matrix structure.

An **entrepreneurial structure** is almost equivalent to the absence of structure, at least in the formal sense and is typically found in small businesses. There is *very* little in the way of job descriptions, and everybody helps out with all the ongoing tasks. Although the absence of formal roles and procedures may be suitable for small organisations, some kind of formal discipline will be needed as the organisation grows.

A functional structure is most people's idea of the 'classical' approach to organisational structure. Different departments are set up to manage the different functions of the business. This is illustrated in the organisation chart below

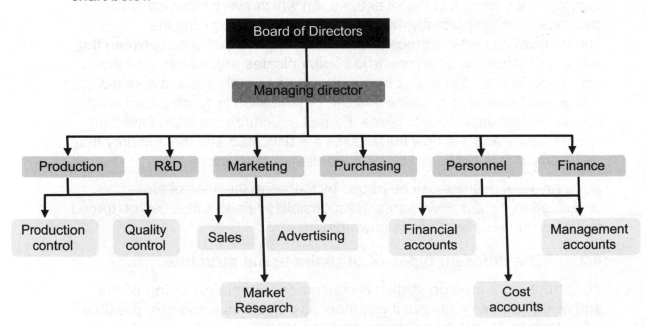

The Board will decide overall company policy. The Managing Director has responsibility for the running of the company and thus is accountable to members of the Board for the implementation of policy. The Board itself is responsible to the shareholders for the success of the company.

Each department head is responsible for the smooth running of their department and has authority to make day-to-day decisions as problems arise. Each head is directly accountable to the Managing Director. Within each department, some authority is delegated to senior staff, e.g. supervisors in the accounting department, team leaders in the production department or buyers in the purchasing department. Such employees are accountable to their department heads.

A product based structure is a way of splitting up the overall business into a number of strategic business units (SBUs) based on products. For example, Procter and Gamble, the manufacturer of household goods, divides its organisational structure in this way. Each of the P&G divisions – food products, toilet goods, paper products, packaged soap and detergents, coffee and industrial food - is headed by a vice-president.

This structure establishes each product or group of products as an integrated unit within the framework of the company. The main functions of production, sales, personnel and finance are apportioned to the relative products. So each product group could have its own specialist in accounting, personnel, etc. Such an organisation allows considerable delegation by top management and clear profit accountability by division heads.

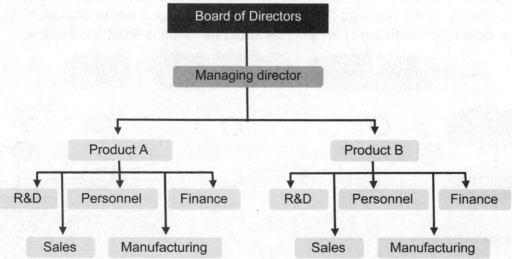

Geographical or territorial structure is a favoured method amongst companies that have wide geographical areas and where it is important that activities in any area should be grouped and assigned to a manager. It is a more suitable method where customer needs or product characteristics are regionally based and when the product itself is not so complex or capital insensitive as to make the establishment of regional operations too costly or impractical.

This would typically happen when the tastes and demands of customers varied greatly between geographical areas and could best be satisfied by local bases. Consider the differing needs of an estate agency chain, which must be geographically based, and that of an insurance agency, which can be centralised.

A matrix structure – in many modern organisations where conventional communication structures either do not exist or are less formal, communication tends to be horizontal, between individuals and departments, rather than the upwards or downward flow assumed by so many to be the normal case. A project team may be set up as a separate unit on a temporary basis to accomplish a specific task and when this is completed, the team is disbanded or members of the unit are reassigned to a new task. The matrix organisation is a combination of functional departments, which provide a stable base for specialised activities and a permanent location for members of staff, and units that integrate various activities or departments on a project team, product, programme or geographical basis. It establishes a grid with a two-way flow of authority and responsibility.

Its great advantage is that it is cross-functional – maintaining functions and the commitment and specialisation of individual departments. At the same time it allows adaptation to change, encourages commitment to the organisation as a whole, improves communication and perhaps most importantly of all, reduces the need for slow, laborious communication up and down the traditional hierarchical structure. This is illustrated below.

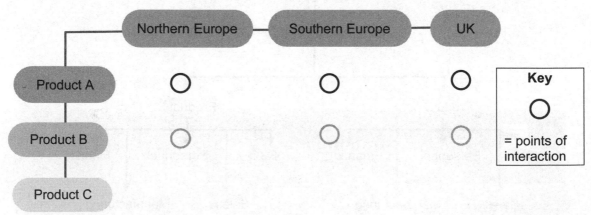

In the above the team working on Product C would be responsible not only to the head of that product, but also to the heads of each geographical region.

4.3 Centralisation or decentralisation?

A method of analysing structures is by reference to the level at which decisions are made. The large company may often be distinguished in character from the smaller ones by the use it makes of centralisation and decentralisation.

Centralisation means that most of the decision-making is undertaken at headquarters. At one extreme is the centralised functional organisation consisting of specialised groups in marketing, sales, engineering, production, R&D, personnel and administration. This is most appropriate for organisations with a limited number of closely related product lines and specialisation means benefits and economies. It becomes less effective as coordination becomes important, the product lines spread and specialisation is not such a significant asset.

In contrast, a divisional structure emphasises a decentralised organisation based on product or market groupings – working to some extent independently of each other. This involves people other than top management, i.e. divisional managers making many of the day-to-day operating decisions. In fact, decentralisation has often been defined as 'the delegation of the freedom to make decisions'.

 Activity 5

Imagine that for your report you need certain information. List the functions within the organisation where you might obtain the following:

(a)   numbers of employees in the company pension scheme

(b)   levels of stock (raw materials held) – volume not value

(c)   comparison of customer orders by territory

(d)   records of the value of finished goods sold in the last month.

---

5   The accounting/finance function

5.1 Internal structure

There are many different approaches to how work is divided and responsibilities allocated within a particular function and the accounts department is no exception. However, dependent upon the objectives laid down for the function and the particular characteristics of the organisation, it is possible to suggest a basic structure:

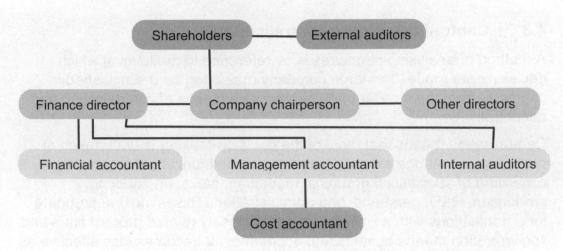

Accountants have to provide information to very diverse groups. The specific needs of each determine whether these can best be served by the financial accounting or the management accounting function of the business organisation.

- **Financial accounting** is concerned with the recording and processing of transactions as they occur. Accounts are kept of all debtors' and creditors' transactions and of all moneys paid by and to the business. Coupled with this will be the preparation of the annual accounts in the forms required for both shareholders and the Inland Revenue and also periodic financial statements (e.g. cash flow statements, debtors and creditors balance, draft monthly profit and loss accounts and balance sheets). For these there will be the need to incorporate adjustments such as for depreciation, asset valuation, accruals and provisions.

- **Management accounting** involves the preparation and presentation of internal accounting information in such a way as to assist management in formulating policies, planning and controlling activities. Based mainly on the information provided by the cost accounts, data is analysed and information is presented to management to provide a basis for decision-making. Associated with this will be the operating of systems of budgeting control and standard costing. As you will know, the preparation of cost accounts involves a separate approach from financial accounting and will thus have a separate role in the accounting function.

Normally other subdivisions of the accounting function include the cashiers' department and the wages department. The cashiers are responsible for all the transactions involving cash, such as receipts from customers, payments to suppliers and payments of wages. The wages department, in addition to the calculation of remuneration due to employees, will also provide basic data for both the financial and costing systems.

The role of internal auditor ideally should be a separate function but is very often part of the accounting function.

5.2 Sections in the accounts department

The financial accounts department will be further divided with a supervisor or manager responsible for each section e.g. sales ledger, purchase ledger, credit control and payroll. Management accounting work will also be divided up with accountants as supervisors of sections responsible for keeping different cost records e.g. materials, production and marketing.

Taking a section of the cost accounts department, we can outline a possible structure:

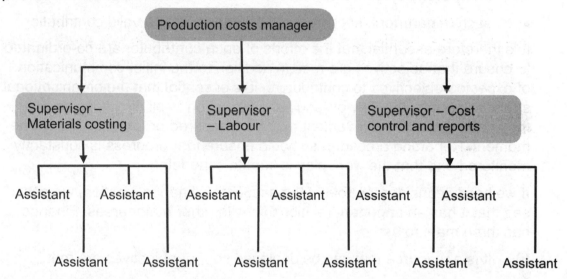

5.3 Location of accounts department

For organisations with different sites the overall policy on centralisation versus decentralisation and organisational structure will have important effects on the location of the accounts departments. In some cases the accounting function may be carried out entirely at the head office; in others each location would be responsible for all its own accounting procedures, with only interim and final financial statements being forwarded to head office.

With centralisation there is the opportunity to employ specialist accounting staff and advanced EDP systems more effectively and economically. When staff are in one central office, supervision may be improved and there is greater flexibility of staff and easier handling of peak loads. However day-to-day control over financial control systems may be lost and there may be delays in the flow of information and documents. In addition head office staff are quite often regarded with suspicion and resentment and there may be the danger of head office becoming out of touch with the peculiar characteristics of the methods of working at each location.

Organisational structure may determine the location of departments. A divisionalised structure with different activities within the group may lend itself to separate accounts departments at each division. On the other hand a major chain of retail stores may install strong control systems at each outlet, with basic data being transmitted daily for processing and reporting by a centrally located accounts department.

5.4 Relationships of the accounting function

Within any organisation (when seen as an entity), departments, sections and individuals must all be organised to ensure that:

- the overall objectives of the organisation are attained

- each department, section and individual makes a valid contribution.

It is therefore essential that the efforts of each contributor are co-ordinated to ensure that objectives are met. In addition to the initial communication of expected objectives to contributors, it is essential that the organisational structure permits the flow of required information in all directions so that the attainment and achievement may be measured or forecast at any one moment. Reporting procedures should ensure that progress is constantly monitored and that the work plan is kept to schedule.

If we briefly consider the role of the accounting/finance function, we can see that it has an important relationship with other major areas. Finance has three main roles:

(i)   It is a resource that can be deployed so that objectives are met.

(ii)   An organisation's objectives are often expressed in financial or semi-financial terms.

(iii)   Financial controls are often used to plan and control the implementation of strategies and financial indicators are often used for detailed performance assessment.

The accounting department can be viewed as having responsibility for handling and processing information within the organisation. This information and any control procedures are provided as a service to the other departments.

Other relationships involving the accounting function include the following:

(a)   The marketing department will rely on an analysis of sales by region, sales person, customer or town in order to formulate an advertising strategy or sales promotion effort.

(b)   There is a relationship between the personnel department and the wages department, because employee details must be updated to cover any changes. This relationship could be extended to include the industrial relations officer, who may be employed by the production department and be responsible for initiating these changes.

(c) The IT department, whether considered part of the accounting function or not, has a very wide span of responsibility in any organisation. Most of the department managers will expect regular reports from this department and must therefore be in constant liaison with the staff to make sure the information is relevant to their current needs. Any suggestions for changes to the system would be negotiated here.

(d) The statistician will have responsibilities for providing information on such things as production output, variations from quality standards, comparisons of efficiency in the sales department, analysis of questionnaires for the market research staff and comparative information on wastage of materials from different suppliers.

6 Organisation review

6.1 Introduction

An organisation review may be undertaken as a specific exercise or as part of a larger project. For example, many large companies often combine an organisation review with a study of management information systems, where changes in the system often require changes in the way things are organised.

Organisation reviews can be undertaken with a small section of a department, a group of units or for the company as a whole. Organisation at section level (for example, bought ledger, sales ledger, costing department) in a company might form part of an organisation and methods (O & M) review with the primary aim of work simplification or cost reduction

6.2 Influencing factors

The existing structure of any organisation may have been the result of careful planning or it may have evolved informally. Factors that may have influenced the present structure include:

- management style
- type of products and services offered and the nature of the inputs required, for example capital or labour intensive
- degree of centralisation and/or the location of premises

- type of skills required and the various characteristics of the employees nature of past growth, for example, by acquisition

- past approach to organisational matters, such as manpower planning or career development

- impact of technological developments

- type of financial ownership.

6.3 Review

Any shortcomings in the structure are likely to be well hidden. This is not because managers deliberately hide such matters but merely that structures are not often carefully planned. It is more likely to be the result of external factors such as the markets in which the firm operates and/or the personal idiosyncrasies of top management. In addition, many so-called business problems often have underlying causes that are more closely related to organisational matters. The key question that must be answered in any organisational review is whether delegation is clear in principle and effective in practice.

A general approach that might include some or all of the following steps:

1. An initial short survey involving the development of a simple checklist with a series of yes/no type questions. Typical subjects to be included are:	<ul><li>objectives of the present departments</li><li>organisation charts</li><li>job descriptions</li><li>means of communication</li><li>salary structure and grading</li><li>use of committees.</li></ul>
2. A critical review to establish whether the present arrangements appear to be satisfactory or whether there is a case for looking at the organisation in more depth and if so in what particular main areas.	

3.	A detailed study assuming that more in-depth work was necessary, which might include:	• collection of facts, such as department titles, names, number of staff, salary costs, ages
		• preparation of organisation charts
		• critical analysis and review of present arrangements identifying all shortcomings and/or weaknesses
		• development of outline proposals and recommendations.
4.	Presentation of proposals involving discussions with management and staff.	

7 Checklist of tasks

- Produce an organisational chart for your company.

- Write a brief description of the structure of your organisation.

- List the key objectives of your organisation.

For the section of your organisation on which you are basing your project, repeat the above three tasks in detail.

8   Test your knowledge

Test your knowledge

1   At what level of activity e.g. primary, secondary or tertiary, would a building society be classified?

2   What type of organisation will have its shares quoted on the Stock Exchange?

3   Give three ways that the size of an enterprise can be measured.

4   Do managers plan their tactics before or after their strategy?

5   In relation to characteristics of good objectives, what does the acronym SMART stand for?

6   Give three examples of non-financial objectives.

7   Do authority and power flow upwards or downwards through the formal organisation?

8   Is a narrow span of control associated with a tall or a flat organisation structure?

9   What type of organisational structure is most people's idea of the 'classical' approach?

10   What are the three main roles of the accounting/finance function?

KAPLAN PUBLISHING

9 Summary

This chapter was an introduction to an organisation's business and should help you understand and differentiate between the nature, characteristics and attributes of different types of organisation.

Since this Unit is assessed by means of a project, you should bear in mind that the purpose of the project is to describe ways of improving a system. Whatever the nature of your particular project, the same basic structure will apply:

- You will be expected to start with a background of the organisation in question (i.e. information such as its business, location, size, goals and aims).

- You should describe the organisational structure. Diagrams are often more convenient than pages of narrative text as you can show sections, departments, chains of command and the span of control.

From this basic structure, you can identify the section that you are researching.

Answers to chapter activities and 'test your knowledge' questions

 Activity 1

A short informal report generally has only two or three sections. The main areas are:

- the name of the person requesting the report
- the title
- an introduction, which might include the background
- the procedure, information, findings and 'overview' of the problem
- the name and position within the company of the writer, and
- the date.

To: Mr Horn

Classification of Cadbury Schweppes

Introduction

This report classifies the organisation in terms of its Standard Industrial Classification, activity, legal form, ownership, control, size and technology.

Procedure

The majority of the information was found on the Internet.

Standard Industrial Classification – this is a method of dividing up products so that each establishment can be allocated to a relevant classification on the basis of its principal activity. Cadbury Schweppes is classified under Food Producers & Processors.

Activity – the group has a large portfolio of chocolate and drinks brands, which it sells in around 25 countries. Their heritage began in 1783 when Jacob Schweppe perfected his process for manufacturing carbonated mineral water in Geneva, Switzerland. And in 1824 John Cadbury opened in Birmingham selling cocoa and chocolate. These two great household names merged in 1969 to form Cadbury Schweppes plc. Since then they have expanded the business throughout the world by a programme of organic and acquisition led growth.

Concentrating on their core brands in beverages and confectionery since the 1980s, they have strengthened their portfolio through almost 50 acquisitions, including brand icons such as Mott's, Canada Dry, Halls,

Trident, Dentyne, Bubblicious, Trebor, Bassett, Dr Pepper, 7 Up and Snapple.

Legal form – Cadbury Schweppes is a public limited company. It has been in existence in different guises for more than 200 years.

Ownership – Cadbury Schweppes is owned by shareholders. The shares are publicly quoted on the Stock Exchange.

Control – as well as control procedures and responsibilities that are normal within a major international manufacturing company, the managers of Cadbury Schweppes aim to ensure that in the course of their business activities they:

- minimise their impact on the environment around the world, working towards the objective of long-term sustainability

- look after the health and safety of their employees

- find opportunities to improve the local environment in the communities in which they operate.

Size – Cadbury Schweppes is organised around four regional operating units supported by six global functions. The four regions are Americas Beverages; Americas Confectionery; Europe, Middle East and Africa (EMEA);and Asia Pacific. The six global functions are human resources; legal; finance; supply chain; commercial strategy; and science and technology.

It is the world's largest confectionery company and employs around 50,000 people.

The US has been its focus of late with acquisitions of Dr Pepper and gum maker Adams now making the US its biggest source of profits.

Technology – Cadbury Schweppes would be classified as a medium to high technology user. During 2004,a new global science and technology strategy was put in place to enable the Group to gain greater advantage in this area. Currently, the function undertakes the investigation of changes to existing products, and the development of new products, packaging and manufacturing processes. This includes rigorously assessing the safety of ingredients and products and the inclusion of any benefit-enhancing ingredients, as well as the development of improved product tastes, textures and physical properties of products which meet or exceed customer expectations while also meeting regulatory requirements of all countries where the product is sold.

The Group uses its own science, technology and innovation facilities as well as those of suppliers. The Group's major facilities in the UK are based in Reading.

Conclusion

Cadbury Schweppes is a large publicly owned major international beverage and confectionery group selling brands around the world.

Martin Murray

Trainee accountant

Accounts department

Date

 Activity 2

Using the acronym SMART, the three components of the Avis objective are:

(i)   Specific – market share is a manageable feature of the organisation

(ii)   Measurable – 20% is a quantifiable yardstick of attainment

(iii) Time bounded – the deadline to complete the objective is within three years.

 Activity 4

The term hierarchy refers to the distribution of authority, responsibility and accountability within the organisation. For example, a bishop has authority over a diocese, while the range of authority of a local clergyman is confined to his or her local parish.

 Activity 5

(a)   Personnel.

(b)   Production.

(c)   Marketing/Sales.

(d)   Accounts.

Test your knowledge

1   A building society would be classified as a tertiary company.

2   A Public Limited Company (PLC) is quoted on the exchange.

3   The size of an enterprise can be viewed in terms of numbers employed, volume of output or sales, assets employed, profits earned or net worth in real terms.

4   Managers generally plan their strategy before their tactics.

5   SMART stands for **S**pecific, **M**easurable, **A**chievable, **R**elevant (or realistic) and **T**ime bounded.

6   Non-financial objectives include wanting to increase market share, extend geographical coverage or develop new products.

7   Authority and power flow downwards through the formal organisation.

8   A 'tall' organisation is one that has a large number of levels in its management hierarchy and a narrow span of control.

9   Most people's idea of the 'classical' approach to organisational structure is a functional structure.

10 Finance has three main roles:

   •   It is a resource that can be deployed so that objectives are met.

   •   An organisation's objectives are often expressed in financial or semi-financial terms.

   •   Financial controls are often used to plan and control the implementation of strategies and financial indicators are often used for detailed performance assessment.

The organisation's environment

Introduction

At this stage in your studies you should be thinking about the system that you are considering for your project. The report will obviously detail the accounting environment, the system, its procedures, personnel and costs. Further detail can cover how the success or effectiveness of the system is measured.

The project is about improving the system and, therefore, you will want to outline what is wrong with the current system in terms of costs, location, resources and the skills of the staff. To explain how you found out the system was not working as well as it might be, you must identify the sources of this information and the methods you have used to identify the weaknesses. Having identified the problem, or problems, you must then continue by looking for alternative solutions and researching the constraints that will apply when you are evaluating these options.

KNOWLEDGE	CONTENTS
1.5 Explain the effect on users of changes to accounting systems caused by: • external regulations • organisational policies and procedures	1 Organisations as systems 2 Critical external relationships 3 External analysis 4 SWOT analysis 5 Checklist of tasks

1 Types of fraud

1.1 Systems

We have already begun to identify the needs of a successful formal organisation. These are:

(a) a system of dividing work into functional groupings, enabling members to specialise

(b) a system of authority of power, so that group members would accept the decisions of supervision and management – this requires leadership to have the appropriate technical skill, charisma and ability to lead

(c) a system of logical decision-making, and

(d) adequate motivational incentives.

The term 'system' can be defined as a set of interacting elements responding to inputs to produce outputs. Every system, whatever its nature and purpose (e.g. central heating system, banking system, payments system) is a way of viewing a group of components or elements and the way in which they interact.

The elements of a system are outlined in the diagram below:

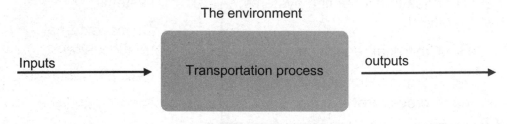

Every system exists within an environment. This is the set of elements that affect the system, but are not controlled by it. The system boundary is the limit of the system; within it is the system and outside it is the environment. A boundary is often a matter of definition. For example, if the system under examination is 'the whole company' then within the boundary will be found the subsystems of the system, for instance, the employees and procedures contained within departments such as production, purchasing, sales and finance. The sub-systems communicate by passing messages between themselves. Outside the boundary is the environment, which includes customers, suppliers, the labour market, shareholders, lenders, competitors and the local community as well as more abstract and indirect influences such as the law and the economy.

If we are concentrating on the finance system, then sales, production and purchasing become part of the environment, and within the system boundary will be found smaller subsystems such as product costing, financial accounting and treasury.

For your project, you may need examples of communication and co-operation at the boundaries of these sub-systems:

- Financial accounting staff responsible for the preparation of the annual accounts might rely on the management accounting staff for data about stock records so as to place a value on closing stocks in the accounts.

- The sales ledger section relies on sales staff to send copies of sales orders or confirmation of goods delivered to customers and on the cashier to pass on information about payments received. It must also co-operate with debt collection staff by helping to prepare monthly statements and lists of aged debtors.

- The purchase ledger section relies on the purchasing department to send copies of purchase orders and confirm the validity of invoices received from suppliers and also inform the purchase ledger staff about any despatches concerning goods received or purchases returned. The section also relies on the cashier to inform it of all payments of invoices.

1.2   The systems approach

The systems that operate within organisations can be viewed in many ways, for example:

- social systems – composed of people and their relationships

- information systems – relying on information to support decisions

- financial systems – emphasising the organisation's cash flows

- economic systems – utilising resources to produce economic welfare.

The systems approach views an organisation as 'a social system consisting of individuals who co-operate within a formal framework drawing resources from their environment and putting their products or services back into that environment'. The enterprise receives inputs of money, manpower and skills and produces outputs in the form of wealth e.g. units of production.

An organised enterprise does not, of course, exist in a vacuum. It is dependent on its external environment and it is part of larger systems such as the industry to which it belongs, the economic system and society. It is also composed of a number of sub-systems, manufacturing, finance, sales and so on. The manufacturing subsystem is interdependent upon the sales sub-system, i.e. a business should only manufacture what it can sell.

The manufacturing cycles depend upon the procurement of human resources (the personnel sub-system) and the provision of funds (finance sub-system). The technical department sub-system examines the feasibility of new products and brings them to a state of completion.

1.3 The organisation as a system

We can describe an organisation as receiving inputs from the environment, transforming them and then exporting the outputs to the environment. The illustration below indicates how the various inputs are transformed through the managerial functions of planning, organising, staffing, leading and controlling.

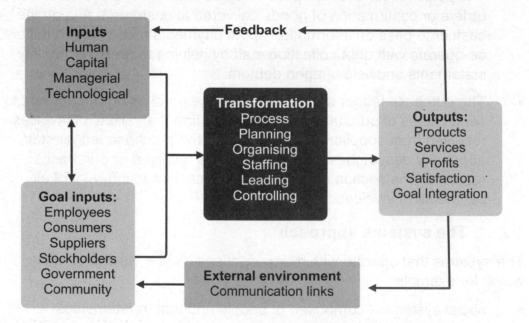

Inputs – the inputs from the external environment may include people, capital, and managerial skills, as well as technical knowledge and skills. In addition, various groups of people will make demands on the organisation. For example, employees want higher pay, more benefits, and job security. On the other hand, consumers demand safe and reliable products at reasonable prices. Suppliers want assurance that their products will be bought. Stockholders want not only a high return on their investment but also security for their money; Government depends on taxes being paid, but also expect the organisation to comply with their laws. Similarly, the community demands that enterprises be 'good citizens', providing the maximum number of jobs with a minimum of pollution.

The transformation process – in a manufacturing organisation this would be the production department; in an insurance company it would be the underwriting department. The production sub-system is the heart of the organisation and all sub-systems are usually oriented towards it.

Management is the sub-system that co-ordinates all of the other sub-systems by means of policies, plans, resolving conflict, etc. It is the task of managers to transform the inputs, in an effective and efficient manner, into outputs.

The communication system – is essential to all phases of the managerial process. It integrates the managerial functions. For example, the objectives set in planning are communicated so that the appropriate organisation structure can be devised. Communication is essential in the selection, appraisal, and training of managers to fill the roles in this structure. Similarly effective leadership and the creation of an environment conducive to motivation depend on communication. It is through communication that the manager determines whether events and performance conform to plans. Thus, it is communication which makes managing possible.

The second purpose of the communication system is to link the organisation with its external environment, where many of the claimants are. It is through the communication system that the needs of customers are identified; this knowledge enables the firm to provide products and services at a profit. Similarly, it is through an effective communication system that the organisation becomes aware of competition and other potential threats and constraining factors.

Outputs – these will vary with the enterprise but include the following – products, services, profits, satisfaction, and integration of the goals of various claimants to the enterprise.

Feedback – some of the outputs may become inputs again e.g. the satisfaction of employees becomes an important human input. Similarly; profits, the surplus of income over costs, are reinvested in cash and capital goods, such as machinery, equipment, buildings, and stock.

1.4 Control systems

We have many control systems such as quality control, stock control and budgetary control. Control is the activity that monitors changes or deviations from those originally planned. The control of an organisation is exercised by managers obtaining and using information.

To get a better understanding of control systems, it is useful to start with an example that is in everyday use – a thermostat. All central heating systems contain thermostats to regulate the temperature of the rooms they are heating. The user sets the thermostat to the required temperature on the dial. There is a thermometer in the system, which measures the temperature of the rooms. The room temperature is continually compared with the pre-set temperature on the thermostat dial. If the room temperature is above the dial temperature, the power (e.g. gas) is switched off. When room temperature falls below the dial temperature, the power is switched on.

The elements of a control system are:

- **Standard** – is what the system is aiming for. In the thermostat system it is the pre-set temperature.

- **Sensor** (or detector) – measures the output of the system. In the thermostat system it is the thermometer.

- **Comparator** – compares the information from the standard and the sensor.

- **Effector** (or activator) – initiates the control action. In the thermostat system it is the switch.

- **Feedback** – is the information that is taken from the system output and used to adjust the system. In the thermostat example the feedback is the actual room temperature

In an organisational system, information about how the system actually performs is recorded and this information is available to the managers responsible for their achievement of the target performance. For effective and accurate control it is essential that timely and efficiently detailed feedback is provided so that corrective action can be taken. This may be a minor operating adjustment or it may involve a complete redesign of the system.

1.5 Control methods

There are a variety of control methods but the two that you will be concentrating on are both quantitative methods. The first type focuses on physical values such as quality control and the second focuses on monetary values such as budgets.

Quality control is the control system of setting quality standards, measuring performance against those standards and taking corrective action when necessary. The standard aimed for will depend on the nature of the product, the market the goods are produced for and the standards achieved by competitors in the same market.

Budgets are statements of the desired future performance of the organisation usually expressed in financial terms and looking one year ahead.

The range of budgets that the organisation needs for its control follows a typical pattern, with forecasts:

- about the probable economic climate in which the organisation will be operating

- about the activity of the company

- on the likely level of sales and production · about the capital expenditure

- about the cash expenditure.

In a budgetary control system the financial performance of a department is compared with the budget. Action is then taken to improve the department's performance if possible. The elements of the control system are:

- **standard:** the budget (e.g. standard costs)

- **sensor:** the costing system, which records actual costs

- **feedback:** the actual results for the period, collected by the costing system

- **comparator:** the 'performance report' for the department, comparing actual with budget (e.g. variance analysis)

- **effector:** the manager of the department, in consultation with others, takes action to minimize future adverse variances and to exploit opportunities resulting from favourable variances.

The opportunity may also be taken to adjust the standard (i.e. the budget) if it is seen to be too easy or too difficult to achieve.

1.6 Systems and procedures

As with most aspects of business administration, there are certain principles that have been built up over a long period. They include the following:

- There should be a smooth flow of work with no bottlenecks.

- Movement of staff should be kept to a minimum.

- Duplication of work should be avoided.

- The best and most effective use of existing specialist attributes should be made.

- Simplicity within systems should be sought. Complications usually lead to misinterpretations and/or mistakes.

- Machines should be used to help staff where appropriate.

Any system must be cost-effective. The benefits should be compared with the cost of implementation and subsequent supervision costs.

The establishment of systems and procedures will ensure that organisational objectives are attained. Data and information are constantly flowing within an organisation, some being generated internally and some stemming from external sources. All of this information must be processed and, to ensure that it is accomplished in the most effective, efficient and economical manner, a system needs to be established.

Although they are not always immediately apparent, every organisation has systems, which are usually referred to as 'office procedures' that outline the operations necessary to perform a task associated with the receipt, recording, arrangement, storage, security and communication of information.

Sometimes these procedures are formalised by the preparation of 'laid-down' or written procedures in an office manual format stating the system, as it should be. These written instructions should indicate clearly what is required to be done, when, where and how. There are, however, advantages and disadvantages associated with manuals. A list of the advantages would include the following:

The preparation requires careful examination of the systems and procedures. This close attention can only be of benefit in that strengths and weaknesses are revealed.

- Supervision is easier.

- It helps the induction and training of new staff.

- It assists the organisation in pinpointing areas of responsibility.

- Once they are written down, systems and procedures are easier to adapt and/or change in response to changing circumstances.

The disadvantages include:

- The expense in preparing manuals both in the obvious financial terms and the perhaps less obvious cost of administrative time.

- To be of continuing use an office manual must be updated periodically, again incurring additional expense.

- The instructions that are laid down in the office manual may be interpreted rather strictly and implemented too rigidly. Within any organisation it is often beneficial for employees to bring a degree of flexibility to their duties to cope with particular circumstances.

1.7 The review of office procedures

Systems should be kept under continuous review and altered as necessary to reflect changes in the organisation, advances in technology, or indeed suggestions from the staff as to how systems can be improved. The decision to review the office procedures could stem from weaknesses that may have already been highlighted (for instance, too much paperwork).

A review may be divided into two parts:

(i)   an overview of the office and the role it plays within the organisation, which will consider:

- the purpose of the office

- what actually happens within the office

- who does what within the office

- the techniques and methods employed by staff in carrying out assigned responsibilities

- the quality of performance

(ii)   a detailed step-by-step examination of the procedures themselves.

The establishment of such information is vital as a first stage. After this a more detailed analysis of the day-to-day routine may be attempted.

 Activity 1 (no feedback)

Does your office incorporate the procedures into some form of office procedure manual, or in the form of a duty list issued to staff? You might like to review the current system for your project.

2   Critical external relationships

2.1   Stakeholder analysis

All enterprises must consider carefully the elements that comprise their environment. A method or model for understanding the relationship between an organisation and its environment is to consider the various groups, both internal and external, that can affect or be affected by the accomplishment of its objectives. Each of these groups has a 'stake' in the survival of an enterprise. Assessing the expectations of stakeholders enables an organisation to gauge whether its objectives will provide the means to satisfy their demands.

Stakeholders can be defined as groups or individuals who have an interest or 'stake' in what the organisation does. They directly influence an organisation and include the following:

- Shareholders – are the owners of companies and the suppliers of any additional risk capital that may be required. They are generally concerned with a steady flow of income (e.g. dividends),possible capital growth and continuation of the business. For example, if an organisation wishes to follow a strategy that will involve a large capital injection, the shareholders will be unhappy if the injection has an adverse effect on their income stream.

- Managers – are generally concerned with pay and status, job security and individual performance measures. If an organisation wishes to follow a strategy that results in a particular department being reduced in size or abolished, the manager of that department is likely to be hostile to the plans.

- Employees – are generally concerned with job security, pay and conditions and job satisfaction. For example, if an organisation wishes to follow a strategy that results in workers being given more responsibility for monitoring quality, the employees may be unhappy unless this increased role is supported by an increase in wages.

- Trade unions – apart from the problems of the employees noted above, unions within an organisation are generally concerned with taking an active part in the decision-making process. For example, if an organisation wishes to follow a strategy that results in a manufacturing plant being closed, the union will be unhappy if it has not been consulted and if there is no scheme for helping the employees to find alternative employment.

- Customers – are generally concerned with receiving goods and services of a reasonable quality and paying a reasonable price for them. For example, if an organisation wishes to follow a strategy that increases the quality of a product at the same time as increasing the price, there may be problems with both existing and potential new customers. Existing customers may not be willing to pay more for the product, while new customers are not attracted to a product that they still view as being of low quality.

- Suppliers – are generally concerned with being paid promptly for goods and services delivered and receiving regular repayments of any capital provided (e.g. banks). For example, if an organisation wishes to follow a strategy that improves working capital management by paying suppliers late, existing suppliers may decide to stop supplying the organisation, leading to the increased cost of finding new suppliers.

- Government and the general public – are generally concerned that the organisation is meeting relevant legal requirements and that it does not harm the outside environment. For example, if an organisation wishes to follow a strategy that relies on increased use of shops based in out-of-town retail centres, this will be affected by government attitudes towards increased road building and society's attitude towards this method of shopping.

2.2 Legislation and regulations

The law constitutes a set of environmental factors that are increasingly affecting organisations and their decision-making. Most of the nations of the world are, or are becoming, regulated economies. Government, or self, regulation of business has four principal aims.

- To protect business entities – e.g. laws putting limits on market dominance by acting against monopolies and restrictive practices and providing financial assistance to selected ailing industries and companies.

- To protect consumers – with many detailed consumer protection regulations covering packaging, labelling, food hygiene and advertising, and much more.

- To protect employees – with laws governing the recruitment of staff and health and safety legislation that regulates conditions of work.

- To protect the interests of society at large against excessive business behaviour, e.g. by acting to protect the environment.

Also at the most basic level, perhaps, laws are passed that enable Government to levy taxes, whereas company law affects the corporate structure of the business and prescribes the duties of company directors.

Managers cannot plan intelligently without a good working knowledge of the laws and regulations that affect their own companies and the businesses they operate in. In addition to those laws that apply generally to all companies, such as laws regulating Corporation Tax or Value Added Tax, there are laws specifically used to deal with individual industries, e.g. Petroleum Revenue Tax in the offshore oil and gas industry.

There is an almost endless list of laws or categories of legislation that affect business enterprises, in domestic, national or international dimensions. The main categories are listed below:

- Local by-laws (planning permission, construction of roads, licences, etc).

- Labour legislation (safety at work, employee protection, redundancy payments, etc).

- The Data Protection Act – the underlying principles behind the legislation are openness, good practice in obtaining and using data, and an opportunity for redress when an individual has cause for complaint. The Act places obligations on those who use personal data. They must be open about that use – through registering with the Data Protection Registrar, and they must follow a code of good practice – the Data Protection Principles.

- Trade union legislation.

- Consumer protection legislation.

- Company legislation.

- Taxation legislation (VAT returns must be submitted at regular intervals. Payroll involves keeping records and submitting returns to the Inland Revenue)

- Anti-trust (monopolies) legislation and rulings.

- Trade legislation (countries restricted for export, etc).

- Business legislation (contract and agency law, etc).

- Social legislation (welfare benefits, etc).

2.3 Regulations affecting accounting practice

The contents and presentation of financial statements that must be presented to a company's shareholders in the UK are influenced by the following regulations:

- The Companies Act 1985 and Companies Act 1989

- Regulations of various types issued by the accountancy profession

- EC directives.

- Tax regulations – where the organisation runs a PAYE system and/or is registered for VAT, these regulations have a significant impact on the timing of accounts work since the returns are required every month for payroll and every three months (generally) for VAT and must be ready on time to comply with these requirements.

- Stock Exchange regulations – companies that are 'listed' commit themselves to certain procedures and standards that are more extensive than the disclosure requirements of the Companies Acts.

2.4 The Companies Act 1985 (CA85)

The accounting requirements of CA85 can be summarised as follows.

Formats – CA85 lays down basic formats for the published profit and loss account and balance sheet. These formats are mandatory only in the accounts of companies (not in those of sole traders, etc).

– CA85 gives valuation rules for fixed and current assets, together with the alternative accounting rules.

Fundamental concepts – CA85 refers to certain fundamental concepts, which must be observed in preparing accounts:

- going concern

- prudence

- consistency

- matching

- separate determination.

True and fair – the overriding principle is that financial statements must show a true and fair view. This is a concept rather than a rule that can easily be defined.

At a basic level, a set of financial statements, which follows accounting standards and fundamental concepts, will prima facie (on the face of it) show a true and fair view.

2.5 Regulations issued by the accountancy profession

To regulate and standardise the preparation of financial statements in the UK, the accountancy profession issues accounting standards.

Accounting standards comprise Financial Reporting Standards (FRSs) issued by the Accounting Standards Board (ASB) and SSAPs adopted by the ASB (having been published originally by the ASB's predecessor body, the Accounting Standards Committee (ASC).

- Compliance with accounting standards is normally required in order to show a true and fair view.

- Standards need not be applied to immaterial items.

- Departure from the requirements of accounting standards is only permitted in exceptional cases where compliance would be incompatible with showing a true and fair view.

- Preparers of accounts must be guided by the spirit and reasoning of standards when applying them.

(a) **The Financial Reporting Council**

To enforce observance of accounting standards, the UK accountancy profession has established a Financial Reporting Council (FRC) made up of about 25 members who are a combination of users, preparers and auditors of financial statements. The FRC then governs two companies as follows:

- The Financial Reporting Review Panel

- The Accounting Standards Board (ASB).

(b) **The Financial Reporting Review Panel**

(c) **The Accounting Standards Board (ASB)**

The ASB has the aim of establishing and improving standards of financial accounting and reporting, for the benefit of users, preparers and auditors of financial information.

The ASB is achieving this aim by the following means:

- developing a conceptual framework (Statement of Principles)
- issuing new accounting standards (or amending existing ones)
- addressing urgent issues promptly.

The ASB identify an area of accounting that may need revision. This may be due to any of the following:

- inadequacy of an existing standard, which permits choices or is vague, thereby producing unsatisfactory results
- non-compliance of UK standards with International Accounting Standards
- improving the basic disclosure rules laid down in CA85.

The ASB will then issue a discussion paper and invite comments from interested parties. The discussion paper will outline the problem and a range of possible solutions.

Following review of comments a Financial Reporting Exposure Draft (FRED) will be issued. This is the proposed accounting standard. Again, comments are invited from interested parties.

The FRS is then issued in its final form, usually subject to minor revisions from the FRED.

Apart from accounting standards, you also need to be aware of Statements of Recommended Practice (SORPS).

SORPs deal with the following issues:

- matters of widespread application, but which are not of fundamental importance
- matters of limited application (i.e. relating only to a specific industry).

SORPs are originally developed by the particular industry involved and then can be endorsed by the ASB. One example is Accounting by Charities.

(d) **Urgent Issues Task Force (UITF)**

The UITF assists the ASB in areas where an accounting standard or Companies Act provision already exists, but where unsatisfactory or conflicting interpretation has developed. It deals with issues that need a fast response to establish best practice.

2.6   Generally Accepted Accounting Practice (GAAP)

The concept of GAAP stems from US accounting. In the UK we publish financial statements, which show a 'true and fair' view. In the US the reference is to conforming to GAAP.

Although GAAP is not often referred to in the UK it comprises the whole set of accounting practices which have authoritative support amongst users of financial statements.

There will be crossovers between accounting standards and GAAP where standards reflect GAAP. However, there may be a GAAP that is not represented by a standard.

UK GAAP extends further than accounting standards alone to include the requirements of the Companies Acts and The Stock Exchange.

 Activity 2

As a supervisor of an accounts section, how might you be involved in the critical external relationships of the organisation?

3   External analysis

3.1   Components

External analysis involves an examination of the relevant elements external to an organisation. It should be purposeful, focusing on the identification of opportunities, threats and strategic choices.

The aim of the external analysis is to identify and understand the opportunities and threats facing the organisation, both present and potential. A threat is a trend or event that will have no strategic response as well as a significant downward departure from current sales and profit patterns e.g. consumers' concern for healthy eating and foods that affect cholesterol represents a threat to the dairy industry. An opportunity is a trend or event that could lead to a significant upward change in sales and profit patterns, given a suitable strategic response.

There are four components of external analysis – customer analysis, competitive analysis, industry analysis and environmental analysis.

(i)   Customer analysis – identifies the organisation's customer segments and each segment's motivations and unmet needs.

(ii) Competitive analysis – covers the identification of current and potential competitors. Some competitors will compete more intensely than others and, although they should be examined in more detail, all competitors are usually relevant to the strategy development.

(iii) Industry analysis – market or industry analysis has two main objectives. The first is to measure the attractiveness of the market and of the individual sub-markets to find out whether competitors will earn attractive profits or lose money. The market will be no place to invest if it is so difficult that everyone is losing money. The second objective is to understand the dynamics of the market so that threats and opportunities can be detected and strategies formed. The analysis will include an examination of the market size, profitability, growth, cost structure, channels, trends and key (or critical) success factors.

(iv) Environmental analysis – important forces outside an organisation and its immediate markets and competitors will shape its operation and thrust. Environmental analysis will attempt to identify and understand emerging opportunities and threats created by these forces. It is important to limit environmental analysis to the manageable and relevant, because it can easily get bogged down with excessive volume and scope.

One approach to carrying out an environmental analysis is to conduct a PEST analysis

3.2 PEST analysis

Organisational performance will be dependent on the successful management of the opportunities, challenges and risks presented by changes in the external environment. The organisation exists in the context of a complex commercial, economic, political, technological, cultural and social world. This environment is more complex for some organisations than for others and an understanding of its effects is of central importance when deciding on strategies. The historical and environmental effects on the business must be considered, as well as the present effects and the expected changes in environmental variables.

The wider environment in which the enterprise and its industry are located can be subdivided into four sectors:

- Political/legal environment

- Economic environment

- Social/cultural environment

- Technological environment.

An analysis of the political, economic, social and technological dimensions, which can influence the organisation, is commonly known as a PEST analysis.

3.3 The political/legal environment

Political influence will include legislation on trading, pricing, dividends, tax, employment, government stability, monopolies legislation, environmental protection laws and foreign trade regulations, as well as health and safety.

The organisation must react to the attitude of the political party that is in power at the time. The government is the nation's largest supplier, employer, customer and investor and any change in government spending priorities can have a significant impact on a business.

Because the addition or removal of legislative or regulatory constraints can pose major strategic threats and opportunities, the organisation needs to know:

- What changes in regulations are possible and what will their impact be?

- What tax or other incentives are being developed that might affect strategy?

3.4 The economic environment

General economic conditions and trends are critical to the success of an organisation. They include interest rates and the availability of credit, inflation, the balance of trade and exchange rates, business cycles, the level of unemployment, disposable income, government subsidies and energy availability and cost.

Economic indicators measure national income and output (GNP), savings, investment, prices, wages, productivity, employment, government activities and international transactions. All these factors vary over time and managers could devote much of their organisation's time and resources to forecasting the economy and anticipating changes because wages, price changes by suppliers and competitors, and government policies affect both the costs of producing products or offering services and the market conditions under which they are sold.

International economic issues may also be important to the organisation. These could include:

(a)   the extent of protectionist measures

(b)   comparative rates of growth, inflation, wages and taxation

(c)   the freedom of capital movement

(d)   economic agreements

(e)   relative exchange rates.

The organisation needs to know what the economic prospects and inflation forecasts are for the countries that it operates in and how they will affect strategy.

3.5 The social/cultural environment

The social/cultural environment includes population demographics, social mobility, income distribution, lifestyle changes, attitudes to work and leisure, levels of education and consumerism.

The social/cultural factors include changes in tastes and lifestyles. They may also include changes in the demographic make-up of a population. For example in Western Europe people are living longer and in many countries the birth rate is falling, leading to an ageing population. This has obvious implications for the types of products and services that organisations may plan to offer. Typical questions that need to be answered include:

- What are the current and emerging trends in lifestyles and fashion?

- What demographic trends will affect the size of the market or its sub-markets?

- Does the trend represent opportunities or threats?

3.6 The technological environment

The level of technology in a particular industry determines to a large extent which products and services will be produced, what equipment will be used, and how operations will be managed. Government institutions, independent research establishments, universities, and large corporations all carry out basic research. Independent entrepreneurs, business firms, and some government agencies carry the developments out of the laboratory and into the marketplace. The environment is influenced by government spending on research, new discoveries and development, government and industry focus of technological effort, speed of technological transfer (i.e. the speed at which knowledge developed in R & D centres can be utilised to fulfil public and private needs) and rates of obsolescence.

This is an area in which change takes place very rapidly and the organisation needs to be constantly aware of what is going on. Technological change can influence the following:

- changes in production techniques

- the type of products that are made and sold

- how services are provided

- how we identify markets.

Technological factors may include changes in retailing methods (such as direct selling via the Internet), changes in production methods (greater use of automation), and greater integration between buyers and suppliers via computer link-ups. The managers would need to know to what extent the existing technologies are maturing and what technological developments or trends are affecting or could affect the industry. The effect of technological development and change includes the following:

- markets and customers analysed more effectively (using sophisticated databases)

- new products and services being developed

- changes in work methods leading to a reduction in production and other costs

- better quality products and services at no increased cost

- products and services available and delivered quicker or more effectively than previously

- employees freed from repetitive work and able to demonstrate more creativity

- short product life cycles – an organisation needs to be innovative.

3.7   PEST checklist

The headings can be used as a checklist when analysing the different influences. The organisation can use the checklist to identify which are the most important at the present time and over the next few years. For example:

Political/legal	Economic
Taxation policy	Interest rates
Foreign trade regulations	Inflation
Environmental protection	Unemployment
Anti-monopoly legislation	Disposable income
Government stability	Business cycles
	GNP trends
	Energy availability and cost
Socio-Cultural	**Technological**
Lifestyle changes	New discoveries
Education levels	New developments
Attitudes to leisure	Speed of technology transfer
Consumerism	Rates of obsolescence
	Government spending on R&D

4 SWOT analysis

4.1 Internal and external appraisal

A SWOT analysis consists of the internal appraisal of the organisation's strengths and weaknesses and an external appraisal of the opportunities and threats open to organisations in competition within the industry. Therefore, strengths and weaknesses are peculiar to an individual organisation but opportunities and threats are open to all organisations within the market place. The purpose of the analysis is to outline the company's present position in the market place.

Strengths are those positive factors or distinctive attributes or competencies that provide a significant competitive advantage that the organisation can build on. These are characteristics of the organisation e.g. present market position, size, structure, managerial expertise, physical or financial resources, staffing, image or reputation. Searching out opportunities that match its strengths helps the organisation to optimise the effects of synergy.

Weaknesses are negative aspects in the organisation e.g. deficiencies in the present competencies or resources, or its image or reputation, which limit its effectiveness and which need to be corrected. Examples of weaknesses include limited accommodation, high fixed costs, a bureaucratic structure, a high level of customer complaints or a shortage of key managerial staff.

Opportunities are favourable conditions that usually arise from the nature of changes in the external environment e.g. new markets, improved economic factors or a failure of competitors. Opportunities provide the organisation with the potential to offer new or to develop existing products, facilities or services.

Threats are the opposite of opportunities and also arise from external developments. Examples include unfavourable changes in legislation, the introduction of a radically new product by a competitor, political or economic unrest, changing social conditions or the actions of a pressure group.

The internal appraisal (strengths and weaknesses) should identify:

- the organisation's strengths that any new project may be able to exploit

- organisational weaknesses that may impact on the project.

The main areas considered would include:

- **products** e.g. age, life span, life cycle stage, quality comparisons

- **marketing** e.g. market share, presence in target segments, identifiable and non identifiable benefits, success of promotions, advertising

- **distribution** e.g. delivery promise performance, depot location

- **production** e.g. age/obsolescence, valuation, capacity

- **research and development** e.g. number of commercially viable products, costs/benefits, relevance of projects

- **human resources** e.g. manpower plan, management in depth, training levels, morale

- **finance** e.g. cash availability, risk exposure, short and long-term funding, contribution levels.

The external appraisal should identify opportunities that can be exploited by the organisation (such as growth in market demand, or new technological possibilities) and should help managers anticipate environmental threats e.g. competitors' actions, declining economy, legislation, etc.

Opportunities and threats could be expected to arise in five main areas – four of which we have already discussed in the PEST analysis. The fifth area is competitors e.g. cheap imports, closure of export markets, potential entrants, sources of raw material.

SWOT analysis is a commonly-used business planning tool. Although the SWOT analysis is most often carried out on an organisation, as part of the strategic planning process, it can be applied to a department, section or project just as easily.

4.2 The SWOT analysis process

The idea is to undertake a more structured analysis so as to yield findings that can contribute to the formulation of strategy. An outline of a SWOT analysis process is shown on the next page.

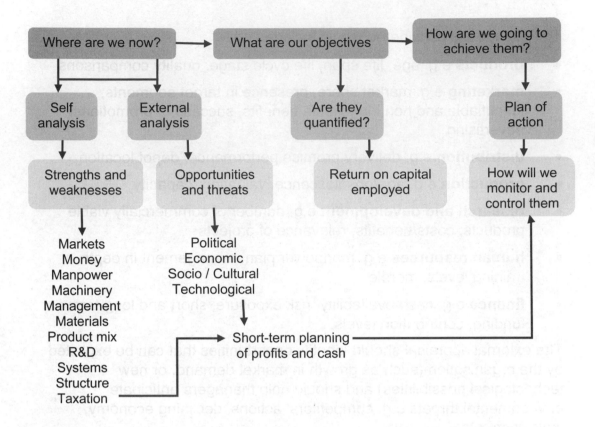

The strengths and weaknesses refer to the internal aspects of the organisation compared both to the expectations of the market place and to the competition i.e. what the organisation is relatively good and bad at doing. The external analysis aims to highlight opportunities and threats i.e. potential constraints for the organisation. In the light of both the internal and external analyses, previously established objectives may be seen as either unachievable or set at too low a level and some of the objectives may have to be modified.

The internal and external appraisals will be brought together and perhaps shown in some form of chart so that potential strategies can be identified. For example, the results below could be from a police force:

Strengths	**Weaknesses**
Committed employees	Under-capacity
Good community links	Reactive approach
New equipment	IT systems
Operational planning	Financial planning systems

Opportunities	**Threats**
Socio-cultural	
New technologies in	Increase in major crime
communications	New legislation
Public expectations	

5 Checklist of tasks

- Write a short paragraph on your organisation's background, history and environment.

- Identify your organisation's main competitors, suppliers and customers or market areas.

6 Test your knowledge

Test your knowledge

1 An organisation's inputs are transformed through certain managerial functions. Can you identify them?

2 Explain quality control as a control system.

3 Outline the elements of a budgetary control system in which the financial performance of a department is compared with the budget.

4 As stakeholders, what are the main concerns of employees?

5 What are the four components of external analysis?

6 One approach to carrying out an environmental analysis is to conduct a PEST analysis. What does the acronym PEST stand for?

7 How can technological change affect the organisation?

8 Which environment analysis includes income distribution, lifestyle changes, attitudes to work and leisure, levels of education and consumerism?

9 Why would you do a SWOT analysis?

7 Summary

This chapter should have given you an overview of the organisation's business in terms of the environment in which it operates and its external relationship in that environment.

The environment of a company is not just the area where it is situated or where it gets its raw materials. It includes society, the government, the law, the economy, customers, competitors, technology and many other factors.

Managers must be aware of how the environment influences the company and how the company affects it. Changes in the environment must be expected and foreseen where possible.

Answers to chapter activities and 'test your knowledge' questions

Activity 1

Critical external relationships that involve the accounting department include investors, customers, suppliers and the government.

Most business organisations exist to provide a return to shareholders. Investors may be institutional, venture capital firms or private investors who own the organisation's shares. Some firms run schemes enabling employees to acquire shares, perhaps at a reduced option price and this may be a responsibility of your section. Banks lend long-term and also provide overdraft finance, giving them an intimate knowledge of the cash flows of the business, which your section might have to produce. Factors often 'buy' a company's debts for a fee in order to collect them. Lease companies enable firms to buy expensive items of equipment.

Businesses have to satisfy customers to generate a return. You may be involved in delivering products and services that live up to expectations; in assuring customers of fair treatment; and in the redress of any grievances, complaints or replacements for any defective items.

Suppliers are stakeholders because the organisation is their customer. You may be involved in developing a long-term relationship with a supplier, ensuring a sufficient volume of business and payment on time.

The government shapes the environment of organisations in many ways. You may be required to understand the issues associated with the minimum wage, discrimination, job security, working hours and/or redundancy payments. Your organisation will probably collect PAYE and VAT and pay corporation tax and there are also legal requirements to produce financial information (for example, annual returns, annual report and accounts).

You may also come across pressure groups. Some companies report on their 'environmental' performance and give statistics relevant to pollution and recycling in their annual report and accounts. This in part is in response to pressure from groups for them to be socially responsible.

Test your knowledge

1   An organisation's inputs are transformed through the managerial functions of planning, organising, staffing, leading and controlling.

2   Quality control is the control system of setting quality standards, measuring performance against those standards and taking corrective action when necessary. The standard aimed for will depend on the nature of the product, the market for which the goods are produced and the standards achieved by competitors in the same market.

3   The elements of the control system are:

- standard: the budget (e.g. standard costs)

- sensor: the costing system, which records actual costs

- feedback: the actual results for the period, collected by the costing system

- comparator: the 'performance report' for the department, comparing actual with budget (e.g. variance analysis)

- effector: the manager of the department, in consultation with others, takes action to minimise future adverse variances and to exploit opportunities resulting from favourable variances.

4   Employees are generally concerned with job security, pay and conditions and job satisfaction.

5   There are four components of external analysis – customer analysis, competitive analysis, industry analysis and environmental analysis.

6   The wider environment in which the enterprise and its industry are located can be analysed by subdividing it into four sectors known as a PEST analysis.

- Political/legal environment

- Economic environment

- Social/cultural environment

- Technological environment

7   Technological change can influence production techniques, the type of products that are made and sold, how services are provided and how we identify markets.

8   The social/cultural environment includes population demographics, social mobility, income distribution, lifestyle changes, attitudes to work and leisure, levels of education and consumerism.

9   You would do a SWOT analysis to outline the company's present position in the market place.

It consists of the internal appraisal of the organisation's strengths and weaknesses and an external appraisal of the opportunities and threats open to organisations in competition within the industry. Therefore, strengths and weaknesses are peculiar to an individual organisation but opportunities and threats are open to all organisations within the market place.

Fraud in an accounting system 5

Introduction

The management of the risk of fraud is a matter for all levels of an organisation. Senior management should strive to create an anti-fraud culture, which should involve the entire organisation. For example, the culture will result in personnel managers considering the security elements of different posts, assessing what backgrounds are not appropriate for potential post holders. The IT department will keep up to date with the techniques of computer hackers, and the measures that can be taken against them.

An important consideration in the implementation of fraud management strategies and policies is the concept of communication. Effective lines of communication, when built in to the organisational structure, allow staff at all levels to pass on their local knowledge of procedures, processes and activities to decision-making senior staff, providing them with insights into possible areas of fraud that they would not have otherwise understood.

KNOWLEDGE	CONTENTS
2.2 Describe the causes of and common types of fraud and the impact on the organisation.	1 Types of fraud
	2 Implications of fraud
2.3 Explain methods that can be used to detect fraud within an accounting system.	3 Detecting fraud
	4 Preventing fraud
2.4 Explain the types of controls that can be put in place to ensure compliance with statutory or organisational requirements.	5 Fraud policy and contingency plans
	6 Checklist of tasks

1 Types of fraud

1.1 Introduction

Fraud can be perpetrated by many groups: third parties, a company's employees, the company's management, suppliers or customers. Because of the risk of embarrassment and resulting reduction in the level of customer or shareholder confidence, much fraud is not reported. Consequently it is difficult to estimate the losses to business, but it is estimated as several hundred million pounds each year in the UK alone. And of the reported frauds, a majority of the worst kind are committed by a company's own employees or managers.

The start of any programme to prevent fraud is first to identify the types of fraud, then to identify the risks of it happening in a particular organisation and next to devise control procedures to prevent it or detect it.

1.2 What is fraud?

No precise legal definition of fraud exists, though many of the offences referred to as fraud are covered by the Theft Acts 1968 and 1978. It is for the court to determine in a particular instance whether fraud has occurred. Auditors need to be alert to conduct that may be dishonest before considering whether it may be fraudulent. The term is often used to describe such acts as deception, bribery, forgery, extortion, corruption, theft, conspiracy, embezzlement, misappropriation, false representation, concealment of material facts and collusion. Fraud comprises both the use of deception to obtain an unjust or illegal financial advantage and intentional misrepresentations affecting the financial statements by one or more individuals among management, employees, or third parties.

Fraud may involve:

- falsification or alteration of accounting records or other documents

- misappropriation of assets or theft

- suppression or omission of the effects of transactions from records or documents

- recording of transactions without substance

- intentional misapplication of accounting policies, or

- wilful misrepresentations of transactions or of the entity's state of affairs.

There are two main types of irregularity which are of concern:

- Theft – dishonestly appropriating the property of another with the intention of permanently depriving them of it (Theft Act 1968). This may include the removal or misuse of funds, assets or cash.

   Some theft, particularly of tangible assets such as computer or telephone equipment, can be opportunistic and may not always involve deception. A theft does not therefore necessarily fit into the general perception of 'fraud'. However, theft carried out by, or involving, departmental staff usually involves some element of deceit such as denial of the offence or concealment when removing the asset from the premises. Cases of theft are therefore included in this analysis of fraud involving departmental staff.

- False accounting – dishonestly destroying, defacing, concealing or falsifying any account, record or document required for any accounting purpose, with a view to personal gain or gain for another, or with the intent to cause loss to another or furnishing information which is or may be misleading, false or deceptive (Theft Act 1968).

1.3 Common frauds

The first step towards combating fraud is to recognise the many different forms that it can take. Although the facts are never quite the same in any two cases, there are always certain features in common.

Theft – any business assets can be stolen, whether by employees or management, acting alone or in collusion with third parties. This may involve the theft of stock, commonly known as shrinkage. Computer equipment is particularly vulnerable here. There are incidences of theft that will go unnoticed because of the scale of the crime. Small amounts of cash taken from the till of a retailer or the petty cash box in an office might not be noticed because the sums involved are not significant enough to have any impact on the organisation. Many employees think nothing of taking pens and paper from the stationery cupboard to stock up their home supply.

There are thefts that are for significant amounts. The last cheques in the company's cheque book can be taken out and the thief can do a passable imitation of a couple of authorised signatures, clear the funds, withdraw and disappear. No one realises until the bank statement comes, so it may be weeks, or months before they realise they are missing a quarter of a million pounds. The theft of intellectual property, perhaps in the form of customer or price lists, also falls into this category. Staff who are sure of not being challenged may submit false expense claims, covering anything from private entertainment to large-scale projects. Theft from a company may also take the form of payroll fraud where payments to former or fictitious employees are diverted to the fraudster's own bank account.

Collusion is a common element in frauds whereby individuals pool their resources to achieve their aims – specialist skills might not be available to the individual acting independently. Employees can collude with customers, with other employees or with friends. In the case of fraud involving collusion with a third party, money may be taken from unsuspecting customers on the promise of spectacular returns or as an advance fee. Or the customer may not be an innocent dupe but may in fact be acting in collusion with the staff member. Such cases may involve the payment of kickbacks or commission from a supplier as a reward for being awarded that contract. These are particularly difficult to detect since the kickback is paid directly to the employee and does not go through the company's books. Sometimes it happens that an employee has an undisclosed interest in a transaction that results in harm to the business because the price of the contract is not the best that the company could get.

There is a great deal of talk about computer fraud but in fact it could be argued that there is no such thing. What is usually meant is that fraud is carried out using a computer rather than traditional methods of paper and pen. The computer is simply the mechanism for perpetrating the fraud. Computers may be used to disguise the true nature of a transaction by manipulating the date records and programs, to hack into an organisation's computer system to steal or manipulate information or for the unauthorised electronic transfer of funds. On the Internet fraudsters may pose as a legitimate business to obtain payment for goods that are either not delivered or are of significantly lower quality. While there are legal obstacles to a successful prosecution, such as jurisdiction and privacy rights, computers also generate a great deal of admissible evidence.

Some companies are seeking to appoint 'computer fraud experts', but are having great difficulty in defining the special skills and experience such a person would require.

Computer fraud may be summarised as the use of information technology resources to commit or conceal a criminal offence or civil wrong. Computer fraud typically includes:

- financial fraud
- sabotage of data and/or networks
- theft of proprietary information
- system penetration from the outside, including denial of service attacks

- unauthorised access by insiders, including employee misuse of Internet access privileges; and malicious software (such as viruses, worms, trojans, time bombs, zombies), which is the leading cause of unauthorised users gaining access to systems and networks via the internet.

False accounting – the main aim of false accounting is to present the results and affairs of the organisation in a better light than the reality. Frequently, there are commercial pressures to report an unrealistic level of earnings, which can take precedence over controls designed to prevent fraud.

Management may occasionally wish to '**window dress**' their balance sheet (i.e. present either a better or worse picture than that which can be fairly presented) by a variety of devices. For example, cheques paid are entered before the year-end but are not sent to creditors until after the year-end. Or the cashbook is kept open for some days after the year-end so that money received after the year-end is included in the cashbook balance. This will give an incorrect impression of the company's credit worthiness to a reader of the accounts.

The owners or managers of the company could '**cook the books**' by:

- a misuse of pension funds

- overvaluing assets

- not writing off bad debts and avoiding the effects on profits and assets

- understating depreciation

- understating expenses

- illegally supporting their own company by purchasing shares to force up their value.

Whatever the purpose of the fraud, the feature common to all cases is the need to falsify records, alter figures, and perhaps keep two sets of books. In every instance, it is only a matter of time before the 'hole' cannot be hidden any longer and the fraud is exposed.

Some of the most dramatic corporate collapses and high-profile fraud trials have been characterised by false accounting used to cover up extensive fraud or theft within the business. Recent times have seen the end of huge multinationals such as Enron and WorldCom, both of which fraudulently inflated their profits by deliberately misstating revenues to disguise mounting losses.

Although the aim is always to present the business in a flattering light, the reasons for doing so can be as varied as the ways in which it is achieved. In some cases the purpose is to deceive the bank into providing more finance. The bank reconciliation may also be manipulated to cover up a theft. The target of the deception may be a customer, who is more likely to be attracted by a successful company, or it may be a regulator whose intervention can be prevented or delayed. Another common practice is the abuse of a slush fund under the discretion of executive management.

False accounting is obviously carried out by insiders – either employees or management who are in a position to override the normal controls and to present figures that are simply not true. By contrast, fraud under the general heading of theft may be carried out by third parties as well as insiders.

 Activity 1

Can you think of three ways that stock can be used to show a false increase in the value of the assets in the company?

1.4 Types of fraud

The following table outlines some of the various types of fraud.

Type of fraud	Examples
False accounting	• Obtaining external financing by falsely improving the results.
	• Raising the share price by false means to aid acquisitions or to help a new issue of shares.
	• Obtaining more business by appearing more successful or less indebted.
	• · Obtaining performance bonuses for managers by inflating profits.
	• Covering up internal theft by altering, adding, falsifying or deleting bank/stock/purchase or other records. A fictitious customer can be created. Orders can be sent, goods despatched on credit and the 'customer' can neglect to pay their bill. The debt is written off.
	• Hiding losses in the hopes that fortunes may reverse. Preventing or delaying intervention by a regulator.

Theft	• Direct theft of cash, stock or assets – theft of stock, commonly known as stock shrinkage, can be significant. Computer equipment is particularly vulnerable.
	• Staff can make private telephone calls (to friends in Australia).
	• Employees can fiddle their time sheets and claim for overtime hours they did not work or claim a higher rate for the job.
	• Employees can claim to have purchased supplies in excess of the actual amount or there is no control on prices charged and the employee could be keeping a percentage of the takings.
	• Theft of intellectual property – customer lists, contract prices, etc.
	• False expense claims – this can be anything from claiming for private entertainment expenses to large-scale projects, and relies on the claimant being sure that the expense will not be challenged. Expenses can also be deducted from takings without prior authorisation and could thus be inflated.
	• Payroll fraud – diverting ex-employee or fictitious employee payments to one's own bank account.
	• Rolling debtors receipts – misappropriating debtors receipts and substituting subsequent receipts. This is where takings are remitted at irregular intervals, and the rate that they are remitted could be kept permanently behind the rate at which they are actually received (known as teeming and lading). It could mean that substantial sums are available to the employee.
Third-party	• Customers ordering goods on credit with no intention of paying – includes some credit card frauds.
	• Kickbacks or commission from a supplier as a reward for awarding the contract to that supplier. These are particularly difficult to detect, since the kickback is paid direct from the supplier to the employee and does not go through the company's books.
	• Collusion with customers to charge lower prices or raise spurious credit notes.
	• Collusion with suppliers to accept under-deliveries of stock.
	• Related party transactions. A company employee or officer has an undisclosed financial interest in a transaction that causes harm to the business, often because the price of the contract is not the best the company could get.

Computer fraud	• Hacking/unauthorised access to bank accounts to transfer funds.
	• Setting up as a legitimate Internet business and obtaining payment for goods that are either never delivered or are of lower quality than advertised.
	• Theft of intellectual property, e.g. engineering drawings, by unauthorised access to a computer.
	• Publishing malicious claims about the company on anonymous bulletin boards, thus affecting the company's reputation.
	• Disguising the true nature of a transaction by manipulation of date records and programs held on a computer.
	• Hacking into an organisation's computer system to steal or manipulate information.

2 Implications of fraud

2.1 Common features of fraud

Except in the case of investment fraud or some consumer scams, most cases of fraud will impact the company profit and loss account or balance sheet. Frequently fraud will become apparent when investigation reveals one or more of the following:

- Credit notes given to customers for undisclosed or inadequate reasons.

- High level of inventory losses accepted without investigation.

- Suppliers insist on dealing with only one employee in the department.

- Discrepancies in petty cash are not investigated or are written off to 'sundry' expenses.

- Payroll summaries are not checked by department heads or by the HR department.

- Excessive habitual overtime worked without relation to workload.

- High levels of sickness absence not investigated.

- Unduly friendly relations between some employees and their suppliers or service providers.

- Faulty goods are not returned to the supplier for credit or credit notes are not chased up.

- Excessive and constant level of returns to suppliers.

- Company assets are not checked against a fixed asset or stock register.

- Inadequate reconciliation of balance sheet accounts.

- Insufficient justification for balance sheet reserves.

- Unusually high levels of despatches or purchases just prior to the period end.

- Employees' expense claims are not checked and authorised by departmental managers.

- Management appears to condone petty fraud because 'everybody knows about it but never does anything about it'.

- Invoices from some suppliers seem high in relation to the goods or services rendered.

- Amounts are written off the sales ledger without authorisation or investigation.

- Management and supervision are remote from those they control.

- Some branches are in reality uncontrolled because of geography or because no manager has become involved in the branch.

 Activity 2

To be in a position to combat fraud, you need to think like a fraudster. Make a list of the ways expenses can be fiddled.

2.2 Effect of fraud

The way the organisation is affected by the fraud depends on the type of fraud perpetrated.

Type of fraud	Implications
Any fraud that is discovered and addressed.	• Negative publicity can damage the organisation irrevocably by affecting the public's perceptions and consumer confidence. • Consideration must be given to what effect any publicity would have on suppliers and customers. Will suppliers withdraw credit? Will customers look elsewhere for their supplies? Whilst publicity will certainly deter other frauds within the company, its effects on outsiders must be managed. If the case goes to court the facts cannot be prevented from getting out. • Fraudsters may be arrested and, depending on the scale and seriousness of the fraud, may face a custodial sentence.
Theft of funds or assets from the organisation.	• Profits are lower than they should be. Because there is less cash or fewer assets the net asset position is weakened. Returns to shareholders are likely to be reduced as a result. • If the working capital is reduced it can be difficult for the organisation to operate effectively. In the most serious cases of fraud, otherwise successful businesses can collapse e.g. Barings.
Misrepresentation of the financial position of the organisation – results artificially enhanced.	• Too much of the organisation's profits may be distributed to shareholders. • Retained profits will be lower than expected, which could result in a shortfall in working capital – making day-to-day activities more difficult to perform effectively. • Investors making decisions based on inaccurate information may not achieve the expected returns. • Suppliers may extend credit while being misled about the financial position of the organisation.
Misrepresentation of the financial position of the organisation – results under-stated.	• Access to loans may be restricted where assets are under reported. • If the organisation is a listed company, and quoted on the Stock Exchange, the share price might fall and market strength might be eroded. • Returns to investors may be reduced unnecessarily.

3 Detecting fraud

3.1 Questions to pose

The starting point for most fraud detection is to ask yourself how someone could go about making money by defrauding your employer. Someone who knows a lot of detail about the way the business works will probably be able to think of several ways in which a suspected fraud could have been committed. For each possible method of fraud a series of questions should then be asked.

- Who might be involved in this fraud?

- Why would this person risk their job, reputation and future livelihood by committing the fraud?

- How would the person attempt to cover up the fraud?

- Where would the loss appear in the company's accounts?

- Would the fraudster need accomplices either inside or outside the company to carry out the fraud?

- What would be the tell tale signs to look for?

- Who is the best person in the company to look for suspicious signs of fraud?

- Is the company's policy to prevent future frauds or punish existing frauds?

- Is the investigation to be kept secret and if so how does this affect the answers to the above questions?

By answering the above questions for each method of perpetrating the suspected fraud, the company will be well on the way to evolving a fraud detection plan with clear objectives. In particular the following questions will have been answered:

- What are the most effective means of detecting whether fraud has taken place?

- Who should lead the investigation into the suspected fraud?

- What should the company do if fraud is confirmed? At what stage, if any, are the police or others within or without the organisation to be informed?

Activity 3

Why might an employee be motivated to act against their company's interest?

3.2 Conditions for fraud

Fraud is found to be more frequent in organisations with some or all of the following characteristics:

- Domineering management with no effective overseeing board or committee.

- Climate of fear or an unhealthy corporate culture.

- High staff turnover rates in key controlling functions. Long-service staff in stores/ purchasing departments.

- Chronic understaffing in key control areas.

- Frequent changes of legal advisers, auditors or professional advisers.

- Excessive reporting leading to insufficient time for analysis of data.

- Remuneration based very significantly on financial performance.

- Inadequate segregation of duties – e.g. where an individual orders goods, approves the invoices and then authorises the payments.

- Low staff morale/lack of career progression/weak management.

- Excessive hours worked by key staff with insufficient delegation of duties.

- Lack of effective procedures in HR, credit control, inventory control, purchasing or accounts departments. Consistent failure to correct major weaknesses in internal control.

- Management frequently override internal controls.

- Rumours that fraud is not dealt with effectively or at all.

- Inadequate internal reporting or management accounting.

- Loss of records or inadequate documentation about transactions.

- Unusual transactions having a large profit effect.

- Frequent transactions with related parties/no checking that suppliers are appropriate.

- Overly secret dealings with certain clients or suppliers.

- Mismatch between profitability and cash flow.

- Excessive pressure to meet budgets, targets or forecast earnings.

- Personnel not required to take their holiday entitlement.

- When an employee is on holiday leave, the work is left until the employee returns.

- Inadequate responses to queries from management, suppliers, auditors or bankers.

- An employee's habits change or their lifestyle is more affluent than would be expected from their employment.

- Lack of common-sense controls such as changing passwords frequently, requiring two signatures on cheques or restricting access to sensitive areas.

Effective fraud detection requires management to be sufficiently knowledgeable about the mechanics of the business and constantly aware of the need to be vigilant against fraud.

3.3 Uncovering fraud

Discovering fraud can be exceptionally difficult and perhaps the majority of frauds both with and without computers are found by accident. Well-operated controls should prevent fraud taking place but, as one of the ways fraud is committed is to circumvent controls, these may be inadequate to discover it is occurring. There are some key ways of uncovering fraud:

- Perform regular control checks, e.g. stocktaking, cash counts. Often computers are used to cover up non-computer frauds. All frauds have a weak point in having to remove what has been taken (cash or other assets).

- Be aware that fraud might be occurring: have an attitude!

- Look out for signs that there may be a problem: late payments, work backlogs, incomplete audit trails, people with an extravagant life-style, people who are 'experts', confused decision making, multiple interlocking companies or deals, strange payments to countries with strict privacy laws, large transfers before public holidays.

- Don't look first for the complex: many frauds exploit simple missing elements of control.

- Look out for managers who say fraud can't happen in their department and say they have trustworthy staff.

3.4 Risk management

Risk management comprises risk assessment (identifying and analysing risk) and risk control (taking steps to reduce risk, provide contingency plans and monitor improvements). Risk management can be seen as a series of steps:

- Risk identification – producing lists of risk items.

- Risk analysis – assessing the loss probability and magnitude for each item.

- Risk prioritisation – producing a ranked ordering of risk items.

- Risk-management planning – deciding how to address each risk item, perhaps by avoiding, transferring, absorbing or reducing the risk (see below).

- Risk resolution – producing a situation in which risk items are eliminated or resolved.

- Risk monitoring – tracking progress toward resolving risk items and taking corrective action.

Risk analysis – no matter what process is used, the method is always the same:

- Identify the asset.

- Ascertain the risk.

- Determine the vulnerability.

- Implement the corrective action.

For example a table could be drawn up with the headings shown below.

Area of risk	Probability	Impact	Controls	Net likely impact	Action
False accounting: Inflation of assets					
Theft: Expense statement frauds					

The risks to and impact on the systems/applications supporting the organisation's operations may be identified as below:

Threats

- Attempts to access private information
- Malicious attacks
- Fraud
- Pranks
- User error
- Natural disasters
- Sabotage
- Systems/applications supporting the organisation's operations interrupted
- Customer loss of confidence
- Sensitive information disclosed
- Assets lost
- Integrity of data compromised
- Critical services & benefits operations halted
- Failure to meet contractual obligations

Potential Damage

Risks can be handled in a number of different ways.

- Ignore the risks and do nothing – appropriate where the effect of the risk is small and the chances of it occurring remote. Remember – sometimes accepting the risk is the appropriate corrective action. · Purchase insurance against the risk.

- Transfer the risk – e.g. arranging for third parties to complete the riskier parts of the project.

- Protect against the risk – arrange for additional staff to be available at critical parts of the project to minimise the possibility of the project overrunning.

4 Preventing fraud

4.1 Prerequisites for fraud

As with any crime prevention strategy, the key to minimising the risk of fraud lies in understanding why it occurs, identifying business areas that are at risk and implementing procedures to address vulnerable areas. Fraud generally occurs when someone has identified an opportunity, a weakness in the company's systems, and believes that the potential rewards will outweigh the risk of being caught.

There are three prerequisites for fraud to occur: dishonesty, opportunity and motive. All three are usually required – for example an honest employee is unlikely to commit fraud even if given opportunity and motive. The motive for fraud is often simply dissatisfaction, based on being passed over for promotion, inadequate pay or a feeling of carrying more than a fair workload. Just giving employees the opportunity to air their grievances and discuss aspirations could be sufficient to reduce this problem. Employees may also be aware of other problems within the organisation and would welcome some forum where they could come forward.

Most frauds should be prevented by an organisation's system of internal controls. However, there are particular controls that deal specifically with the prevention of the three prerequisites.

Dishonesty will be prevented by careful scrutiny of staff. The fight against fraud should start even before a new employee joins the company. References must be checked thoroughly. Take particular care where temporary employees, particularly those supplied through an agency, are to be employed permanently. Screening and reference checking are frequently overlooked in these circumstances. Fraud will be reduced in a culture of: · severe disciplinary procedures for offenders · moral leadership by management.

Opportunity will be prevented by:

* separation of duties

* input and output controls on computer processing

* control over and testing of new computer programs

* physical security of assets and computer hardware sound internal controls

* controls over forms and documentation, e.g. cheques.

Motivation to commit fraud will be prevented by:

- good employment conditions (e.g. pay)

- instant dismissal where appropriate

- sympathetic grievance procedures.

Most of the above controls are standard internal controls on preventing fraud. In addition to controls to prevent fraud it is important to have a system for detecting fraud covering such areas as:

- an audit trail

- logging of access to files, terminals, books and records

- good documentation of accounting procedures and programs.

Employees and third parties should be encouraged to report their suspicions of fraud or other irregular activity without fear of reprisal. In fact, where the report is made in good faith, the whistleblower is now protected by law.

4.2 Prevention

Prevention of fraud is a two-stage process:

1   ensure that opportunities for fraud are minimised (fraud prevention), and

2   ensure that potential fraudsters believe they will be caught (fraud deterrence).

Fraud prevention – means examining all the key company systems and viewing them with the mindset of a potential fraudster. The review will bring to light a number of weaknesses in the current systems that could be exploited by a fraudster. Having identified the weaknesses in the current systems, the company must then change those systems by introducing new or different controls.

Simple controls are often the most effective and frequently require little management time or effort. For example:

- credit notes over a threshold amount must be explained to and authorised by a senior independent manager before issue.

- inventory write-downs must be investigated before authorisation by an independent manager.

- key balance sheet accounts must be reconciled monthly and the reconciliation reviewed regularly by senior managers.

- fixed assets must be tagged and checked periodically – this can often be combined with the regular testing of electrical and lifting equipment.

- ensure that no goods or assets leave a site without a despatch note or other documentation.

- sickness absence must be monitored and controlled.

- wherever practical, duties must be segregated so that no one person is responsible for both approving expenditure and authorising payment. physical and electronic access to sensitive areas and procedures must be restricted.

- employees must take their vacation entitlement and the work of employees on vacation must be covered by others.

- all employees' expense claims must be authorised by their immediate managers before payment.

- new employees must be screened and their references must be checked.

The introduction and enforcement of controls like these will reduce the opportunities for fraudsters. The controls themselves warn potential fraudsters that management is actively monitoring the business and that in turn deters fraud.

Fraud deterrence – only when potential fraudsters believe fraud will be detected and when whistle-blowers believe they will be protected will there be an effective deterrence of fraud. The most effective ways of detecting fraud have been found to be:

- Internal controls.

- Internal audit.

- Management review.

- Whistle-blowers.

- Change of management. · Anonymous tip-offs.

- Outside information.

- Security of passwords.

- External audit.

- Access/exit controls – operating effective access controls within the premises is obviously essential. Never underestimate the role of security tags, CCTV cameras or other surveillance equipment. Pay particular attention to access controls over computer systems, which should include the rigorous use of passwords, firewalls and other measures to prevent or detect hacking into the system. Significant amounts of information are now held in databases and other formats to aid communication within companies. If not properly managed, this concentration of information constitutes an increased risk.

Fraud is difficult to prevent and detect, but all organisations should institute basic controls. These include:

- segregation of duties (often lost with computerised systems) · employment of honest staff

- a control log or audit trail of all transactions carried out.

 Activity 4

Lots of passwords are very basic. There are top ten password charts published in magazines. Can you guess what the most popular ones are?

5 Fraud policy and contingency plans

5.1 Fraud ethics policy

A fraud ethics policy is intended to show the company's desire to be open and honest in all its dealings, internally and externally. It should be clear that the company values integrity and effort, not merely financial performance, in all dealings with staff, customers and suppliers. It is important to emphasise that the policy applies consistently to all staff, whatever their level. Failure to comply with the policy will be considered a disciplinary offence.

What is considered acceptable and unacceptable behaviour may vary between countries and cultures, therefore specific guidance should be given on this, with reference to the core values of the organisation. The company should give its definition of fraud and provide a detailed list of examples of actions that it considers to be fraud, for example theft of any company property, forgery or alteration of any document such as a cheque, destruction or removal of records, falsifying expense claims, disclosing confidential information to outside parties without authority, or use of company assets for personal use.

The company should explain that unless authorised, personal interests in outside organisations should be avoided. Employees may not act as a director, officer, employee or partner of any other organisation outside the group. Relationships with parties of another organisation should be disclosed to management, who should then ensure that the individual is not involved in any activity in the area of the conflict of interest. If employees find themselves in a position where there is a conflict of interest, this must be disclosed immediately.

The company must make it clear that employees may not accept gifts to a value in excess of what is laid down in the ethics policy. Employees should be advised to use discretion and common sense if accepting modest gifts. All gifts received must be reported and recorded by the company. A similar policy should exist for giving gifts to customers and for entertainment.

The policy should state that employees have a duty of confidentiality to the company and its clients. Information received in the course of employment must not be disclosed to persons outside the group. Information received must not be used for an employee's own benefit or the benefit of others. The policy should make it clear that employees are obliged to report suspicions of fraud or irregular activity.

Finally, the fraud ethics policy must state that all suspicions and reports of fraud will be treated seriously and investigated. The fraud contingency plan will be implemented and appropriate action taken, which could include police involvement.

 Activity 5 (no feedback)

Check whether your company has a fraud policy statement. There may be opportunities for improvement in the system relating to the policy.

5.2 It's fraud – what now?

When the unthinkable happens and fraud is suspected, what do you do next? Whom should you tell and whom should you not tell? Who should investigate and what powers would the investigators be able to exercise? What should you do with regards to the suspect? What are you going to do with any information that is obtained? How can the organisation go about getting its money back?

When faced with the suggestion that fraud has been perpetrated against them, companies react in different ways. For some, it is critical that no hint of the matter ever comes to light; they only want to recover the lost funds. Others believe that to maximise the impact of their corporate code of ethics, action should be taken and should be seen to be taken against the perpetrator and that this is more important than recovering the money.

Few companies have established and agreed procedures for handling suspected fraud. Yet, if the suspicion and supporting evidence are handled in the wrong way, considerable damage can be done to the organisation's finances and reputation.

5.3 Fraud contingency plan

Many organisations have disaster recovery procedures in place in the event of fire, bomb explosion or major computer failure. Few have established and agreed procedures for handling suspected fraud. Yet, if the suspicion and supporting evidence are handled in the wrong way, considerable damage can be done to the organisation's finances and reputation.

A fraud contingency plan provides the route map that enables the company to undertake an investigation that meets its objectives and protects its interests. This plan identifies fraud risks in each area from management, employees, third parties or through collusion; implements appropriate controls; determines who will lead the investigation as well as the objectives and powers of the investigation team; and decides on how to work with the police and handle publicity.

In the initial stages, an investigation is likely to be undertaken by company personnel and/or external investigators, perhaps forensic accountants. At a later stage it is of particular benefit to use private organisations and forensic specialists to establish and assess the facts, which can then be handed over to the police in the event of a criminal prosecution.

No matter how suspicion was aroused, it is essential to ascertain as soon as possible who is implicated. Where the suspect is an employee, the designation and position of the suspect may determine the financial damage that could be caused, the reputation damage that could result if the matter became known publicly, the parties to be informed and the action to be taken.

Fundamental to any investigation is the documentary information, which may be what first aroused suspicion, and will subsequently provide the evidence that an irregularity has occurred. It is essential to ensure that this information cannot be destroyed, altered or removed from the company's control.

Internal and external publicity must be managed in order to avoid scare mongering, while those who need to know are kept informed. A carefully managed media strategy can help to deflect criticism and concerns about the organisation's stability.

Activity 6

Someone in your organisation should be aware of the 'latest' fraud scams so that precautions taken can be as up-to-date as possible. Did you know that it is possible to park your van near a building, pick up radio waves from the air and read what is on the MD's computer screen? It is also easy to buy a machine that reads and writes the magnetic strips on credit cards. What could you do with a fax card plugged into the computer?

6 Checklist of tasks

Start by identifying any opportunities for fraud in your chosen section. Include any past examples of fraud if appropriate. Detail all current procedures in place to reduce opportunities of fraud taking place.

Identify current weaknesses in the systems in place relating to fraud, and suggest improvements.

7 Test your knowledge

 Test your knowledge

1   Explain the term 'window dressing'.

2   The information systems security is based on three elements. What are they?

3   Identify five types of false accounting.

4   Give an example of collusion.

5   List as many types of computer fraud that you can.

6   How would you go about uncovering fraud?

7   Outline the four ways that risks can be handled.

8   What are the three prerequisites for fraud to occur?

9   What areas would be covered in a fraud policy statement?

8 Summary

This chapter has identified the risks and common indicators of fraud. You should understand how to evaluate a system and identify potential risk areas and be able to suggest ways of detecting and avoiding incidences of fraud. Detection of fraud is rare and unlikely to be experienced by students, so you must concentrate in your project on how the systems in your place of work prevent fraud and can help in detecting fraud.

Answers to chapter activities and 'test your knowledge' questions

 Activity 1

The ways of artificially inflating the value of stock include the following:

- Instead of being written off, obsolete or damaged stock may be shown at cost on the balance sheet.

- Records can be falsified at the stock count, i.e. generating stock that does not actually exist.

- Returns to suppliers may not be recorded or suppressed until after the year end stock count.

- Similarly with deliveries to customers – the reduction in stock may not be recorded or suppressed until after the year end stock count.

 Activity 2

This list could be really long, but here are a few to start you off:

- You can claim for a meal that you did not have.

- You could take someone with you on business and both stay at the hotel at the company's expense.

- You could use the free 'park and ride' service but charge for parking the car in the city centre.

- You could travel in a group and share petrol costs but claim individually for mileage allowance.

- You could claim for tips that you did not give.

KAPLAN PUBLISHING

Activity 3

There may be a variety of reasons, including:

- envy and resentment of the success of other employees

- frustrations that their own high expectations of rewards or recognition have not been achieved

- greed and selfishness (some employees consider this form of extra earning capacity as a perk)

- the intellectual challenge of beating the system or of having fun.

 Activity 4

The top ones include – FRED (because it is easy to type in), SECRET, PASSWORD, naughty words and people's names.

 Activity 6

If you plug a fax card into your personal computer so that you can send faxes, you could prepare a document, scan someone else's signature in, scan in their company's letterhead, programme the little ID that a fax machine normally sends at the top of each fax and send off a completely bogus fax giving whatever instructions you want.

 Test your knowledge

1   Window dressing is a type of false accounting. Management may occasionally wish to 'window dress' their balance sheet (i.e. present either a better or worse picture than that which can be fairly presented) by a variety of devices such as keeping the cashbook open for some days after the year-end so that money received after the year-end is included in the cashbook balance or entering cheques paid before the year-end but not sending them to creditors until after the year-end. This gives an incorrect impression of the company's credit worthiness to a reader of the accounts.

2   The information systems security is based on three elements. The people and the data/information elements and the physical elements, which acknowledge that the operation of computer equipment can be severely impaired where it is subject to events such as fire, flooding and improper environmental conditions, e.g. heat.

3   Examples of false accounting include:

- Obtaining external financing by falsely improving the results.

- Raising the share price by false means to aid acquisitions or to help a new issue of shares.

- Obtaining more business by appearing more successful or less indebted.

- Obtaining performance bonuses for managers by inflating profits.

- Covering up internal theft by altering, adding, falsifying or deleting bank/stock/purchase or other records. A fictitious customer can be created. Orders can be sent, goods despatched on credit and the 'customer' can neglect to pay their bill. The debt is written off.

- Hiding losses in the hopes that fortunes may reverse.

- Preventing or delaying intervention by a regulator.

4   Collusion is a common element in frauds whereby individuals pool their resources to achieve their aims – specialist skills might not be available to the individual acting independently. Employees can collude with customers, with other employees or with friends. Examples are:

The price, quantity or quality of goods sold to a customer can be manipulated to defraud the company.

An employee could write off a debt or issue a credit note and get something in return.

An employee could arrange for a supplier to falsify their invoice and show more goods or services than were received. Fictitious supply of goods or services.

5   Computer frauds include:

- Hacking/unauthorised access to bank accounts to transfer funds or to steal or manipulate information.

- Setting up as a legitimate Internet business and obtaining payment for goods that are either never delivered or are of lower quality than advertised.

KAPLAN PUBLISHING

- Theft of intellectual property.

- Publishing malicious claims about the company on anonymous bulletin boards, thus affecting the company's reputation.

- Disguising the true nature of a transaction by manipulation of date records and programs held on a computer.

6   Uncovering fraud means performing regular control checks, e.g. stocktaking and cash counts, being aware that fraud might be occurring and looking out for signs that there may be a problem e.g. late payments, work backlogs, incomplete audit trails, people with an extravagant life-style, people who are 'experts', confused decision making, multiple interlocking companies or deals, strange payments to countries with strict privacy laws, large transfers before public holidays.

7   Risks can be handled in a number of different ways. You can ignore the risks and do nothing – appropriate where the effect of the risk is small and the chances of it occurring remote. You can purchase insurance against the risk. Alternatively, you can transfer the risk – e.g. arranging for third parties to complete the riskier parts of the project or protect against the risk – arrange for additional staff to be available at critical parts of the project to minimise the possibility of the project overrunning.

8   There are three prerequisites for fraud to occur: dishonesty, opportunity and motive.

9   The areas covered in a fraud policy statement could include an allocation of responsibilities for the overall management of fraud, such that all those concerned are fully aware of their individual responsibilities, and so that accountability can be ensured. It could also include a manual of formal procedures to which staff must adhere if a fraud is discovered. This is required so that continuity of action results, and so that the actions of staff in such a situation are planned and well thought out, rather than ad hoc and ill conceived. It necessarily follows that where a manual of formal procedures exists, staff must be adequately trained to identify fraud or, better still, work to prevent it.

Internal control

Introduction

Control is a management function, which ensures that plans are followed and objectives are achieved. In this chapter we are going to describe some formal systems of control although the principles also apply to more informal and one-off control measures e.g. a supervisor coaching a team member who is not performing to standard. It forms a relatively large part of the syllabus for the ICAS unit.

The integrity of the data i.e. avoidance of mis-statement of assets and liabilities, income and expenditure and the safety of the assets are the two main aims of accounting controls. Much of your report may concern accounting or administrative controls.

KNOWLEDGE
Be able to identify and use the appropriate accounting system to meet specific organisational requirements.
3.1 Identify weaknesses in accounting systems.
• potential for errors.
• exposure to possible fraud.
3.2 Explain how an accounting system can support internal control.
3.3 Identify ways of supporting individuals who operate accounting systems using training, manuals and written information.
3.4 Explain the value and benefit to the organisation of different types of systems and software.

CONTENTS

1. Internal control systems
2. Internal controls in the purchases system
3. Internal control in the sales system
4. Internal control in the payroll system
5. Analysis of cheque payments
6. Analysis of cash receipts
7. Checklists of tasks

1 Internal control systems

1.1 Internal control

The Auditing Practices Board defines an internal control system in their Auditing Standard SAS 300 to comprise the control environment and control procedures.

The **control environment** is the overall attitude, awareness and actions of directors and management regarding internal controls and their importance in the entity.

The **control procedures** are those policies and procedures in addition to the control environment which are established to achieve the entity's specific objectives and maintain the orderly and efficient conduct of business.

It is possible to identify eight categories of internal controls. These controls are applicable to both computerised and non-computerised environments.

(i) **Organisation** – there must be a well-defined organisational structure showing how responsibility and authority are delegated.

(ii) **Segregation of duties** – a fundamental form of control in any enterprise is the separation of responsibilities so that no one person can fully record and process a transaction. This can be achieved by ensuring that the custodial function, the authorisation function, the recording function and the execution function are kept separate. (The mnemonic CARE might be useful to you in remembering these four functions.)

(iii) **Physical controls** – these are concerned with the custody of assets and records and are concerned with ensuring that access to assets and records is only permitted to authorised personnel.

(iv) **Authorisation and approval** – all transactions require authorisation or approval by a responsible person. Limits on authorisations should be set down in writing.

(v) **Arithmetical and accounting** – these controls include those that check the arithmetical accuracy of records such as control accounts, cross totals, reconciliations and sequential controls over documents.

(vi) **Personnel** – the proper functioning of the system depends upon the employment of well-motivated, competent personnel who possess the necessary integrity for their tasks.

(vii) **Supervision** – an important aspect of any control system is the existence of supervisory procedures by the management.

(viii) **Management** – these are controls exercised by the management outside the day-to-day routine of the system. Examples are the use of monitoring procedures through the use of budgetary control and other management accounting techniques as well as the provision of internal audit procedures.

(You may find **SPAM SOAP** a useful mnemonic to remember these eight categories of internal control.)

1.2 Internal checks

Internal checks can be described as one of the features of internal control. They are procedures designed to ensure that:

- All transactions and other accounting information that should be recorded have been recorded.

- Any errors or irregularities in processing accounting information are highlighted.

- Assets and liabilities recorded in the accounts do actually exist and are recorded at their correct amount.

The essence of an internal check is to ensure that no one person carries too much responsibility and that each person's work is reviewed or checked by another. This is achieved by a division of responsibilities. The absence of internal check leads to errors remaining undiscovered and can also lead to fraudulent acts, which are committed because the fraudster feels free of any form of supervision.

1.3 Internal audit

The internal audit is an independent appraisal function carried out by specially assigned staff. Auditing Standard SAS 500 issued by the APB defines internal audit as 'an appraisal or monitoring activity established by management and the directors for the review of the accounting and internal control systems as a service to the entity. It functions by, amongst other things, examining, evaluating and reporting to management and the directors on the adequacy and effectiveness of components of the accounting and internal control systems'. Internal audit may also be viewed as having a problem-solving function whereby impartial advice is given to management on all aspects of policy.

The Institute of Internal Auditors (IIA) state that internal audit 'assists members of the organisation in the effective carrying out of their responsibilities. To this end, internal auditing furnishes them with appraisals, recommendations, counsel and information'.

There are five different types of internal audit:

(i)   Operational or 'value for money' audit – monitors the organisation's performance at every level to ensure optimal functioning according to pre-determined criteria. It concentrates on the outputs of the system and the efficiency and effectiveness of the organisation.

(ii) Systems audit – tests and evaluates the internal controls to determine what reliance can be placed on those controls to ensure resources are being managed effectively and information provided accurately.

(iii) Transactions audit – sometimes called a financial audit seeks to ensure that the assets and liabilities exist and are safeguarded. This audit only uses substantive tests.

(iv) Social audit – investigating social matters such as the environmental impact of the business.

(v)   Management investigations – assessing management's performance.

1.4   Audit tests

There are two types of test that are used by auditors in the course of their work:

* Compliance tests – are tests of controls and provide evidence as to whether or not the controls on which the auditor wishes to rely were functioning adequately during the period under review.

* Substantive procedures (or substantive tests) – are those tests of transactions, account balances and the existence of assets and liabilities and their valuation e.g. stocks, fixed assets and debtors and other procedures such as analytical review, which seek to provide audit evidence as to the completeness, accuracy and validity of the information contained in the accounting records or in the financial statements.

1.5   Functions associated with internal audit

The tasks carried out by internal audit staff vary widely from business to business. The following activities are usually regarded as being within the province of the internal auditor:

* Reviewing systems and controls, financial or otherwise – establishing adequate accounting and internal control systems is a responsibility of the directors and/or senior management. Internal audit is often assigned responsibility for reviewing the design of systems and processes, monitoring their operation and recommending improvements.

* Special investigations, and the prevention and detection of errors and fraud.

- Examination of financial and operating data, and testing transactions and balances – this may include a review of the means used to identify, measure, classify and report information as well as specific enquiry into individual items including detailed testing of transactions, balances and procedures.

- Review of the operation of non-financial controls and the efficiency of business systems – looking at the effectiveness of operations.

- Review of implementation of corporate policies, plans and procedures – complying with laws, regulations and other external requirements.

1.6 Internal control questionnaires (ICQs)

As their name suggests, internal control questionnaires (ICQs) are checklists of questions that are designed to discover the existence of internal controls and to identify any possible areas of weakness. The questions are framed so as to discover any situation where there is no subdivision of duties between essential functions, where controls do not exist, or where the aspects of managerial supervision that are so essential to efficient operations are deficient.

An important feature of the ICQ is the way in which questions are phrased; an affirmative answer indicates a strength and a negative answer a weakness. An identified weakness in an ICQ can be cross-referenced to the part of the report concerned with evaluating that particular aspect of the system.

1.7 Internal control evaluation

An internal control evaluation (ICE) summary may be used in conjunction with ICQs or in substitution for them. The principal difference between an ICQ and an ICE is that the latter concentrates on the most serious weaknesses that could occur within a system through the use of 'key' questions. The answer to the key question depends upon an evaluation of desirable features of the system, which are set out in a number of follow-up questions. For example, the answer to a key question like 'Can liabilities be set up for goods or services which are either not authorised or received?' depends upon satisfactory answers to various follow-up questions, some of which are exemplified below:

- Is there adequate segregation of duties between authorising, recording, custodial functions and execution?

- Is the issue and authorisation of purchase orders controlled?

- Are goods inspected and are prenumbered goods received notes prepared?

2 Internal controls in the purchases system

2.1 Internal control objectives

All orders for goods and services should be properly authorised. Goods and services should be ordered in accordance with the purchaser's needs and on the most favourable terms that can be obtained.

All goods ordered should be received in a satisfactory condition with evidence of their receipt, which can be used as a basis for entries in stock records and recording the liability arising from such transactions.

Control should be established over the process of returning goods and making claims on suppliers.

Purchase invoice documentation should be validated before a liability is recorded.

The validated transactions should be recorded accurately in the accounting records.

2.2 Overall supervisory controls

If an internal control system is to work satisfactorily, there must be certain overall disciplines which enable the framework of controls to be maintained. In particular, there must be segregation of duties and appropriate supervision.

- Segregation of duties means that the persons who raise orders should be independent of the ledger keeping function, the stock recording and control subsystem and the cheque drawing/approval/signing functions.

- Supervision means that there must be overall systems of review by a responsible official.

2.3 Internal control questionnaire

The internal control questionnaire is a useful tool for identifying the main internal controls that exist in an organisation. An internal control questionnaire will be used as the basis for questioning the members of staff who operate the system under review to identify what controls are in place.

Note that the internal control questionnaire outlined below is a fairly detailed questionnaire which is designed to assess a fairly 'advanced/ideal' system. In many smaller organisations, it will not be possible or even necessary to have a system which contains many of these features.

You will notice that the questionnaire is designed such that if a question is answered with a 'yes', it means that the system is satisfactory; if the question is answered with a 'no', it means that the system is unsatisfactory. However, a 'no' does not necessarily mean that there is a major failure of internal control, as this can only be assessed in relation to the needs of the organisation under review.

Below we outline a typical internal control questionnaire for the purchases system.

Purchases and payments to suppliers		
Client: Normanton Ltd		
Year end: 30 September 20X6	Prepared by: B E Mignano	
Cycle: Purchases	Date: 7.9.X6	
	Yes/No or N/A	Flowchart reference
1 To ensure that all orders are raised to minimise errors Are the orders raised in the order/purchasing department which is independent of all other departments? Are the orders requisitioned by a user department which is separate from the ordering department and stores? Are orders raised on authorised order forms which are pre-numbered serially and sequentially controlled? Is the supplier's price list checked to ensure that the correct quality and quantity of goods are being ordered at the correct price? Is a supplier's file maintained which will confirm details of discounts? Are all orders issued checked regularly to ensure that they have been fulfilled? Are unfulfilled orders checked to ensure that they are being satisfactorily progressed by the supplier? Is the official order signed by a responsible official?		

2   To ensure that goods received are correctly controlled

Are goods received in a stores department that is independent of the user and purchasing departments?

Does the organisation use official goods received notes?

Is the goods received note correctly filled in when an order is received and signed off by a responsible official?

Are the goods received notes sequentially prenumbered and is there control over them?

Is the delivery note which accompanies the goods from the supplier signed and returned to the supplier?

Is a copy of the delivery note sent by the supplier retained and filed?

Is the goods received note raised by the company matched and filed with the delivery note sent by the supplier?

3   To ensure that invoices received are valid and agree with the goods delivered

Are the invoices arithmetically checked?

Is the invoice compared to the purchase order and quantities, qualities and prices checked?

Is the invoice compared to the goods received note and supplier's delivery note to ensure that the correct quantities and quality were received?

Is the invoice stamped with a 'grid' so that the above checks are correctly evidenced on the face of the invoice?

Is the invoice correctly coded so that goods received are allocated to the correct nominal ledger code?

Are the invoices received allocated an internal sequential number and filed sequentially?

4   To ensure that payments to suppliers are correctly made

Are the persons who sign the cheques different from those who handle the authorisation of the invoices?

Are there two responsible officials who act as cheque signatories?

Is close control maintained over the custody of the cheques?

Are all cheques issued in sequential order?

Are spoilt or cancelled cheques retained?

Are all cheques stamped 'A/C payee'?

Are cheques presented for signature with relevant authorising documentation, e.g. an authorised invoice?

Is the number of the cheque used to pay the invoice written on the face of the invoice?

If BACS are used to pay suppliers, do two responsible officials sign the BACS authorisation?

Does company policy forbid the use of cash to pay suppliers' invoices?

 Example

Illustrative case study – a purchases system

The following brief case study will illustrate some of the points that have just been studied and which you may choose to adopt when researching your project. You should pay particular attention to the strengths and weaknesses of the internal controls that are present in the system.

Miller Ltd

Miller Ltd is a company engaged in pharmaceutical manufacturing. The purchasing department is managed by Mr Wurm, the buyer, and his assistant Walter Green. The value of purchase contracts placed annually is about £3 million. When goods are required the stock records clerk (Frederica) sends a purchase requisition to Mr Wurm, who gets Walter to type out an order form. Walter enters a serial number, sequentially-numbered after the last purchase order, and photocopies the order. The original is sent to the supplier and the copy is kept in a file.

When the goods arrive, they are taken into stock and the supplier's despatch note is sent to Walter from the goods inwards supervisor. Walter then marks off the items received on the order and sends the despatch note to the stock records section, who use it to write up the stock ledger and file it in chronological sequence.

(a) What weaknesses does the system possess?

(b) What outline recommendations would you make to improve the system? You may assume that the company has enough manpower to implement your recommendations.

Solution

(a) **Weaknesses in the system**

(i) The purchase orders are not multipart, prenumbered documents (the numbers are added manually). As a result of this weakness, unauthorised orders can be placed. The lack of original documentation makes the system susceptible to loss or irregular alteration.

(ii) The orders are neither priced, nor are they checked by Mr Wurm before they are despatched.

(iii) Mr Wurm does not sign the orders as the company's authorised signatory.

(iv) There is no goods received note system to evidence the arrival of goods.

(v) The acceptance of goods in the goods inwards section is done without reference to the purchase order; they are only matched up later by Walter.

(vi) There is no review of outstanding purchase orders in order to chase up unfulfilled orders.

(b) **Recommendations**

(i) The purchase orders should be a three-part document and sequentially-controlled. Unissued order pads should be kept under lock and key. Sequential control should then be maintained over books of purchase orders in issue. Spoilt and unused copies should be retained and the completeness of the sequential numbering monitored frequently.

(ii) The purchase orders should be priced by reference to suppliers' catalogues before despatch. This enables the amount eventually invoiced by the supplier to be checked.

(iii) Purchase requisitions should be checked before being processed. Similarly, purchase orders should be signed by Mr Wurm as evidence of authority before being despatched. This ensures that unauthorised purchases cannot be made.

(iv) A copy of the purchase order should be sent to the goods inwards department in order to provide authority for the acceptance of the goods.

(v) When goods arrive they should be checked against the copy purchase order and evidenced on a pre-numbered, three-part goods received note (GRN). One part (top) of the GRN should be used to update the order file i.e. to indicate which orders have been fulfilled and which are still outstanding. The second part can be used to write up the stock ledger. The third part can be kept as a master copy in serial number order.

(vi) Mr Wurm should review the order file weekly and check on the position of outstanding orders.

 Example

Illustrative case study – cash payments

Melchior Manufacturing Supplies Ltd

At monthly intervals the purchase ledger clerk of Melchior Manufacturing Supplies Ltd, Mrs Thorborg, lists the ledger balances. She then compares them with a file of suppliers' statements. Those statements that agree with the list of balances are extracted and placed in a file. Those that do not agree with the listed balances are left in the original file.

Mrs Thorborg then prepares a list of payments for all the suppliers who have sent statements as follows.

(a) Where the statement agrees with the balance, the statement is attached to the list.

(b) Where there is a disagreement, Mrs Thorborg computes a 'round sum amount' (which is generally slightly less than the balance on the ledger) and enters this amount on the list of payments. She leaves these statements in the file. The list of payments is then passed to Mr Lehmann, the assistant accountant, who writes out the cheques. The cheques, list and statements are then sent to Mrs Turner, the commercial director, who signs them after checking against the statements (where these are attached) and the list. The cheques are then passed to the managing director, Mr Widdop, the other signatory, who signs the cheques and sends them back to Mr Lehmann, who then posts them to the parties concerned.

Required:

The internal auditors have made various comments regarding the poor quality of the accounting controls. Identify those areas that you think would have been likely to attract adverse comment from the internal auditors.

Solution

Matters likely to cause adverse comment from the auditors:

(a)   Mrs Thorborg appears to operate in a most lackadaisical fashion in that she:

   (i)   does not appear to claim cash discounts for early payment

   (ii)   makes no attempt to reconcile bought ledger accounts

   (iii)   makes round sum payments and is therefore likely to aggravate the problem of account balances that disagree

   (iv)   does not attach invoices for payment; thus there is no attempt to identify specifically the transactions that are being settled and the same invoice could therefore be paid twice.

(b)   There is a lack of evidence for the first cheque signatory, as Mrs Turner does not see the statements for balances that disagree.

(c)   Mr Widdop does not receive supporting evidence for payment. Consequently he may not notice errors or be aware of any lapses in control.

(d)   The signed cheques are sent to Mr Lehmann who could suppress or alter them for his own benefit.

(e)   The payment of invoices or statements does not alert the company to errors made by the supplier. Thus it is possible to pay for items not ordered and charged to the company in error.

 Activity 1

Segregation of duties reduces the risk of intentional manipulation or error and increases the element of checking. Which functions should be separated?

3 Internal controls in the sales system

3.1 Internal control objectives

Overall objectives

Customers' orders should be properly controlled and recorded so that no losses of business opportunity are allowed to occur.

Controls should exist over goods delivered so that proof of delivery is obtained and all deliveries are accurately charged to the customer

All claims made by customers should be validated and all goods returned to stock properly evidenced.

All invoices and credit notes should be validated before entry in the records.

Procedures should exist to ensure that invoices are paid for, overdue debts are followed up and bad debts promptly identified.

No sales should be made to non-creditworthy customers.

Overleaf we give some examples of the controls that might be put in place to achieve these objectives.

3.2 Specimen internal control questionnaire Sales and trade debtors

Client:	Normanton Ltd		
Year end:	30 September 20X6	Prepared by: B E Mignano	
Cycle:	Purchases	Date: 7.9.X6	
		Yes/No or N/A	Flowchart reference
1	**To ensure that all orders received are processed in such a way that keeps errors to a minimum**		
	Are persons responsible for preparation of sales orders independent of credit control, custody of stock and recording sales transactions?		
	Are standard forms used to record orders?		
	Are sales orders pre-numbered?		

	Do sales order clerks check the goods ordered are available in quantity and quality required?		
	Are standard prices, delivery and payment terms in written form for the use of sales order clerks?		
	Are special orders (special qualities, quantities, prices) authorised by a responsible official?		
2	**To ensure that sales orders are not accepted in respect of a bad credit risk**		
	Is the credit controller independent of the sales order clerks?		
	Are new credit customers vetted for creditworthiness by reference to independent persons or organisations?		
	Are orders from existing customers checked for payment record, sales ledger balance and credit limit?		
	Are credit limits set by responsible officials for all credit customers?		
	Is the credit approval evidenced on the sales order by the signature of a responsible official?		
	Is the work of a credit control clerk independently checked?		
3	**To ensure that goods are only despatched to customers after proper authorisation**		
	Is warehouse/despatch department independent of sales order preparation, credit control and invoicing?		
	Do warehouse personnel release goods from the warehouse on the basis of sales orders signed by authorised sales order and credit control personnel?		
	Is the despatch of goods evidenced by the preparation of a goods despatch note?		
	Are goods despatch notes pre-numbered?		
	Are two copies of the goods despatch notes sent to the customer for one to be returned as evidence of receipt?		
	Is a copy of the despatch note sent to a stock control department to update stock records?		

	Is stock counted periodically and compared with stock records?		
4	**To ensure that all goods despatched are invoiced at authorised prices and terms**		
	Is sales invoicing independent of sales order preparation, credit control, warehouse and despatch departments?		
	Are copies of sales orders received by sales invoicing?		
	Is a sequence check carried out on sales orders?		
	Is a sequence check carried out on goods despatch notes?		
	Are goods despatch notes matched with sales orders and unmatched orders followed up?		
	Do invoicing clerks have details of current prices, terms and conditions, including special agreements with particular customers?		
	Are sales invoices independently checked before despatch?		
5	**To ensure that all sales invoices are properly recorded in individual customers' accounts in the sales ledger**		
	Is the sales ledger clerk independent of sales order preparation, credit control, warehouse, despatch and sales invoicing?		
	Is a sales ledger control account maintained independent of the sales ledger clerk?		
	Are differences between extracted list of sales ledger balances and control account balances investigated by a responsible official?		
	Are monthly statements of amounts outstanding prepared and despatched to customers?		
	Is an aged debtor listing prepared and reviewed by a responsible official?		
	Are sales ledger balances made up of identifiable sales invoices and other items?		
	Are bad debt write-offs and discounts authorised by a responsible official other than the sales ledger clerk?		

Example

Illustrative case study – a sales system

Gustavus plc

Gustavus plc sell a variety of electrical equipment on a wholesale basis to some 1,500 credit customers. Cash sales are not a feature of the business.

Sales orders are received by telephone and are recorded on a prenumbered order form in two parts. Part 1 is sent to the customer as acknowledgement of the order. Part 2 is used by the manager of the sales office as an action copy. He authorises the order after checking the account balance with the accounts department to ensure that the credit limit is not exceeded. The order is then passed to the warehouse where the goods are picked and sent to despatch.

The order form is then passed to the invoice typing section in the sales office and three-part invoice sets are typed. Each set is numbered by reference to a number register and the top copy is given to the customer with the goods at the collection point. The second copy is an accounts copy and the third is filed in the customer file in the sales office. There are no other procedures in relation to sales order processing.

Comment on the weaknesses inherent in the sales system. Solution

Weaknesses in the system

- There is no separation of duties between the functions of recording and authorisation of sales orders.

- The validation procedures appear to be inadequate as there is no evidence of formal procedures such as validation of prices and stock availability.

- There are no procedures to ensure that the customer signs for the goods collected which would serve as proof of delivery.

- Invoices are not prenumbered; this is a serious control weakness as transactions can be suppressed without trace.

- Invoices are not checked for arithmetical accuracy before being despatched.

- There are no procedures for dealing with unsatisfied orders.

- There are no procedures to update the order file with details of orders despatched to customers.

4 Internal control in the payroll system

4.1 Internal control objectives

The payroll cycle embraces the following:

- maintenance of payroll
- authorisation of hours worked
- payroll preparation
- distribution of pay
- payroll approval
- cheque signing, and
- identifying liabilities to third parties for payroll costs and paying these when due.

The objectives of the key internal controls in the payroll cycle are as follows.

(a) Wages and salaries are computed for the client's employees only and in accordance with authorised rates of pay and conditions.

(b) Wages and salaries computed should be in agreement with records of work performed, i.e. overtime claims, bonus calculations, etc.

(c) Payroll is correctly computed and paid to the appropriate employees.

(d) All records of transactions are accurately maintained within the accounting system.

(e) There are controls to ensure that all payroll deductions, PAYE income tax payable, National Insurance Contributions, etc are computed and paid over on the due dates.

4.2　Internal control questionnaire Payroll

Client:	Normanton Ltd	
Year end:	30 September 20X6	Prepared by: B E Mignano
Cycle:	Purchases	Date: 7.9.X6

		Yes/No or N/A	Flow-chart reference
1	**Fundamental controls of a payroll system**		
	Is a permanent record kept for each employee containing details of engagement, dismissal, changes in rates of pay, etc?		
	Are these details and any changes in details evidenced in writing by a responsible official?		
	Are timesheets kept for each employee giving details for each payment period of normal hours and overtime hours worked?		
	For piecework employees, are details kept of amounts produced as a basis for payment?		
	For each payment period, are the calculations which make up gross pay checked for each employee against the timesheets and records of rates, etc?		
	Is the calculation for the total amount of the payroll checked for each payment period?		
	Are all payments for overtime approved by a responsible official?		
2	**To ensure the correct preparation and payment of the payroll**		
	Does a responsible official formally approve the total payroll by signing it?		
	Where employees are paid by cheque or BACS, does a responsible official check the total amount being paid to each employee?		
	Where wages are paid by cash, do two responsible officials authorise and sign the cheque to raise the cash?		
	Is the cash securely transported from the bank and securely held on the premises?		

	Does a responsible official oversee the correct cash being placed into each wages packet?		
	Are unclaimed wages securely held in the company's premises until collected?		
3	**Controls over accounting for payroll**		
	Are payroll liabilities reconciled with the source total payroll (i.e. PAYE and NIC deductions included)?		
	Is PAYE and NIC paid on the due date?		
	Do adequate procedures exist to ensure that payroll is analysed and entered in the appropriate nominal ledger accounts?		

 Example

Bingham

You have been asked by the senior in charge of the audit of Bingham Manufacturing Limited to describe certain aspects of the work you will carry out in auditing the company's wages system. Employees of Bingham Manufacturing are paid on the basis of hours worked and quantities produced. The hours worked are recorded on clock cards and the quantities produced are confirmed by the foreman. Wages are paid in cash each Friday for the previous week's work. Appointment of employees is authorised by the managing director, and the personnel department maintains employees' records and their rates of pay. The cashier is separate from the wages department.

Previous years' audits have highlighted weaknesses in internal controls in the company's wages system. This has allowed an employee in the wages department to perpetrate a fraud by creating fictitious employees on the payroll and misappropriating the wages. Some of your audit tests have been designed to detect whether this fraud is still taking place.

A 'starters and leavers' test is carried out to ensure that employees are not paid before they commence employment or after they have left.

Task

State the principal controls you would expect to exist in a wages system and explain their purpose.

Solution

(a) **Controls**

The principal controls in a wages system and their purpose would include the following.

There should be a proper division of duties in the wages system. Employees who calculate wages should not be responsible for making up the wage packets.

There is proper control over custody of cash for wages and unclaimed wages.

Wages are only paid to employees for work done i.e. not in advance. Employees are paid at a rate authorised by management.

There is appropriate authorisation over employee appointment and dismissal.

Deductions are correctly calculated and paid promptly to the relevant authorities i.e. HM Revenue and Customs and pension companies.

Payments are made to employees actually registered with the company.

The transactions are correctly recorded in the books of account, including the allocation of the wages expense between sales, manufacturing, administration, etc.

The aim of these controls is to ensure that employees are paid at authorised rates for work done, that the transactions are recorded accurately in the accounting records, that the employees and other authorities are paid the correct sums and that the risk of fraud and error is minimised.

(b) **Employees' existence check**

In checking the existence of employees the following techniques can be used.

The signature of the employee signing for his or her wage can be checked to the record in the personnel department. The signature of the employee in the personnel records should have been obtained when the individual started employment in the company. For the purposes of the exam everyone has signed a contract.

The employee can be checked to the annual return made to HM Revenue and Customs (for PAYE and National Insurance purposes), and there may be notifications from HM Revenue and Customs of changes in the employee's tax code. If the employee has just joined the company (and had previously been employed by another organisation), there should be a notification from the former employer of the individual's tax code, gross pay and tax paid to date.

The employee should have a National Insurance number which may also be used to verify existence.

The department manager could acknowledge a list of individuals employed in his department. This is difficult to obtain when a large number of staff are involved.

(c) **Starters and leavers test**

The purpose of a starters and leavers test is to ensure that employees are neither paid before they start nor after they have left the company's employment.

To carry out this procedure, I will select two payrolls, say three months apart, and compare the names on the payroll. Where the name appears on both payrolls, the employee has been paid for the full three-month period. Where the name appears on the first payroll and not the second, this is a 'leaver', and where the name appears on the second payroll and not on the first, this is a 'starter'. Starting and leaving dates should then be verified by examining the relevant personnel records.

I can then ensure that they have been paid for the correct period by checking the dates on the payroll and their P45s.

(d) **Review techniques**

The analytical review techniques I can use in auditing the wages system will include the following.

The gross and net wages, PAYE and National Insurance will be compared for each month and with the previous year. Any unusual changes can be identified and investigated.

The average wage per employee will be calculated and any significant changes will be investigated. The ratio of income tax and National Insurance to gross wages will be checked. This would be expected to be around 20%.

A sample of payrolls will be scrutinised and any large amounts will be investigated.

The returns to HM Revenue and Customs will be test checked to the payroll. This will include monthly PAYE and National Insurance payments, and test checks of annual returns for individual employees.

The computations on the payroll will be test checked, including the calculation of the deductions and the sum of each employee's pay to the total. I will check that the total gross pay is equal to the total net pay plus the deductions. These checks may be very limited where the wages system is computerised and the wages programs have been shown to be reliable.

The analysis of the wages expense (e.g. sales, production, administration wages) will be test checked from the payroll to the nominal ledger and the total for the year will be compared with previous years. Any significant changes will be investigated.

 Example

Burnden Limited

Burnden Limited manufactures a range of components and spare parts for the textile industry. The company employs 150 hourly-paid workers and 20 administrative staff, including the three directors of the company. There are two wages clerks who deal with the weekly payroll of the hourly-paid employees. They are directly responsible to the assistant accountant.

The company uses a computerised time clock at the factory gate to record the hours worked by the production employees. Each employee has a card with a magnetic strip with his own identification code on it. This card is inserted in the computerised time clock on the arrival and departure of each worker, whereupon it records on the card the hours worked. The cards are collected weekly by the wages clerks, who simply insert them individually into the microcomputer, which then reads them and prepares the payroll. The production manager keeps the unused clock cards in a locked cabinet in his office.

Wages are paid one week in arrears. The wages clerks compile the payroll by means of the microcomputer system, and pass the payroll to the assistant accountant who scrutinises it before drawing the wages cheque, which is passed to one of the directors for signature. Any pay increases are negotiated locally by representatives of the employees. If any alterations are required to the standing data on the microcomputer, then the wages clerks amend the records. For example, when a wage increase has been negotiated, the rates of pay are changed by the wages clerks.

The cheque is drawn to cover net wages and the cashier makes arrangements for collecting the cash from the bank. The wages clerks then make up the wages envelopes. Whenever there is assistance required on preparing wages, the assistant accountant helps the wages clerks. The payment of wages is carried out by the production manager who returns any unclaimed wages to the wages clerks who keep them in a locked filing cabinet. Each employee is expected to collect his unclaimed wages personally.

New production employees are notified to the wages department verbally by the production manager and when employees leave, a note to that effect is sent to the wages department by the production manager. All statutory deductions are paid to the appropriate authorities by the chief accountant.

Administrative staff are paid monthly by credit transfer to their bank account. The payroll is prepared by the assistant accountant and the bank credit transfers are authorised by a director. Any increases in the salaries of the administrative staff are notified to the assistant accountant verbally by the chief accountant. The employment of administrative staff is authorised by the financial director.

You have recently been appointed the auditor of Burnden Limited for the year ended 31 December 20X8 and have just started your interim audit. You are about to commence your audit evaluation and testing of the wages system.

Task

Describe the weaknesses in the present wages and salaries system, and suggest, with reasons, improvements which could be made to the system (assuming that the only controls are those set out above).

(a) **Weaknesses and improvements**

The weaknesses in the company's present wages and salaries system and suggestions for improvements are as follows.

There are two wages clerks dealing with the production payroll. To improve control within the wages department, the duties of these clerks should be rotated during the year. Neither of the clerks should be responsible for all functions in the department.

Personnel records should be kept for each employee giving details of engagement, retirement, dismissal or resignation, rates of pay, holidays etc, with a specimen signature for the employee. It does not appear that these records are maintained at present and they would be essential in the event of failure or corruption of the computer system.

The production manager verbally notifies the wages department of new employees. As he also controls the unused clock cards and pays out the wages he could introduce a fictitious employee. It is important that there is written authorisation from the chief accountant for the appointment and removal of all employees. The unused clock cards should also be kept in a secure place by someone other than the production manager. They should be issued weekly by a responsible official.

The wages clerks appear to amend pay rates without any authorisation. Changes in rates of pay should be authorised in writing by an official outside the wages department.

The clocking-in and out procedures do not seem to be supervised. There should be supervision of the cards and timing devices.

The production manager pays out wages alone. It would be preferable if the two wages clerks paid out the wages. A surprise attendance at the payout should be made periodically by an independent official. It would also be preferable that an employee should not be allowed to take the wages of another employee without written authorisation. Unclaimed wages should be recorded immediately in a register and held by someone outside the wages department until claimed or until a predefined period after which the money should be rebanked.

The payroll is not authorised. It should be signed by the person preparing it. The director should check that it has been authorised before signing the wages cheque. He should also sign the payroll. Further, the payroll should be carefully scrutinised by the assistant accountant who should carry out random checks on rates of pay, amendments to employees etc.

Access to the computer payroll system does not appear to be restricted. Access should be controlled by passwords which should be changed regularly.

A manual back-up system should be available in the event of computer failure.

There is a security risk in drawing large amounts of cash from the bank and keeping this on the premises. If possible, the company should transfer the employees onto a bank giro transfer system.

There are weaknesses in the monthly payroll. The assistant accountant should sign the payroll as preparer and the director should authorise the bank credit transfer only after checking an authorised payroll. Salary increases should be notified in writing by the chief accountant after authorisation by a director. Personnel records should be kept as for production staff and appointments and dismissals should be authorised only by directors.

If any overtime is worked it should be authorised by the production manager.

(b) **Audit tests**

The audit of the wages and salaries system would be conducted using both tests of control and substantive procedures. Tests of control would be as follows.

Observe wages payout for adherence to procedures.

Test authorisation and control over payroll amendments e.g. test increase in pay rates to authorisation, new employees to personnel records.

Examine evidence of checking payroll calculations.

Examine evidence of approval of payrolls by a responsible official.

Examine evidence of independent checks on payrolls.

Test authorities for payroll deductions e.g. trade union subscriptions.

Test controls over unclaimed wages. Substantive procedures would be as follows.

Select a sample of clock cards and agree the hours worked. A computer would be required to do this.

Select a sample of wages and salaries records and check the following:

- rates of pay to appropriate documentation
- calculation of gross pay
- calculation of statutory and non-statutory deductions
- calculation of net pay.

Check the additions on a sample of payrolls and agree the total net pay to the cash drawn or, for salaries, agree net pay to bank credit transfer form.

Vouch a sample of leavers and joiners in the period to the personnel records and appropriate authorisation ensuring that leavers have been removed immediately from the payroll.

Test posting of payroll totals to nominal ledger.

Check that the statutory and non-statutory deductions have been paid over correctly and on time.

Review weekly wage totals and obtain explanations for significant variations.

5 Analysis of cheque payments

5.1 Introduction

Cheque payments are an important part of the system for incurring expenditure and so we note the internal controls in this context. It is necessary to remember the fundamental principle of internal control; namely, the need for a division of duties between authorisation, custodial, recording and execution functions.

5.2 Desirable internal controls

(a) Division of duties

(i) The persons who sign cheques should be different from the authorisation, recording and custodial functions.

(ii) There must be two responsible officials who act as cheque signatories. If pre-printed cheques are in use, or a cheque signing machine is installed, the control over the issue and custody of cheques must be closely supervised by a responsible official who is different from the recording or custodial function.

(b) Custody

(i) All cheques should be issued in sequential order and their sequence should be controlled.

(ii) Unused stocks of cheque books must be kept under lock and key.

(iii) Spoilt or cancelled cheques must be retained.

(iv) All cheques should be crossed 'A/c payee only' to minimise the chance of fraud if the cheque is lost.

(c) Authorisation

(i) No cheque should be prepared without supporting documentation, e.g. an approved invoice, a signed payroll or an authorised cheque requisition.

(ii) The cheque signatories' authority should be laid down in writing and be in accordance with the bank mandate.

(iii) The system of cheque payments must be supervised by a responsible official who will oversee the preparation of regular bank reconciliations and carry out spot checks thereon.

6 Analysis of cash receipts

6.1 Introduction

The cash receipts system is an important part of the income cycle. It is necessary to consider the internal control aspects of this part of the system. As with cash payments, one should consider the importance of a proper subdivision of duties between authorisation, custodial and recording functions.

6.2 Internal control

(a) Custodial procedures

(i) All post should be opened by at least two responsible officials.

(ii) All cheques and postal orders should be crossed restrictively to the company's bankers.

(iii) A cash diary should be maintained of daily amounts of cash received.

(iv) All monies received should be banked intact on that business day.

(b) Separation of duties

(i) The persons who are responsible for opening the post, preparing the paying-in details and controlling the sales ledger should be separate functionaries.

(ii) There should be an independent check on cash receipts by a suitable official who can spot-check the details in the cash diary with the paying in records.

(c) Recording controls

(i) The entries in the cash receipts book should be proved by regular bank reconciliations.

(ii) The bank reconciliations should be reviewed and spot-checked on a regular basis by some responsible official remote from the recording functions.

7 Checklist of tasks

- Choose an area of your organisation's systems (purchases, sales or payroll) and produce an internal control questionnaire based on the company's systems.

- Identify the answers to the questions, which illustrate the most serious weaknesses in the system.

8 Test your knowledge

Test your knowledge

1 Can you identify four of the eight categories of internal control?

2 Internal checks are a feature of internal control. What are they designed to ensure?

3 Describe the essence of an internal check.

4 What is an operational or 'value for money' audit?

5 Briefly explain the two types of test that are used by auditors in the course of their work.

6 What are ICQs?

7 An internal control evaluation (ICE) summary may be used in conjunction with ICQs or in substitution for them. What is the principal difference between an ICQ and an ICE?

9 Summary

This has been a very important chapter and in some ways goes to the heart of the analysis of the accounting systems.

The division of responsibilities is a key element to internal control and you should always be aware of any shortcomings in this respect when analysing a system.

The internal control questionnaire is a very good way of gaining information about a system and its shortcomings. When doing your project, it is a technique which you should seriously consider employing.

Answers to chapter activities and 'test your knowledge' questions

 Activity 1

The functions include:

- Authorisation
- Execution
- Custody
- recording
- systems development and daily operations.

 Test your knowledge

1 You could choose any four of the following types of internal control: organisation, segregation of duties, supervision, management, physical controls, authorisation and approval and personnel. The proper functioning of the system depends upon the employment of well-motivated, competent personnel who possess the necessary integrity for their tasks.

2 Internal checks are designed to ensure that all transactions and other accounting information that should be recorded have been recorded, any errors or irregularities in processing accounting information are highlighted and assets and liabilities recorded in the accounts do actually exist and are recorded at their correct amount.

3 The essence of an internal check is to ensure that no one person carries too much responsibility and that each person's work is reviewed or checked by another. This is achieved by a division of responsibilities. The absence of internal checks leads to errors remaining undiscovered and can also lead to fraudulent acts, which are committed because the fraudster feels free of any form of supervision.

4   An operational or 'value for money' audit monitors the organisation's performance at every level to ensure optimal functioning according to pre-determined criteria. It concentrates on the outputs of the system and the efficiency and effectiveness of the organisation.

5   There are two types of test that are used by auditors in the course of their work:

- Compliance tests are tests of controls and provide evidence as to whether or not the controls on which the auditor wishes to rely were functioning adequately during the period under review.

- Substantive procedures (or substantive tests) are those tests of transactions, account balances and the existence of assets and liabilities and their valuation e.g. stocks, fixed assets and debtors and other procedures such as analytical review, which seek to provide audit evidence as to the completeness, accuracy and validity of the information contained in the accounting records or in the financial statements.

6   As their name suggests, internal control questionnaires (ICQs) are checklists of questions that are designed to discover the existence of internal controls and to identify any possible areas of weakness. An important feature of the ICQ is the way in which questions are phrased; an affirmative answer indicates a strength and a negative answer a weakness.

7   The principal difference between an ICQ and an ICE is that the latter concentrates on the most serious weaknesses that could occur within a system through the use of 'key' questions.

Information systems

7

Introduction

Even in the best managed organisations there will sometimes be problems because there can never be in total control over people and circumstances. Contingency planning is carried out at a number of levels. We could say that backing up computer files is a form of contingency planning. We back up in case something happens to the original.

Your ICAS unit report may contain case histories of how contingencies, problems and crises were handled with an explanation of what you learnt from the experience.

KNOWLEDGE	CONTENTS
3.2 Explain how an accounting system can support internal control.	1 Information systems controls
	2 Integrity controls
	3 Contingency control
	4 Assessing and managing risk
	5 Checklist of tasks

1 Information systems controls

1.1 Risks to information systems

Definition

The British Computer Society defines security as 'the establishment and application of safeguards to protect data, software and computer hardware from accidental or malicious modification, destruction or disclosure'. Security is the protection of the system from harm. It relates to all elements of the system, including hardware, software, data and the system users themselves.

There are three basic concerns relevant to the computerised information system. Security should maintain:

(i)   the availability of the computerised service itself

(ii)   the integrity of the data that it processes and stores, and

(iii)   the confidentiality of the data before, during and after processing.

Controls are procedures or system features that help to ensure that the system operates in accordance with the requirements of the organisation and the user. The issue of the information system's security is based on the following three elements:

- physical – the operation of computer equipment can be severely impaired where it is subject to events such as fire, flooding and improper environmental conditions, e.g. heat

- people as a threat, and

- the data/information that might be lost or damaged.

The security measures adopted should perform the following functions:

- the avoidance or prevention of loss

- the deterrence of as many threats as possible

- easy recovery after any loss

- identification of the cause of any loss after the event, and

- the correction of vulnerable areas to reduce the risk of repeated loss.

1.2 General controls

General controls relate to the environment within which computer-based systems are developed, maintained and operated and are generally applicable to all the applications running on the system. Such controls may include the following.

- Personnel recruitment policies to ensure honesty and competence.

- Segregation of duties between different types of job, to minimise tampering with programs or data.

- Proper training programmes for new staff and for new systems developments.

- Physical security of hardware and software against accidental or malicious damage.

- Authorisation procedures for program amendments and testing.

- Basic physical security against natural disasters or thefts.

- Back-up procedures (maintaining copies of files off-site, back-up facilities).

- Access controls.

- Hardware controls (e.g. firewalls and anti-virus checkers).

- Measures to ensure the system is not accessed during data transmission (hacking).

- Controls to ensure that the computing resources are used efficiently.

- Security of confidential data against loss and unauthorised access.

1.3 Data security

A critical element of effective data protection is the need for security. There is a range of issues that should be considered:

- the nature of the personal data and the harm that would result from access, alteration, disclosure, loss or destruction

- the place where the personal data is stored · reliability of staff having access to the data.

Data security measures involve different aspects:

- physical security, such as the security of disk storage facilities, from flood as well as unauthorised access

- software security, such as maintaining a log of all failed access requests, and

- operational security, with regard to such things as work data being taken home by employees, and periodic data protection audits of the computer systems.

Under the terms of the **Data Protection Act 1998**, the need for privacy is recognised by the requirements that all personal data on individuals should be held only for clearly designated purposes. Accuracy and integrity must be maintained and the data must be open to inspection. Only legitimate parties can access data and information must be secured against alteration, accidental loss or deliberate damage. Furthermore, the Act states that data must be obtained fairly, to precise specifications and must not be kept for longer than required.

1.4   Physical security

Computer systems consist of a mixture of electronic and mechanical devices that can be severely impaired when they are subject to events such as fire, flooding, and improper environmental conditions. As well as covering these threats, physical security also covers the prevention of theft and accidental or malicious damage caused by external parties or internal staff.

The organisation must assess the physical risks applicable to them, and put in place appropriate controls. These controls may be designed to detect the risk or may be designed to prevent it, and might include the following.

- *Fire systems and procedures* – systems of fire alarms, heat and smoke detectors can alert staff to the risk or presence of fire in time for preventive action to be taken. The fire control system might also trigger automatic fire extinguishing equipment, though the use of water sprinkler systems in offices with computer hardware is inappropriate due to the damage they can cause to electrical equipment.

- *Location of hardware* away from sources of risk - the siting of computer facilities in areas susceptible to flooding or natural disasters is common sense, but there are other controls that may be less obvious e.g. locating equipment where it cannot be seen through windows from a public area may reduce the risk of theft.

- *Regular building maintenance* – attention to roofs, windows and doors will reduce the risk of water penetration and make forcible entry more difficult. Training - staff should be given copies of relevant policies and procedures, and trained in the implementation of them. Specific training should cover evacuation drills, fire control and fighting, safe behaviour, first aid, how to deal with a bomb threat and general risk identification and management.

- *Physical access controls* – there are a number of steps that can be taken to prevent the access of unauthorised persons to computer facilities. Examples include security guards to check identification and authorisation, CCTV, using badge readers or coded locks on access doors from public areas and electronic tagging of hardware.

Environmental threats can come from extremes of temperature, excessive humidity and interruptions or inconsistencies in the power supply. The mechanisms that can be used to control the computer environment include heating and air-conditioning systems, smoothed power supplies and uninterruptable power supplies (UPS).

1.5 Individual staff controls

No matter what the size of organisation, or the type of hardware involved, where activities are undertaken that are important to the commercial fabric of the organisation, individual staff functions must be specifically defined and documented where they involve data processing of any form.

This is vital, as it may be the only control in smaller organisations that will prevent, minimise or lead to the detection of fraudulent manipulation of data during processing, destruction of data, the accidental incorrect processing of data and unauthorised access to personal or confidential data that may be in contravention of the Data Protection Act 1998,or may be otherwise unlawful.

It is necessary to restrict access to the system, to protect the confidentiality of the software and data. Access must be limited to those with the proper authority, and a number of controls are available. These include the physical access controls that we have already outlined as well as the following:

- Logical access system – unauthorised people can get around physical access controls and gain access to data and program files unless different controls are used to deter them. Measures such as identification of the user, authentication of user identity and checks on user authority are alternative ways of achieving control.

- Personal identification – the most common form of personal identification is the PIN (personal identification number), which acts as a form of password. Users should be required to log in to the system using a unique user name and a password that is kept secret and changed frequently. Other, more sophisticated personal identification techniques that are coming into use include fingerprint recognition, eye retina 'prints' and voice 'prints'. Usage logs – the system should be designed to automatically record the log-in and log-off times of each user, and the applications accessed. Periodic checks should be made for unusual patterns, such as a day-shift worker accessing the system at night.

- Storage of CDs, removable disks and tapes in secure locations – given that one of the risks that the organisation is trying to counteract is the physical destruction of the installation, it is sensible to put in place controls to ensure that back-up data is stored in a fire-proof environment on-site, and occasionally some form of master back-up is removed from the installation site completely.

1.6 Controlling environmental risks

Environmental threats can come from extremes of temperature, excessive humidity and interruptions or inconsistencies in the power supply.

The best way to control these risks is to isolate the computer system from the outside world by placing it in a specially designed computer room or building. Obviously this is possible for a large central computer, but not for personal computers. The mechanisms that can be used to control the computer environment include the following.

- *Heating and air-conditioning systems* – although not possible for portable hardware, computer equipment should be stored and used in an environment protected from extremes and changes of temperature and humidity. Smoothed power supplies – equipment can be purchased to smooth out any variations in voltage and current from the power supply. Such problems arise as a result of poor quality electricity supply, or the use of other equipment that draws a lot of power (such as heating) or introduces sharp 'spikes' to the supply (such as a kettle switching on or off).

- *Uninterruptable power supplies (UPS)* – the risk of losing power due to failures or disaster can be eliminated by the purchase of UPS equipment. This is a storage battery that automatically takes over when the mains power fails, giving the user sufficient time to save their work and exit the system. An auxiliary generator can be connected to the power supply, for use in cases when the mains power fails.

Some buildings with a lot of computer equipment have a dedicated power circuit for its use, often identified by coloured sockets or different plug shapes. Commonly, this circuit will be protected by a sophisticated UPS with smoothing and a backup generator.

KAPLAN PUBLISHING

Activity 1

You are a trainee management accountant in a small manufacturing company. Your head of department is going to a meeting and has asked you to provide some information for him.

Write a briefing report for the head of department which:

(a) examines the factors that you consider most affect the security of an organisation's computer systems

(b) identifies ways in which the risks associated with computer security might be successfully managed.

2 Integrity controls

2.1 Sources of error

It is important to identify how errors might occur during the operation of a system other than as a result of failing to establish proper administrative controls. Errors will fall into the following classes:

1 **Data capture**/classification errors – these occur before data is ready for input to a system and arise because of:

- incorrect classification of data (e.g. allocating a production cost as an administrative cost)

- assessment/measuring mistakes (e.g. recording the arrival of ten tons of raw material when only nine tons was delivered)

- incorrect spelling (of a customer's name)

- transposition (recording a receipt as £50,906 instead of the actual figure of £90,650).

2 **Transcription errors** – these arise during the preparation of data for processing. For example, data which has been written down previously or which is passed on orally may be incorrectly recorded on data input forms.

3 **Data communication faults** – if the system operates over a wide area network (WAN) then the original input at the terminal/PC may become corrupted during transmission either during online processing or where the information is stored in a batch file and transmitted over the WAN later for processing. Similar issues need to

be considered for local area networks (LANs) but far fewer problems arise due to the greater level of resilience inherent in LANs.

4   **Data processing errors** – these can arise due to programming error, system design and/or data corruption on the system itself.

Because the above errors are likely to occur throughout the life of a system, with varying degrees of seriousness, we must take specific measures to identify when they occur and to ensure that corrections are made to the data, either before or after processing has occurred.

2.2   System activities

The purpose of the controls is to ensure as far as possible that:

- the data being processed is complete
- it is authorised
- the results are accurate
- a complete audit trail of what was done is available.

The areas in which we would expect controls to be assigned to provide protection to the system are concerned with input, file processing and output.

Input activities	File processing activities	Output activities
• data collection and preparation • data authorisation • data conversion (if appropriate) • data transmission • data correction • corrected data re-input	• data validation and edit • data manipulation, sorting/merging • master file updating	• output control and reconciliation with predetermined data • information distribution

Controls in these areas are vital and must deal with errors or problems as they arise instead of delaying their resolution to a later processing stage. Inaccurate data represents a waste of both computer time and human effort and may lead to further unforeseen errors occurring and misleading final results.

2.3 Data integrity

Data integrity means completeness and accuracy of data. For decisions to be made consistently throughout the organisation, it is necessary for the system to contain controls over the input, processing and output of data to maintain its integrity.

While computer systems are made up of physical items, the input of data and the output of information is designed for the benefit of human beings and is subject to their interpretation. Security risks arise where input and output occurs. Risks may arise due to innocent events such as running the wrong program, or inadvertently deleting data that is still of value to the organisation.

More importantly, as more and more systems consist of networks of computers either in the form of Local Area Networks and/or Wide Area Networks, the risks of unauthorised users hacking into those systems increases significantly.

This type of activity is referred to as 'hacking' and encompasses anything from the unauthorised accessing of personnel information to the manipulation of important accounting or other financial information.

Many of the security controls described in the previous section will have some effect on data integrity. Data controls – should ensure that data is:

- collected in full and with accuracy

- generated at the appropriate times

- kept up-to-date and accurate on file, and

- processed properly and accurately to provide meaningful and useful output.

Information can only be reliable if the underlying data is also reliable. Controls should be exercised to ensure that data could only be derived in the first instance from properly identified and responsible data providers. In order to remain reliable, such data must subsequently be processed and maintained in an adequately controlled environment.

Input data can get lost or it might contain errors. Human error is usually the biggest security weakness in the system. Controls ought to be applied to reduce the risk. The extensiveness of the input controls will depend on the method used to process the input data and the cost of making an error. If the consequences of input errors would be costly, the system should include more extensive controls than it would if the cost of making an error was insignificant.

(a) **Input controls** – will be designed with a view to completeness, authorisation, accuracy and compliance with audit needs. The controls will use the following techniques:

Verification – determines whether the data has been properly conveyed to the system from the source (unlike validation which is concerned with whether the data is correct or not).This procedure is normally carried out by a system user to check the completeness and accuracy of data. The main types of error found in data verification are copying errors and transposition errors, e.g. where a value £369,500 might have been entered as £365,900. Similarly, transposition errors in the text might be found where a customer's name might have been entered wrongly (Smtih instead of Smith).Various checks are used including:

- Type checks – every entry must comply with the prescribed format, e.g. dates may be defined as consisting of 2 digits, 3 alphabetic characters and 2 further digits such as 04DEC04. Any other form of input will result in an error.

- Non-existence checks – data fields requiring entry may have a separate validation table behind them such that the data being input must exist on that table, e.g. a supplier account number must exist already before the system will accept that number on an invoice.

- Checks for consistency – where data is originally entered and does not require on-going maintenance, the fact that it is still consistent with the original data input should be checked within an appropriate timescale, e.g. batch totals should not be altered once input, payee codes for suppliers paid by BACS should be confirmed by print-out against source data on a half-yearly basis.

- Duplication/repetition checks – the system may check, for example, that only this invoice has been received from a supplier with the supplier's invoice number currently being input.

- Range checks – a minimum and maximum value could be established against which input can be checked.

- Input comparison between document and screen.

- Checking batch and hash totals.

- One-for-one checks between data lists.

Validation is the application, normally by the computer software, of a series of rules or tests designed to check the reasonableness of the data. Computers are unable to check the completeness and accuracy of data, as they are unable to see or read the source data. Instead, they must be programmed with rules and tests to apply to data to check its reasonableness. Techniques used in validation include:

- Comparison of totals, e.g. checking that the total of debits equals the total of credits on a journal voucher.

- Comparison of data sets, e.g. a one-for-one check between two computerised files of data to identify and reject any differences.

- Check digits – are commonly used in supplier, customer and account numbers. The computer would perform the calculation on the code input, and compare the digit calculated with the check digit input.

- Sequence numbers – often documents such as invoices, orders and credit notes have sequential numbers to avoid omission of a document. The software can be programmed to reject any document that is out of order, or to periodically report any missing documents.

- Range checks – the computer might be programmed with an acceptable range for each piece of data, e.g. if products are priced between £3.49 and £12.99, the sales system might be told to reject unit prices lower than £3.00 and higher than £20.00.

- Format checks – the software might be programmed to expect certain data to be alphabetic, numeric or a combination of the two. A numeric field would then reject the letter O being input instead of the number 0, or the letter l (lower case L) instead of the number 1 File controls – should be applied to make sure that:

  - correct data files are used for processing

  - whole files or data on a file are not lost or corrupted

  - unauthorised access to data on files is prevented

  - if data is lost or corrupted, it can be re-created.

(b) **Processing controls** – should ensure the accuracy and completeness of processing. Data processing errors can arise due to programming error, system design and/or data corruption on the system itself. Because these errors are likely to occur throughout the life of a system, with varying degrees of seriousness, specific measures should be taken to identify when they occur and to ensure that corrections are made to the data, either before or after processing has occurred.

Programs should be subject to development controls and to rigorous testing. Periodic running of test data is also recommended. Other processing controls include the following:

- standardisation – structured procedures for processing activities

- batch control documents – information about the batch that is entered prior to processing

- double processing – repeat of processing with comparison of individual reports.

Data communication/transmission control – if a system operates over a WAN, then the original input at the terminal/PC may become corrupted during transmission, either during on-line processing or where the information is stored in a batch file and transmitted over the WAN later for processing. Similar issues need to be considered for LANs but far fewer problems arise due to the greater level of resilience inherent in LANs.

Controls are necessary where data is transmitted in any form. The less sophisticated the techniques used for transmitting data, the higher the level of separate controls that need to be designed to identify errors and ensure that incorrect data is not processed.

(c) **Output controls** – these are controls to ensure that the produced output is checked against the input controls to ensure completeness and accuracy of processing. The system output, particularly in hard copy form, must be controlled so that the recipient receives complete and accurate information. There are a number of features that can be built into each report to ensure this.

- Batch control totals – the totals of accepted and rejected data. Exception reports – reporting abnormal transactions that may require further investigation (e.g. a report of all employees paid more than £3,000 in a particular payroll run).

- Start of report/page number/end of report markers – it should be impossible for a user to receive a report with pages missing without realising immediately. This is often used in error reports, where careless staff might 'lose' some pages from a report of the errors they have made. Nil return reports – if there is nothing to report, a report should be produced that says so. This is particularly important for error, exception and security control reports. A person committing a fraud might steal the report that showed evidence of their action, then claim there was no report produced because there were no items to report.

- Distribution lists – the header of each report should show the distribution list for the report, the number of copies, the copy number and the planned recipient of the report.

(d) **Application controls** – can be incorporated in the software of the system to ensure that applications preserve the integrity of data. These controls include the following:

- *Passwords* – are a set of characters that may be allocated to a person, a terminal or a room, which have to be keyed into the system before access is permitted. They may be built in to the system to allow individual users access to certain parts of the system but not to others. This will prevent accidental or deliberate changes to data.

- *Authorisation levels* – certain actions may require a user to have authorisation attached to their user-name. This type of control is commonly used for the production of cheques. Authorisation is also often necessary when rolling forward the system defaults at the end of a month or year, due to the complicated nature of correcting such a move when it is done in error.

- *Training and supervision* – staff should receive adequate training to prevent them from making the most common mistakes. They should also be made aware of any tasks that they should not attempt.

- *Audit trails* – software should be written in such a way that a clear logic exists in the sequence of tasks it performs, and data at different stages of processing is kept rather than being over-written. In this way the sequence of events can be evidenced for the benefit of any observer trying to check that the system works correctly.

Activity 2

Controls are invariably incorporated into the input, processing and output stages of a computer-based system.

(a)   State the guidelines which should normally be followed in determining what controls should be built into a system.

(b)   Identify and briefly describe one type of control which might be used to detect each of the following input data errors:

(i)   Errors of transcription resulting in an incorrect customer account code.

(ii)   Quantity of raw material normally written in pounds weight but entered in error as tons.

(iii) Entry on a despatch note for a product to be despatched from a warehouse which does not stock that particular product.

(iv)   A five-digit product code used instead of a six-digit salesman code.

(v)   Invalid expenditure code entered on an invoice.

2.4   Systems integrity

Systems integrity relates to the controlling and monitoring of the system in order to ensure that it does exactly what it was designed to do. Factors include:

- project management
- operations management
- systems design
- personnel
- procedure control
- hardware configuration.

These factors are all relevant to the system achieving what it was designed to do.

Some of the controls that we have already discussed in earlier chapters are applicable to the integrity of the system. There is an overlap with control measures that apply to security of the system and to system integrity because, obviously, the loss of security to a system will result in the loss of integrity of the system also.

KAPLAN PUBLISHING

(a) **Administrative systems**

Administrative controls relate to personnel and support functions. For some positions, segregation of duties is a security requirement involving division of responsibility into separate roles. The selection process for personnel (both recruitment for new staff and movement within an organisation) should reflect the nature of the work. If sensitive information is handled, positive vetting might be applied. Staff should all have detailed job descriptions, with those responsible for control clearly identifiable. Other controls include job rotation, enforced vacations, system logs and supervision.

Administrative procedures should be clearly documented and adhered to. These include health and safety procedures, especially fire drills, the operation of a 'clean desk' policy, logging document movements and the filing or shredding of documents.

The physical security of the site is vital. Visitors need to be authorised and accompanied whilst in the building. Access to more sensitive facilities can be controlled by devices such as magnetic swipe cards. Placement of hardware should ensure that the screens and documents are not visible to the 'passer by'. Access to specific terminals can be restricted by the use of devices such as passwords.

Procedures to be followed in the event of interruptions to processing should be documented and observed. Computer-based information should be backed up frequently, with the copies stored in separate locations, in fire-proof safes. Recovery plans should identify procedures for all eventualities from the retrieval of a corrupt file through to complete system failure due to, for example, fire. These plans should clearly identify the people responsible to effect the procedures.

(b) **On-line and real time systems**

In this kind of processing, transactions are input as and when they arise. There is no attempt to accumulate and batch similar transactions. This gives rise to particular control problems. Traditional batch controls are not normally applicable, while the number of people inputting transactions from widely scattered terminals makes security difficult to ensure.

The following controls may be used in on-line and real time systems.

- Using passwords with a logical access system.

- Transaction log – the totals of data on the transaction log (which may be a daily or weekly log) can be matched to movements on master file control accounts.

- Supervisory controls, i.e. regular physical supervision by management. This is particularly important for situations where there is a lack of segregation of computer operator duties.

- Physical restriction of access to terminals – terminals may be kept in separate locked buildings or offices. The terminals themselves may require a key to be inserted before the terminal can be used.

- Documentation of transactions. All transaction or input documents should be recorded and signed or initialled by appropriate personnel within the user department. Pre-numbering of documents is also important so that sequence checks can be performed, and reports of duplicated or missing data can be produced.

Matching transactions to master file data. An on-line system enables full matching of transaction data to master file data.

(c) **Systems integrity in a network environment**

The complexity of local and wide area networks allows for many more breaches of security than a single computer and each breach can, of course, involve many computers. The main risks on a networked system are:

- hardware/software disruption or malfunction.

- computer viruses – usually unwittingly distributed by opening an infected e-mail message, but also catchable from infected floppy disks and CDs. Once the virus comes into contact with a system it replicates itself onto the system and lies dormant until either the use of the system, some defined event or transaction or a certain date activates it. The replication of the virus makes it very difficult to find its original source.

- unauthorised access to the system – hacking is usually associated with people who are not employees of the organisation, but who gain access to an organisation's data for mischievous or malicious intent. However, in its widest term – a person who gains access to a computer without permission – it can also be applied to company employees themselves. Hacking has been made possible by organisations using always-on broadband telecommunications networks that are accessible to the hacker via powerful workstations and modems.

- electronic eavesdropping – which has become more of a risk as more organisations implement wireless network configurations.

Possible controls include many that we have already discussed and some that are specific for the risks outlined above. They include:

- Physical access controls – the use of strict controls over the locking of the rooms in which the computers are located and the distribution of keys to authorised personnel only. This is vital where the computers are used either to access sensitive data files or to alter or develop programs. Secondly, machine access – the restriction of access to and use of computers by keys, cards and badges.

- User identification – this includes the positive confirmation of the identity of the user and the proof of his or her identification (authentication). The former includes the input of the name, employee number and account number. The latter includes the input of something that is known (e.g. passwords, question-and-answer sequences), or something that is possessed (badges, cards), or something personal to the user (e.g. finger print, hand or voice features, signature).

- Data and program access authorisation – after identification of the user, the type of privileges are checked to ensure that the user has the necessary authority. Privileges cover the type of files and programs that can be accessed, and the activities allowed during access. The user is denied access if he or she is not specifically authorised.

- Program integrity controls – ensure that unauthorised access and alterations cannot be made to programs.

- Database integrity controls – controls and audit techniques that protect database management systems software and data against unauthorised access, modification, disclosure and destruction.

- Anti-virus software – (regularly updated with new releases) detects known viruses and destroys them. Each common virus will be known and identifiable by the anti-virus software. However, it must be recognised that such software only protects against known viruses. All emails, removable disks and CDs should be checked before they can be used internally. Most organisations implement stringent internal procedures to make sure that unauthorised disks and CDs are not used within the organisation. Failure to comply with these requirements usually leads to disciplinary action, including dismissal.

- Surveillance – the detection of security violations by direct observation, by review of computer logs or by use of the operator's console to display current program and data usage.

- Communication lines safeguards – while impossible to fully protect communication lines, controls such as encryption, phone tap and bug checks should go a long way to prevent penetration of the system via the communication lines.

- Encryption – is a control to translate a message into coded form using a code key that is only known to the sender and recipient of the message. This is a useful control for preventing eavesdropping, particularly in a wireless network.

- Firewalls – are security devices that effectively isolate the sensitive parts of an organisation's system from those areas available to external users.

- Administrative considerations – procedures that ensure that controls and safeguards are effective in preventing, deterring and detecting unauthorised or fraudulent systems data and program access and modification.

 Activity 3

On a number of occasions, you will be aware that a new virus has been reported that might be spread by e-mail and do considerable damage. Opening the e-mail will run the virus, and might also forward it to all the addresses in your address book. Next time this happens, carefully make a note of all the steps your organisation has taken to deal with this contingency. What would you do if you suspected an e-mail you had been sent contained a virus?

3 Contingency control

3.1 Disaster affecting the computer system

In computing terms, a disaster might mean the loss or unavailability of some of the computer systems. In a modern business there are few areas unaffected by computing, and consequently few that will not suffer if its performance is impaired. Also, risks are increasing; an organisation now has to cope with the risks of hacking, virus infection and industrial action aimed at the computing staff.

Losses that can be expected due to the non-availability of computer systems increase with time; it is therefore important to make plans to keep downtime to a minimum.

Management commitment is an essential component of any contingency plan because it will almost certainly involve considerable expense. Various stand-by plans must be considered; the choice will depend on the amount of time that the installation can reasonably expect to survive without computing.

The key feature of any disaster recovery plan is the regular back up of data and software. If, at the time of disaster, there are no back-up copies, then no amount of stand-by provision will replace them.

The contingency plan must specify what actions are to be taken during a disaster and during the time that computer systems are unavailable up to the time that full operations are restored. The plan must be as detailed as possible; should state who is responsible at each stage, when it should be invoked, and where copies may be found. The more care that is taken with a contingency plan, the better the organisation will be able to survive a computing disaster; it also concentrates the mind on computer security and the risks faced, with an increased likelihood that counter measures will be installed which will reduce the risks.

3.2 Contingency controls

Contingency controls are those which correct the consequences of a risk occurring, rather than preventing or reducing the risk. It is the process of planning for catastrophes, and in the computing environment this usually means the breakdown of the computer system. For organisations that rely upon their computer systems to carry on their business the loss of those systems, even for a short period, can be disastrous, therefore good contingency plans should be put in place.

The plan should include:

- standby procedures – so that essential operations can be performed while normal services are disrupted

- recovery procedures – to return to normal working once the breakdown is fixed

- management policies to ensure that the plan is implemented.

A number of standby plans merit consideration and are discussed below. The final selection would be dependent upon the estimated time that the concern would function adequately without computing facilities.

- Distributed support, where computing is spread over several sites so that, if one site is lost, the others can cope with the transferred work; this approach implies compatibility and spare capacity to cope with the loss of the largest installation.

- Reciprocal agreement with another company. Although a popular option, few companies can guarantee spare capacity, or continuing capability and compatibility, which attaches a high risk to this option.

- A more expensive, but lower risk, version of the above is the commercial computer bureau. This solution entails entering into a formal agreement, which entitles the customer to a selection of services.

- Empty rooms or equipped rooms. The former allows the organisation access to install a back-up system, which increases the recovery time but reduces the cost. The latter can be costly, so sharing this facility is a consideration.

- Relocatable computer centres. This solution involves a delay while the facility is erected and assembled and also larger computers cannot usually be accommodated.

The effectiveness of the contingency plan is dependent on comprehensive back-up procedures for both data and software. The contingency plan must identify initial responses and clearly delineate responsibility at each stage of the exercise – from damage limitation through to full recovery.

3.3   Backing up

Information on your computer is vulnerable: hard disks can fail, computer systems can fail, viruses can wipe a disk, careless operators can delete files, and very careless operators can delete whole areas of the hard disks by mistake. Computers can also be damaged or stolen. For these reasons backing up your data is essential. This involves making copies of essential files, together with necessary update transactions, and keeping them on another computer, or on some form of storage media so that copies can be recreated. Your organisation will have procedures and you will have been taught how to do this.

To ensure that you can back up easily you will probably have your own 'workspace' – an area of a disk that contains your work. This helps segregate your unique work from files or information that are held by a number of people.

It is important to get into the habit of backing up in different ways for different reasons to increase the reliability of your backed-up data. You should consider backing-up:

- when you have done a large amount of work over a short period – in which case you should back up all the contents of your 'workspace'

- when you have completed a major body of work – you should clean up the directory containing the files (to get rid of files that are not needed) and just back up that directory

- on a regular basis, back up your whole 'workspace' and the essential system files.

Where the data is maintained by batch processing, the Grandfather/ Father/ Son method of backing-up will be used. The principle of this method is that at any point in time the last two back-ups made should be available plus all of the batches that have been processed since the older of the back-ups was made. These would be in the form of master and data tapes that would be separately labelled and stored. Once the Grandfather tape becomes older than that, it can be re-used as the latest tape for back-up purposes and becomes the Son.

These days, where it is more likely that the data is maintained on-line, data will be backed-up each day, so that if the normal storage medium fails, the information is available for the system to be restored to the last point of data entry prior to the back-up being taken. Copies of all data files should be taken on a frequent and regular basis and kept off-site or in a fireproof safe. The data can then be restored in case of data loss or corruption.

Software backup – copies of system software and applications should also be taken and stored off-site. Thus the computer system can be re-created on new hardware in case the building is damaged or destroyed. Software can also be restored in case it becomes corrupted or accidentally deleted.

Procedures to be followed in the event of interruptions to processing should be documented and observed. Computer-based information should be backed up frequently, with the copies stored in separate locations, in fireproof safes. Recovery plans should identify procedures for all eventualities from the retrieval of a corrupt file through to complete system failure due to, for example, fire. These plans should clearly identify the people responsible to effect the procedures.

Activity 4

List and give a brief explanation of the control techniques and safeguards to protect a system where multiple users have access to centralised data through terminal devices at remote locations linked to a central computer system via telephone lines or other communication links.

3.4 Advantages and disadvantages of contingency planning

The main argument in favour of contingency planning is that it places the management team in a better position to cope with the change by eliminating or at least reducing the time delay (and hence lost profits) in making a response to an emergency. The emergency may be a lost opportunity or a definite threat. Specific reserve plans help managers to respond more rationally to the event. A crisis can lead to decisions being made within a very short time span and without full information. Early evaluation of the demands of low probability events and the alternative remedies allows more detailed consideration and consequently should reduce the likelihood of panic measures.

Although contingency planning does force managers to consider unlikely events that can result in beneficial spin-offs, it can also result in negative attitudes. Events with low probabilities may be threats and focusing attention on these threats could be demoralising and demotivating.

4 Assessing and managing risk

4.1 Managing risk

In general terms, risk would be taken as meaning anything that could cause the organisation to make a financial loss. It can be defined as the 'chance of bad consequences'. The types of risk include disasters outside the control of the organisation, poor trading, mismanagement, errors because of human or machine problems and misappropriation of resources, physical assets or intangible assets.

You must understand the concept of risk and how it may be assessed in the planning of controls within an organisation.

The following step-by-step process is a useful framework for the risk assessment process:

- Identify risks.

- Quantify risks.

- Identify counter measures (some of the possibilities are listed below).

- Cost counter measures.

- Choose which counter measures are required. · Draw up contingency plans.

- Implement the plan to manage the risk.

- Monitor, review and update the plan.

- Constantly watch for new risks – encourage all staff to report situations where they feel there might be a risk.

The counter measures that an organisation can adopt include the following possibilities:

- Transfer the risks (by means of an insurance policy) – limited liability is another way of transferring risk.

- Decide to live with the risks, if the counter measures cannot be justified. Modify a system so as to eliminate the risks.

- Reduce the probability of risk by introducing controls e.g. two signatures on payments.

- Reduce the exposure to risk by removing the organisation from risky situations.

- Adopt measures that reduce the cost associated with a risk (e.g.by ensuring an adequate back-up system).

- Enable recovery by implementing recovery procedures appropriate to the situation e.g. relocation plans and computer disaster recovery plans.

5 Checklist of tasks

- Produce a flowchart of existing procedures in your section, with a narrative.

- Highlight any control issues you can detect in the current system.

6 Test your knowledge

Test your knowledge

1   Why do organisations adopt security measures?

2   Describe the three elements of the information system's security.

3   Outline the terms of the Data Protection Act.

4   What are usage logs?

5   Identify four of the techniques used in data validation.

6   What do you understand by the term 'data integrity'?

7   What sort of documents need sequence controls?

8   To maintain systems integrity, what types of control may be used in on-line and real time systems?

9   What type of control is encryption?

7 Summary

Computer systems require special attention in any organisation for two reasons. Firstly, the fact that the audit trail through a computer system is not visible as in a manual system may lead to problems of control. Secondly, any errors in a computer system of a systematic nature can have a very serious impact on the accuracy of the records, whereas in a manual system the damage is likely to be far more localised to one specific area.

You should therefore ensure that the computer systems of an organisation are very well controlled with tight security over all the key functions.

Answers to chapter activities and 'test your knowledge' questions

 ## Activity 1

BRIEFING REPORT

To: Head of Department
From: Trainee management accountant
Date: 2nd November

Security of an organisation's computer system

The factors, which most affect the security of an organisation's computer system, can be divided into three groups – physical, systems and human.

Physical aspects – these relate to the security risks to which the computer hardware is exposed. These risks mainly come from outside the system and include theft, fire, dust, humidity, flooding and wind and earth movement damage to the building housing the computer.

Systems aspects – these relate to risks, which are inherent in the system itself and include loss of data, loss of software and possibly damage to equipment, all caused by system malfunctioning brought about by either hardware or software failure or errors.

Human aspects – these include risks from inside and outside the organisation and risks arising from both intentional and unintentional actions. For example a large multi-user networked computer system is at risk from outside 'hacking' as well as from employees within the organisation. Unintentional damage to equipment, data and software etc may be caused by accidents e.g. spilling drinks into equipment, accidental changes to data e.g. correcting the wrong file or deleting a file, running the wrong software, forgetting to run a particular process etc. Intentional aspects include setting up fake accounts, causing unauthorised payments either as credit or cheques to be made, allowing favourable discount terms to particular clients and damage such as the deletion or corruption of data files and software.

Managing the risks associated with computer security

Managing the risks associated with computer security involves reducing the risks and the effects to the lowest possible levels. Three stages are necessary.

Risk assessment – a full examination of all the risks in the three groups above is made. Particular types of computer systems and particular locations and environments each have their own problems. The risks are, of course, different for a centralised system as against a distributed computing system.

Another factor is the importance of the work being done on the computer. For example if a personnel department computer went down, it would not be as serious as if the computer monitoring a production line failed and there would not be such a need to get the personnel computer up and running again quickly.

Risk minimisation – this comprises the actions, which may be taken when the risks to a computer system have been assessed. These actions include both taking physical and system precautions and providing fall-back and remedial measures. The list of actions includes:

- securing the building(s) housing equipment with bars, strong doors, locks, monitoring systems, access control, etc.

- provision of an environment suitable for reliable computer operation, having clean air at the correct temperature and humidity and an electrical power supply that is both continuous and smooth

- strict control of the quality of new software and on any modifications required to existing software

- vetting of all computer staff appointments and the taking out of 'fidelity guarantees' with suitable insurance companies

- access control for the system from terminals, etc. This will normally involve a system of passwords changed on a regular basis

- a high level of training and education of computer staff

- automated operating procedures with built in checks (probably utilising job control language 'programs') so that operators do not have to trust to memory and are given minimum scope for error

- fully documented systems and procedure manuals including precise statements of actions to be taken for system recovery after breakdowns · provision of standby facilities and a reciprocal processing agreement with another organisation.

(If the computer failed and it was expected that it would not be repairable for quite some time, then back-up disks would be transferred and processing carried out on the other organisation's computer, overnight or at the weekend – and vice versa.)

Risk transference – it is impossible to eliminate all risks, but it is possible to transfer the element of uncovered risk to another party through the medium of insurance i.e. in the event of a computer catastrophe, the losses caused would be covered by insurance.

Activity 2

(a) Systems controls should be designed according to the following guidelines.

- All transactions should be processed.

- All errors in transactions should be reported. Errors should be corrected and re-input. Fraud should be prevented.

- The likelihood of error should be estimated. This will depend partly on the location in which the source document is prepared and the type of person originating it.

- The importance of errors should be assessed. In accounting systems, 100% accuracy may be required. In other systems (e.g. market surveys), a degree of error may be acceptable.

- The cost of control should be considered in relation to the cost of an error. The cost of 100% accuracy is, in practice, usually too high. The controls should not interfere unduly with the progress of work. The controls should be as simple as possible, and acceptable to users. Auditors should be consulted and the system designed to meet their requirements.

(b) Incorrect customer account code

This should be detected by a check digit. The account code would include an extra digit derived by calculation from other digits. On input to the computer, the program would perform the calculations and, if the digit derived was not the check digit, an error would be reported. The system selected should minimise the possibility of undetected error.

Raw material quantity

This should be detected by a reasonableness check. Upper and lower limits would be set, outside which a quantity should not lie. Since the entry of tons instead of pounds would result in a value 2,240 times as big as the correct one, it would be detected.

Product not stocked

This would be detected by an on-file check. On input, the despatch note details would be referred to the stock master files, which would indicate that the product was not held in the warehouse shown.

Five-digit product code

This would be detected by a format check. The validation program would have parameters for the size of fields, and would report the product code as being a digit short

Invalid expenditure code

This would be detected by a range check. The validation program would have parameters showing the upper and lower values of expenditure codes. Comparison of the code with the parameters would reveal that it was not in the permissible range.

 Activity 3

Did you note that your organisation has anti-virus software? Does the information systems department give you clear instructions on the procedure to adopt? If a machine was infected, what happened?

You would not open the e-mail under any circumstances but should contact the IS department immediately. They should be able to identify and remove the virus. In some situations you might have to delete it yourself. This means deleting it from your inbox and then deleting it from your 'deleted items' folder.

 Activity 4

The control techniques and safeguards used to protect a system where multiple users have access to centralised data through terminal devices at remote locations linked to a central computer system via telephone lines or other communication links are as follows.

- **Terminal physical security** – this covers two aspects. Firstly, terminal room access – the use of strict controls over the locking of the rooms in which the terminals are located and the distribution of keys to authorised personnel only. This is vital where the terminals are used either to access sensitive data files or to alter or develop programs. Secondly, terminal machine access – the restriction of access to and use of terminals by keys, cards and badges.

- **User identification** – this includes the positive confirmation of the identity of the user and the proof of his identification (authentication). The former includes the input of his name, employee number and account number. The latter includes the input of something that is known (e.g. passwords, question-and-answer sequences), or something that is possessed (badges, cards), or something personal to the user (e.g. finger print, hand or voice features, signature).

- **Data and program access authorisation** – after identification of the user ((b) above), the privileges he has as to what he can access (files and programs) and what he can do during access have to be checked to ensure that he has the necessary authority. The user must be denied access if not specifically authorised.

- **Surveillance** – the detection of security violations by direct observation, by review of computer logs or by use of the operator's console to display current program and data usage.

- **Communication lines safeguards** – while impossible to fully protect communication lines controls such as encryption, phone tap and bug checks should go a long way to prevent penetration of the system via the communication lines.

- **Encryption** – the transformation of a message or of data for the purpose of rendering it unintelligible to everyone but the correct users who are able to translate the message back to its original form. Program integrity controls – controls, which ensure that unauthorised access and alterations cannot be made to programs.

- **Database integrity controls** – controls and audit techniques, which protect database management systems software and data against unauthorised access, modification, disclosure and destruction.

- **Administrative considerations** – procedures, which ensure that controls and safeguards are effective in preventing, deterring and detecting unauthorised or fraudulent systems data and program access and modification.

Test your knowledge

1   They adopt security measures to avoid or prevent loss; to deter as many threats as possible; for easy recovery after any loss; to identify the cause of any loss after the event; and to correct vulnerable areas to reduce the risk of repeated loss.

2   The information systems security is based on three elements. The people and the data/information elements and the physical elements, which acknowledge that the operation of computer equipment can be severely impaired where it is subject to events such as fire, flooding and improper environmental conditions, e.g. heat.

3   Under the terms of the Data Protection Act 1998, the need for privacy is recognised by the requirements that all personal data on individuals should be held only for clearly designated purposes. Accuracy and integrity must be maintained and the data must be open to inspection. Only legitimate parties can access data and information must be secured against alteration, accidental loss or deliberate damage. Furthermore, the Act states that data must be obtained fairly, to precise specifications and must not be kept for longer than required.

4   Usage logs are part of the system, which is designed to automatically record the log-in and log-off times of each user, the applications accessed and any applications or files where access has been denied. Periodic checks are made for unusual patterns, such as a day-shift worker accessing the system at night.

5   The techniques used in data validation include comparison of totals, comparison of data sets, check digits, sequence, range checks and format checks.

6   Data integrity means completeness and accuracy of data. For decisions to be made consistently throughout the organisation, it is necessary for the system to contain controls over the input, processing and output of data to maintain its integrity.

7   Documents such as invoices, orders, petty cash vouchers and credit notes need sequential numbers to avoid omission of a document.

8   The following controls may be used in on-line and real time systems.

- Using passwords with a logical access system.

- Transaction log – the totals of data on the transaction log (which may be a daily or weekly log) can be matched to movements on master file control accounts.

- Supervisory controls, i.e. regular physical supervision by management. This is particularly important for situations where there is a lack of segregation of computer operator duties.

- Physical restriction of access to terminals – terminals may be kept in separate locked buildings or offices. The terminals themselves may require a key to be inserted before the terminal can be used.

- Documentation of transactions. All transaction or input documents should be recorded and signed or initialled by appropriate personnel within the user department. Pre-numbering of documents is also important so that sequence checks can be performed, and reports of duplicated or missing data can be produced.

9   Encryption is a control to translate a message into coded form using a code key that is only known to the sender and recipient of the message. This is a useful control for preventing eavesdropping, particularly in a wireless network.

Improving the system

Introduction

This chapter should cover all of the areas within an organisation that you might investigate when looking for ways of improving the effectiveness of an accounting system. In general, you can look at three issues. Firstly, what the system or department is trying to achieve, including quality which is specifically referred to in the standards. Secondly, how well it achieves what it sets out to do and whether it can be more efficient and effective and lastly, the risks of error.

New methods might involve a new department structure, changes in planning and control systems, recommending computerisation of some activities, changing the equipment or changing the methods of working or documents used.

SKILLS
1.1 Identify an organisation's accounting system requirements.
1.2 Review record keeping systems to confirm whether they meet the organisation's requirements for financial information.
1.3 Identify weaknesses in and the potential improvements to the accounting system and consider their impact on the organisation.
1.4 Identify potential areas of fraud arising from lack of control within the accounting system and grade the risk.
1.5 Review methods of operating for cost effectiveness, reliability and speed.

CONTENTS
1 Systems and procedures
2 Improving effectiveness
3 Analysing the work process
4 Flowcharting
5 Cost-benefit analysis and cost control
6 Performance management and appraisal
7 Training
8 Disciplinary procedures
9 Appraising the working environment
10 Checklist of tasks

2.1 Make recommendations for changes to the accounting system in an easily understood format with clear rationale and an explanation of assumptions made.

2.2 Identify the effects that any recommended changes would have on the users of the system.

2.3 Enable individuals who operate accounting systems to understand how to use the system to fulfil their responsibilities.

2.4 Identify the implications of recommended changes in terms of time, financial costs and benefits and operating procedures.

1 Systems and procedures

1.1 Principles

The establishment of systems and procedures will ensure that organisational objectives are attained. The system will involve activities and procedures for **processing information** together with all the documents needed to convey the information to the right people and to control the activities. These principles of systems are equally applicable to the checking of existing procedures and to any alteration to those existing procedures or to the introduction of new procedures.

(a)   There should be a smooth flow of work with no bottlenecks.

(b)   Movement of staff should be kept to a minimum.

(c)   Duplication of work should be avoided.

(d)   The best and most effective use of existing specialist attributes should be made.

(e)   Simplicity within systems should be sought. Complications usually lead to mis-interpretations and/or mistakes.

(f)   Human efforts should be aided by machines where appropriate.

(g)   Procedures and systems should be designed to facilitate the application of the management by exception principle.

(h)   Any system must be cost-effective. The benefits should be compared with the cost of implementation and subsequent supervision costs.

1.2 The flow of information

Information, even if it originates from outside the organisation, must be processed within the organisation. The flow of information will determine both the system and the documentation required within that system. Whether it originates externally or internally, systems evolve from an examination of the stages involved in typical business transactions, and the documentation generated.

The diagram below shows an overview of an accounts department and the typical information flows involved:

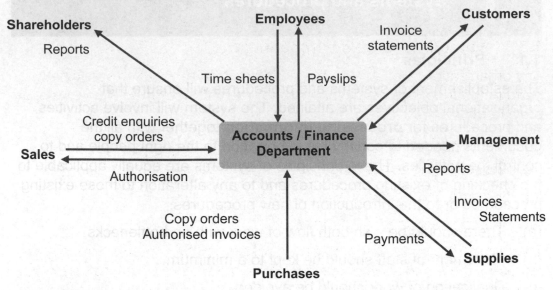

A procedure is a chronological sequence of required actions for performing a certain task. Procedures often cut across departmental lines e.g.in a manufacturing company the procedure for handling orders will almost certainly involve the sales department (for the original order), the finance department (for acknowledgement of receipt of funds and for customer credit approval),the accounting department (for recording the transaction), the production department (for the order to produce goods or authority to release them from stock) and the transport department (for determination of route and shipping). The advantages of procedures for routine work include the following:

- Procedures should prescribe the most efficient way of getting a job done.

- There is no need to exercise discretion in routine tasks.

- Staff will find jobs easier to do when they are familiar with established procedures.

- Prescribed procedures ensure that a task of a certain type will be done in the same way throughout the organisation.

- The work will be done in the same way even when a different person starts in a job or takes over from the previous holder.

- A written record can be kept in a procedures manual so that people unfamiliar with how a job should be done can learn quickly and easily by referring to it.

- Procedures reduce the likelihood of departmental friction because disputes between departments about who should do what and when, should be avoided.

1.3 Establishing office procedures

Any organisation needs a number of different administrative services to perform the functions necessary for it to operate efficiently. These services provide for:

(a) the receipt of information

(b) the recording and arrangement of information

(c) the storage and security of information

(d) the communication of information.

The term 'office procedures' means, in essence, the systems. Procedures represent the summation of a series of operations necessary to perform a task associated with the receipt, recording, arrangement, storage, security and communication of information. Thus administrative systems and office procedures are very closely related.

If procedures need to be established it is essential to adopt a logical, co-ordinated and organised approach. In practice, the establishment of office procedures rarely means completely new procedures; it is more likely to refer to the adaptation of existing procedures. With a new organisation, management can really only set up a provisional system which will need to be reviewed after an initial period and probably changed. Thus the examination of the establishment of procedures will concentrate on the revision of approaches existing within the organisation at the time that the review is undertaken.

A review of existing procedures may be divided into two parts:

1   The first part is a general overview of the office as a whole and the role it plays within the organisation – this will consider: · the purpose of the office

- what actually happens within the office · who does what within the office

- the techniques and methods employed by staff in carrying out assigned responsibilities

- the quality of performance.

2   The second part is a more detailed step-by-step view of the procedures themselves when a thorough examination of 'who does what, when, where and how' must be undertaken. The steps involved in such an analysis include:

- determining the purpose of the review exercise – for example, stemming from the overview, it is likely that weaknesses may have already been highlighted (for instance, too much paperwork)

- examining the procedure's current techniques and methods, and inspecting and analysing existing forms and documentation

- creating a record of the operations involved and revealed by the two steps above

- converting the steps in these operations into some form of chart description (e.g. flowcharts)

- examining each individual step closely to ascertain its effectiveness or inefficiency

- endeavouring to determine other methods and techniques

- determining the most suitable of the options on offer

- altering the chart obtained in the work above to show the effect of the new methods and techniques upon the procedures

- initiating trial runs for test purposes

- developing new, re-designed job specifications for staff

- implementing the new procedure

- ensuring that the new procedure is monitored and modified where necessary.

1.4   Clerical work procedures

Clerical work procedures comprise a series of operations carried out to perform certain tasks within an office. So, for example, there would be a range of procedures in an accounts department varying from, say, preparation of final accounts to passing purchase invoices for payment.

If we consider the latter, we know that there is a series of operations which have to be carried out: for example, receive invoice from purchases office, check invoice stamp correctly completed, check invoice against purchase order, confirm payment arrangements, forward to cashiers' department. In this case, the procedure is likely to be carried out at the same time by the one clerk. It must be remembered, however, that this would be a subroutine of the overall procedure as there would have been, for example, a system to deal with the receipt of the purchase order, another to build up information on payment arrangements, and so on. For a complete picture, details would be noted of each operation, who performs it, where and when, and the other departments concerned.

1.5 The procedures manual

The implementation of procedures is of immense benefit if formalised in writing. This is normally achieved by the preparation of 'laid-down' or written procedures in a procedures manual format, stating the procedures, as they should be carried out:

(a) an outline of the operation to be carried out within the procedure

(b) title of person with overall responsibility for the procedure (not the name of the person currently holding the post)

(c) systems or methods of dealing with the work

(d) the title and department of the member of staff performing each stage of the procedure (again not the individual by name)

(e) sample forms and entries

(f) sample calculations

(g) timetable of various stages and cut-off dates

(h) details of exceptions to be reported and methods of reporting these

(i) sample of any final output

(j) distribution of final output

(k) methods of initiating changes.

Separate manuals may be maintained for each procedure, but where there are only a few procedures carried out in an office, these may all be included in an office manual. These would then be preceded by introductory sections on the organisation, the product range, the organisation chart for the department and details of the various posts within the department.

It may be that the system does not in fact function according to the 'laid-down' procedure. It is then the job of the supervisors to ensure that systems are in fact followed.

Systems should be kept under continuous review and altered as necessary to reflect changes in the organisation, advances in technology, or indeed suggestions from the staff as to how systems can be improved.

The written instructions will clearly indicate what needs to be done (when, where and how), and how procedures within the system as a whole interact. If the written format is poorly constructed and presented, one cannot complain if the systems and procedures are invalidated when attempts are made to implement and operate them.

Advantages of procedures manuals

(a)   In order to prepare an office manual, it is necessary to examine the systems and procedures carefully. The close attention paid to the systems and procedures can only benefit the organisation, in that strengths and weaknesses are revealed.

(b)   Supervision is easier.

(c)   It facilitates the induction and training of new staff.

(d)   It assists the organisation in pinpointing areas of responsibility.

(e)   Having been written down in the first place, it is easier to adapt and/or change systems and procedures in response to changing circumstances.

Disadvantages of procedures manuals

(a)   There is an associated expense in preparing manuals both in the obvious financial terms and the perhaps less obvious cost of administrative time.

(b)   To be of continuing use, an office manual must be updated periodically, again incurring additional expense.

(c)   The instructions as laid down in the office manual may be interpreted rather strictly and implemented too rigidly. Within any organisation, it is often beneficial for employees to bring a degree of flexibility to their duties to cope with particular circumstances.

 Activity 1 (no feedback)

Consider the procedures in your office and see how they compare with the guidelines given.

2 Improving effectiveness

2.1 Introduction

When we think about how we are going to improve the effectiveness of any system, the steps are to:

- analyse the feedback of actual versus the planned or budgeted results for the period

- clarify any strengths and weaknesses

- suggest remedial action and amend plans to revise the whole process in order to achieve the objectives of the department more effectively and efficiently.

For example the continuous nature of corporate planning uses the feedback from budgetary control to revise the budgets. In this context it should be noted that the term 'budgets' means performance budgets (units sold, production, percentage of waste product, number of customer returns, etc) as well as financial budgets.

2.2 Culture

> **Q Definition**
>
> Culture can be defined as 'the way we do things around here'. The effectiveness of an organisation is strongly influenced by the organisational culture, which dictates the way in which the management functions of planning, organising, controlling, staffing and leading are carried out.

The essence of a culture is that the values, attitudes and beliefs within the company are shared and accepted. Some organisations, for example, IBM and Marks & Spencer, have deliberately set out to create a culture that is conducive to customer satisfaction and company growth.

The culture of an organisation is influenced by the style of management that, in turn, influences the management/staff relationships and helps to promote higher performance. If we consider three main management approaches, then we can recognise that each will give rise to different cultures.

Paternalistic management approach – typified by the Quaker companies e.g. Cadbury Schweppes – where the company sets out to be a caring employer and looks to staff to reciprocate in a similar, fair manner. This approach is based on the belief that a satisfied worker is an effective performer. The company establishes itself as the source of important rewards and staff can be induced to work harder out of a feeling of gratitude. This general style promotes a culture of people 'being comfortable and well regarded'. Staff tend to be loyal, good timekeepers and interested in their work but there is little real effort to raise productivity.

Scientific management approach – is encountered in some sales-based organisations and manufacturing companies. The approach is based on the belief that a person will be induced to work if rewards and penalties are tied directly to performance – all rewards follow, and are conditional upon personal performance. A culture stemming from this approach would tend to put practical results above people factors. Success and failure would be clearly measurable, and carry individual responsibility.

The human relations management approach – believes that people derive satisfaction and motivation from doing an effective job – ego, pride, etc, are involved. Such an approach works best in ideas and management areas where there is freedom in deciding how to do the work. It is also heavily dependent upon group pressures and norms. As you would expect, the culture here has a high regard for individuals. Staff tend to be treated as individuals and senior management are readily accessible.

However, companies rarely fall neatly into one category; for example, most large companies will have aspects of all three.

2.3 SWOT analysis

When an organisation, or just a small section of it, wishes to improve its effectiveness, it can carry out a SWOT analysis, as described earlier in this text. SWOT stands for strengths, weaknesses, opportunities and threats. The analysis consists of the internal appraisal of the strengths and weaknesses of the organisation, sometimes called a position audit and an external appraisal of the opportunities and threats that it faces.

The analysis requires an understanding of both the environment and the resource capabilities of the organisation.

If we apply the same principle to the accounting system under scrutiny we must appraise the environment of the accounting system and the resource capabilities, processes, procedures and documentation within the department. The analysis may highlight strengths or weaknesses in any of the following:

- resources – both human and mechanical
- design of processes, procedures and controls

- systems e.g. computer system
- location and layout of office
- relationships with other departments.

The environment may offer opportunities and/or threats:

- It may offer threats (to the well-being of the organisation, such as damaging Government legislation or, say, national action by trade unions) and opportunities (for exploitation, such as growth in market demand, or new technological possibilities).Technological improvements in computing could be seen as an opportunity for the accounting system if it led to faster processing.

- It is the source of organisational resources (human resources come from outside the organisation, as do funds and supplies generally). Difficulty in recruiting staff of the right calibre could be a threat to the accounting system.

2.4 Management information systems

A management information system (MIS) is one that 'collects and presents management information in order to facilitate control'.

Some form of management information systems will exist whether they are planned or not. If they are not planned, managers will devise their own ways of finding the information they need. These are likely to be inefficient, as there will be duplication of effort and a tendency for managers to keep their information to themselves rather than communicate it widely. This will result in lost opportunities. Management information is not confined to accounting information (although accounting information is usually more formal and better-developed than other information areas). Information within a system is used in three principal ways:

- to keep records (historic information)
- to supply management information (current information)
- to forecast (for planning, budgeting, etc).

For many organisations, the management information system represents a significant investment. At the development stage of the system, management determine future information needs and desires, but over time the system procedures may need appraising to make sure that they are meeting the objectives set initially. When appraising the management information system, the real question of performance centres around what the user wants from the system, and what the user is getting. So there is a comparison between planned and actual system behaviour, assessment of the extent to which system objectives have been achieved, and a consideration of overall system behaviour.

The evaluation or appraisal process should:

- assess system operational performance

- verify system objectives and how realistic they are compare planned and actual performance

- establish the extent to which the agreed objectives have been achieved.

The aspects that are assessed and measured are:

- error reports created by the system

- performance characteristics

- turnaround and response time

- machine usage

- data input volumes, paper handling

- output reports: accuracy, necessity, punctuality.

Reference to the costs and benefits, expected and achieved, is made during the evaluation.

2.5 Types of improvement

Performance measurement aims to establish how well something or somebody is doing in relation to the planned activity and desired results. That 'something' may be a machine, a factory, an organisation or a section within the organisation. That 'somebody' may be an individual employee, a manager or a group of people.

By measuring performance over a range of indicators, managers can identify areas that could be improved. Possibilities include:

Productivity – this is the quantity of the product or service produced in relation to the resources put in, for example so many units produced per hour or per employee. It defines how efficiently resources are being used.

Efficiency – labour costs are traditionally reported by rate and efficiency variances against standards. Qualitative measures of labour performance concentrate on matters such as ability to communicate, interpersonal relationships with colleagues, customers' impressions ('so and so was extremely helpful/rude'), and levels of skills attained.

Effectiveness – an effective department is one that does the right things and is thus able to satisfy the needs of its client group.

Quality – the number of items returned by customers as faulty can measure the quality of output. The quality of a service could be measured by the level of complaints or by favourable reaction. For example, asking trainees to complete an assessment form when the course has finished could monitor the quality of a training course. The training manager's performance could be assessed on the basis of the responses. It would be far more difficult to measure actual achievement in terms of improved performance, as there are so many other variables involved.

Working environment – is concerned with internal issues such as efficiency or employee well being.

3 Analysing the work process

3.1 Work study

One means of raising the efficiency of an operating unit is to study what is being done at present and by what methods and to reorganise the work where it is beneficial to do so.

Work study, sometimes known as work simplification, is concerned with the examination of human work in its total context. Its aim is to:

- help improve general efficiency

- reduce expenditure, improving the cost/benefit relationship

- assist management in the evaluation of staff and systems.

It is essential, in order to achieve cost-effectiveness, to examine the way in which an activity is carried out to ensure that maximum effect is obtained with the minimum of effort. Work study covers the techniques of method study and work measurement and examines human work, investigating the features that affect the efficiency and economy of the situations being reviewed in order to bring about improvements.

- Method study is the systematic recording and critical examination of existing or proposed ways of doing work, as a means of developing and applying easier and more effective methods and reducing cost. It is used to find ways to eliminate the unnecessary or of doing something it has not done before or of improving something it is already doing. In general, 'better' ways are ways that involve less work, reduce waiting time, remove the need for special skills, produce better results or make more efficient use of resources.

- Work measurement is a group of techniques for determining how long a specified task should take given a stated set of circumstances. All tasks take time. Just how long depends on the task itself and the length of time it requires, the physical conditions under which it is done, the machines, equipment and tools used, the method employed and the operator.

The main objectives of work study are as follows.

- the analysis, design and improvement of work systems, work places and work methods

- the establishment of work standards for determining requirements in manpower and equipment, assessing performance, planning operations, costing operations, products and services, and paying workers

- the development and application of job evaluation schemes based on job descriptions

- the specification of work facilities, layout, space utilisation and material and traffic flows

- the economic evaluation and optimisation of alternative combinations of personnel, materials and equipment

- the development of procedures for the planning and control of work and material usage

- the development of procedures for presenting information to management about work performance.

The obvious application of work-study is in production, where it was first developed, but the technique is now applied almost universally. It is also applied to office work, although the term organisation and methods (O&M) is then used to describe it.

3.2   Organisation and methods (O&M)

The objectives of O&M are to determine the way in which work should be organised and what methods should be adopted, or to review and improve existing methods, so that effort, time, materials and machinery will be used to greater advantage. O&M frequently involves the design of procedures and the supporting documentation.

The principal aim of O & M may therefore be described as the elimination of waste. This includes waste of time, human effort and skills, equipment and supplies, space and money. Eliminating waste will increase productivity, reduce administrative costs and improve staff morale and satisfaction by:

- ensuring that organisation structure is as efficient and simple as possible

- checking that procedures are effective, and achieve their objectives

- cutting out unnecessary operations and streamlining the rest

- co-ordinating tasks so there are no overlaps or gaps

- using staff and equipment to the full, so that there is even work flow and no idle time

- using office space effectively

- simplifying the planning, measurement and control of work

- standardising forms and practices for greater integration.

New methods might involve changes in planning and control systems, a new organisation structure, changing the numbers and location of equipment such as telephones, computer terminals and filing cabinets; recommending computerisation of some activities; or changing methods of working or documents used.

An O & M study may arise from:

(a) a computer system feasibility study which recommended that improvements should be made without computerisation

(b) the introduction of new products, services or equipment (c) the identification of problems such as:

- bottlenecks causing unbalanced workflow

- idle workers or equipment

- poor morale, indicated by trivial complaints or absenteeism escalating costs

- excessive errors and rejected work

- inconsistent earnings, where the earnings of employees are not related to output.

3.3 Method study

The aim of method study is to ensure that the work to be done makes the best use of the available resources. The procedure for doing this uses seven fundamental steps.

(i) **Select the work to be studied** – this is largely dictated by the whole work-study programme. Within that programme it is naturally best to start with activities where the need for improvement is most urgent or where the benefits likely to be obtained are the greatest in relation to the time and effort expended.

(ii) **Collect the facts** – when the order of priorities has been determined, the next step is to decide what information is required. Everything relevant that can be measured should be measured whether it is time, distance, temperature or humidity, and the records of any trials undertaken should be kept. Direct observation is more reliable than opinions.

(iii) **Record the** facts – the three traditional techniques are observation, interview and questionnaire. The scope and the means for making improvements can be more easily seen if the information collected is depicted in charts or diagrams.

(iv) **Examine the facts** – the 'examine' step refers to the critical and systematic examination of each feature of existing methods, a process that is greatly facilitated by the charts and diagrams referred to in step (iii). Each operation is subjected to the following questions:

- *Why?* – What is achieved? Is it necessary? Can it be eliminated?

- *When?* – Is there any advantage in changing the sequence of, or combining operations?

- *Where?* – Is it being done in the best place?

- *Who?* – Would it be better if someone else did it?

- *How?* – Is it being done in the best way? Is there any scope for new techniques or equipment? What about the workplace layout and the principles of motion economy?

(v) **Develop a better method** – the critical examination carried out during the 'examine' stage is almost certain to reveal opportunities for improvement.

(vi) **Install the better method** – it is during the installation stage that unexpected difficulties can arise. Even where training is provided workers can experience difficulty in changing over to new methods of working. However, people usually overcome these initial difficulties if their assistance and co-operation has been sought at an earlier stage.

(vii) **Check results** – it is up to management to take whatever steps are necessary to maintain the new method and to sort out any difficulties encountered.

 Activity 2

What sources of data will be used in an O&M study?

3.4 Work measurement

Generally work measurement is undertaken to:

- establish the relationship between costs and productivity
- highlight the reason for deteriorating performance
- prepare for system changes
- prepare for new system implementation.

Performance measurement methods are generally concerned with quantity, quality and time spent on work produced. The term 'measurement' implies that a particular performance is to be measured against some form of required standard. The methods of measurement therefore involve the setting of standards to provide a yardstick for comparison. The main problem is that some methods are less precise than others. Measurement must have specific (and useful) objectives, such as:

- comparing results from the current system with an intended alternative
- finding out why costs are rising or why productivity is falling
- identifying errors and their overall effects
- identifying bottlenecks and idle time that could be more efficiently organised
- evaluating the worth of an employee for wage setting.

Quality control is concerned with reducing the frequency of errors. Errors are not only wasteful in terms of time but, on occasions, can be very costly. An error in, for example, a purchase order may result in perhaps the wrong quantity of the wrong product being delivered at the wrong time. The cost in time, effort and money in rectifying the situation could be considerable.

If an unreasonable number of errors are occurring then action must be taken to identify the area of responsibility. It is, perhaps, understandable that even the most conscientious individual may make an occasional error and again a form of cost/benefit analysis should be applied.

The matter of time allowed is closely connected with quality control. The longer an individual has in which to perform a task then the higher the quality expected – but, of course, time is not unlimited.

Before the quality or quantity of work can be measured, a standard must not only be available but that standard must be set. The process goes through a cycle of establishing quality standards and procedures, monitoring actual quality and taking control action when actual quality falls below standard.

The main ways in which those responsible for setting standards can obtain the necessary information are:

- personal observation and timings – a trained observer should make repeated observations over a period of time to record the time taken to complete a particular task

- estimates from managers and supervisors, and/or employees actively engaged in the task – estimates here may be relied upon if the work is of a repetitive nature and the supervisor is experienced. Such estimates would not be suitable where duties are varied

- activity sampling – this is a technique designed to establish the proportion of a work period spent by an employee on each of a number of different activities

- the completion of time/diary sheets by individuals recording which tasks have been accomplished and how long each task took. This is also well suited to measuring the usage of machines thus establishing idle time or breakdown time.

Once standards have been set it is necessary to employ them as yardsticks against which the performance of an individual, section or department can be measured.

3.5 Quality control

Quality control is essential because people are prone to errors and mistakes. Errors need to be corrected – this takes time and therefore costs money. For example a document with lots of mistakes will need to be re-keyed or altered and this will take time – productivity effectively decreases and costs per unit, given that it has taken more time than it should have, will also increase. Sometimes errors are not spotted until it is too late – the document containing the error may have been sent to a third party and might well involve additional correspondence and/or telephone calls to resolve the problem.

The benefits of quality control include:

- reductions in costs of scrap or re-working

- reductions in complaints

- enhanced reputation for products/services

- feedback to designers and engineers about the performance of products and the machines required to produce them.

There are three main methods to ensure that quality of output is controlled, each being a logical extension of the other. They are:

- 100% checking
- random sampling
- partial checking.

100% checking is probably the most foolproof of all methods but at the same time the most expensive in terms of time and money. It involves a variation on the theme of proofreading and involves checking words and figures on a one-for-one basis. It should only be used for work of the greatest importance.

Random sampling is a modification of the 100% checking method. Here samples of work are selected at periodic intervals and usually checked completely from start to finish. The problem of determining the optimum cost/benefit relationship is important under this method. If sampling is undertaken too frequently then the cost/benefit relationship will deteriorate. If sampling occurs only rarely then no reliance of any value will be placed upon the results.

Partial checking is a compromise between 100% checking and random sampling. It involves checking only the most important portion of the work and assuming that if such vital sections are accurate then the remainder of the work is likely to be of the required standard. Partial checking is the most commonly employed method and is easily operated by supervisors.

 Activity 3

Explain how quality can be managed.

3.6 Causes of errors

Another aspect of quality control is the identification of why errors occur – once the cause is known steps can be taken to eliminate the causes of errors. The most sensible approach to the elimination of errors involves the implementation of a system, which will necessitate the identification of the causes as soon as the errors have been made. If the causes are not identified then errors will continue and may indeed increase in frequency.

Errors are usually caused by one or more of the following three factors:

- **The fault of the worker** – the most common causes are haste, carelessness, lack of the correct attitude, lack of method in working, lack of back-up/associated knowledge, inexperience and general standard of education.

- **The fault of management** – may be due to defective or lack of training, poor recruitment policies, lack of organisation, lack of supervision and control or wrong attitude towards workforce.

- **The working conditions** – errors may be due to poor ventilation, heating etc, bad lighting, too much noise/too many distractions or poor furniture, decor and general surroundings.

In an ideal world it would be possible to identify all causes of errors and to take action to prevent them. Unfortunately, an error-free world does not exist and most organisations are content to set a pre-determined level of error tolerance. Each group of tasks will have different levels of error tolerance and account must be taken of this. It may well be possible to eliminate nearly all errors by 100% checking but this is often not cost-effective. It is this aspect of cost-effectiveness, which is the key to the determination of an acceptable level of error tolerance.

4 Flowcharting

4.1 The purpose of flowcharting

The purpose of flowcharting is to reduce a procedure to its basic components and to emphasise their logical relationships, so that a connected pattern of activity can be traced from the beginning to the end.

The technique is simple but unfortunately flowcharting in practice lacks a uniform terminology, both in the descriptions of types of flowchart and in the symbols to be used.

The flowcharts dealt with in this chapter are called 'system flowcharts' or 'document flowcharts'. System flowcharts or document flowcharts depict, in outline, the sequence of events in a system showing document flow and the department or function responsible for each event.

One of the advantages of flowcharts is that their construction enables you to identify the division of responsibilities or lack of it. This is achieved by using separate columns for the various people involved in the operations.

In what follows we are adopting very simple conventions that will be helpful in the analysis of systems.

4.2 Flowcharting conventions

Document (e.g. sales order)

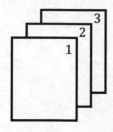

3 parts or copies of a document

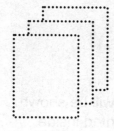

Documents appearing for second or
subsequent time

Check or inspection of operation

Document flow

File with letter in the centre

Information flow

4.3 Annotation

To distinguish between filing methods it is possible to mark a file with the letter as follows:

A – alphabetical order

N – numerical order

D – date order

Thus  represents a file in alphabetical order

Thus 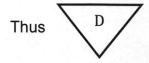 represents a file in date order

4.4 'Ghosting'

When a document appears in the system for the first time it will be shown as a solid square symbol with the name of the document printed inside. Normally there is no need to show the document again, its progress can be seen by following the document flow line, but where the document is carried forward to another chart or when copies that have previously been processed together are split up, it is useful to repeat the document symbol with dotted lines as shown.

> Invoice

4.5 Illustration of a flowchart – sales

We do not suggest that you produce over-complicated flowcharts that track every document, file and information flow in detail. These can be produced but the detail can be a barrier to comprehending the main elements and weaknesses of a system.

If you do use a flowchart, keep the chart simple and use plenty of narrative to explain how the chart works.

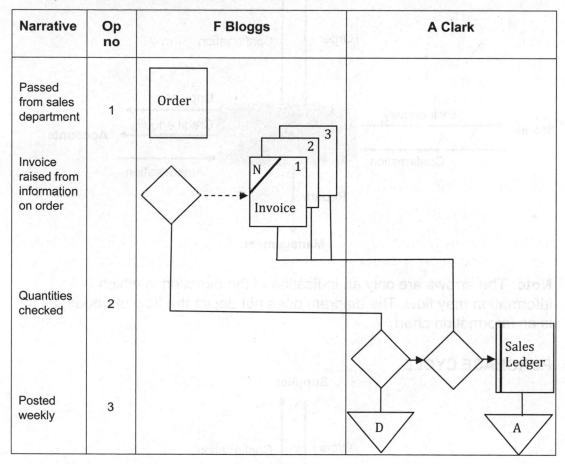

Narrative	Op no	F Bloggs	A Clark
Passed from sales department	1		
Invoice raised from information on order			
Quantities checked	2		
Posted weekly	3		

We will now interpret this simple flowchart.

When an order is received it is passed to F Bloggs. F Bloggs, on receipt of the order, raises a three part pre-numbered invoice.

The order and all three copies of the invoice are sent to A Clark for the quantities to be checked. One copy of the invoice will be sent to the customer, the order and second copy of the invoice will be filed in date order and the remaining copy will be posted on a weekly basis by A Clark to the sales ledger and filed in alphabetical order.

4.6 Use of flowcharts

Information flowcharts will determine both the system and the documentation required within that system. Two separate information flowcharts are shown below.

SALES CYCLE

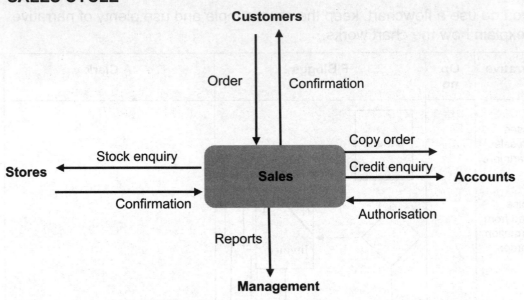

Note: The arrows are only an indication of the direction in which information may flow. The diagram does not depict the flow of goods, as it is an information chart.

PURCHASE CYCLE

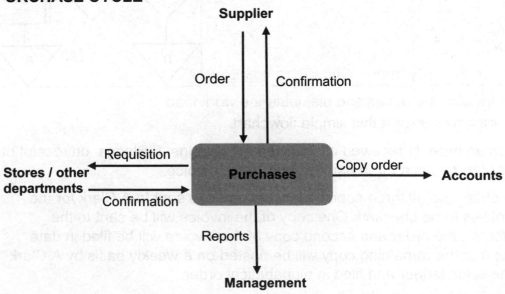

Study of charts by an experienced investigator will reveal where there are problems such as bottlenecks, duplication of work, etc. Dependent on the type of problem being considered, there may be a special type of chart, e.g. a string diagram that examines movement in an office. Other approaches could be as follows.

4.7 Appraisal of clerical work procedures

Your project might be the opportunity to examine the current procedures in your section and make recommendations for any changes. Initially the procedure should be examined in detail, probably using charts. The work being done should be analysed in depth. Of each operation, and the procedure as a whole, the following questions could be asked:

- Is this operation essential?

- Is the information used?

- What for?

- Is the information already provided elsewhere? · Can the method of working be simplified? · Would new technology be appropriate?

- Are there any bottlenecks?

- Is work fairly divided between staff?

- Are the correct grades of staff employed for each stage? · Does the work flow correctly?

- Would a change in office layout be helpful? · Are the correct instructions given to staff?

Recommendations might suggest revisions to organisational structure or procedures. These might include the following:

- reorganise the office layout to smooth the workflow or increase productivity through improving employee morale

- re-allocate duties and distribute the work load

- change IT configuration – by introducing networking · re-design or eliminate forms

- establish or revise procedures

- improve control mechanisms to cut down errors in or abuse of the system

- reduce staff.

4.8   Display design

Use of forms – An important part of the work in the accounting function is the completion of forms. Many of the procedures discussed depend on the practicability of the forms used and it is evident that the better the form, the greater the aid to achieving efficiency within the systems.

Many of the questions we asked of procedures could equally be asked of forms, and in fact this approach should be an integral feature of any clerical work procedure review. Typical questions might be as follows.

- Is the form really necessary?
- Could an existing form serve the same purpose?
- Could existing forms be combined to reduce paperwork?
- Are all the copies in a set necessary?
- Are there sufficient copies in a set?

When a new form is being designed or an old one being revised the following factors should be considered:

- Who will complete the form?
- Under what type of conditions will the form be completed?
- Who requires the information and for what purpose?
- Are additional copies required?
- How long will the form be kept?

All these factors need to be considered to ensure that the right person receives the right information.

Wherever possible a standardised approach should be taken throughout the organisation. This may lead to economies in printing and filing procedures and efficiency of staff completing forms throughout the organisation may also be improved. On designing a form, the following principles should apply: · It must contribute to the objectives of the procedure and the content and layout must take account of any other stages in a procedure.

- It should have a title for its purpose and, where appropriate, a code reference.
- The name of the organisation should appear on forms that go outside the undertaking.
- Items should appear in a logical sequence.
- As much information as possible should be pre-printed and, where required for control purposes, forms should be consecutively numbered.

KAPLAN PUBLISHING

- Adequate space should be allowed for entering information, including signatures.

- Wherever possible, answers should be in the form of marking, e.g. tick against one of several conditions.

- The quality of the paper used will be determined by the amount and style of handling and the type of entries i.e. handwriting, stamp impression. Top quality paper should only be used for prestige documents.

- A pleasing appearance should be aimed for with a minimum variety of fonts used.

- If required, instructions for completing the form should be incorporated.

- Where forms are prepared in sets the distribution should be marked on each copy and different colours used to aid identification.

- Form size should be standard e.g. A4 wherever possible, to assist filing.

User/computer interface design – The user interface design covers screen layout and dialogue design. The types of dialogue to choose from are:

- menu selection

- questions and answers

- form filling

- natural language

- command languages.

Dialogue design considerations include:

- user needs consistent and logical messages

- user should receive rapid responses

- user problems and dialogue effectiveness should be logged by the system

- user should be encouraged, not discouraged, by dialogue which is simple to comprehend

- dialogue must be user- (not analyst-) oriented

- system must be able to validate and edit

- user should be monitored and guided (perhaps by menu-driven progress)

- errors must be clearly indicated

- dialogue must be able to adapt to user speed and awareness
- user must be able to question in order to seek guidance.

If the user is a specialist a more coded dialogue may be adopted, whereas a casual user requires simple dialogue.

The dialogue must be devised so as to satisfy special needs (the keyboard may require special keys, such as 'debit entry'). Various graphics-oriented displays provide differing aspects of the same item (e.g. 3-D).

Visual display design – This can be either text or graphic display. Graphics displays are a feature of most business applications and offer these advantages: · the emphasis on relationships

- disclosing previously unobserved facts
- focusing interest.
- graphics may be used in three ways:
- information graphics (presenting to the user) · report graphics (in printed page format)
- presentation graphics (printing out directly to a transparency for projection).

The design of visual displays is linked to the dialogue adopted. When the VDU is activated for data entry, the user is shown a menu presenting various options that prompt him or her to select the next keyboard operation. So, the visual display has to be clear, unambiguous and free of distractions, such as unnecessary details.

Some visual displays appear as forms that have to be completed; fields needing completion are highlighted by adoption of colour, and so on. The designer specifies the display required in the form of a layout sheet, and the programmer is then responsible for providing it. The beneficial results when users participate in system design may be:

- it is ego-enhancing and builds users' self-esteem
- it is challenging and intrinsically satisfying
- the user becomes more knowledgeable and is better trained in the use of the system
- the solution to the problem is better because participants know more about the system than the computer department staff members · the user retains much of the control over operations.

Activity 4 (no feedback)

You should take the opportunity to study several of the many forms that you encounter and ask yourself if you consider them well or badly designed.

Activity 5

What are the principles of form design?

5 Cost-benefit analysis and cost control

5.1 Financial evaluation of information systems change projects

In order to convince managers to accept that proposed changes to an information system are worthwhile, it is necessary to demonstrate that the project is 'cost-beneficial'. This means that the benefits of the changes outweigh their expected costs.

Cost-benefit analysis focuses on the balance between expected costs and benefits of a proposed system. Although non-financial benefits can be considered, economic feasibility should assess costs and benefits in financial terms.

5.2 Costs of information system changes

Tangible costs associated with developing and running information systems can be classified into one-off costs (e.g. development, buying new equipment) and on-going costs (e.g. maintenance, replaceable items). Tangible costs are easy to quantify and can be related directly to development and operation of a system. However, information systems often incur intangible costs that are much harder to quantify or to relate back to specific systems. Examples of intangible costs include:

- staff dissatisfaction if systems are poorly specified or implemented

- the cost of increased staff mistakes and reduced performance during the learning period after a new system is implemented

- opportunity costs. Whenever money is invested in one area of the company, the opportunity to invest in another area is foregone

- lock-in costs. Purchasing a particular solution can bind a company to a particular supplier, reducing its ability to take advantage of future developments from other providers.

5.3 Benefits of information system changes

Benefits can be classified into tangible and intangible benefits. A selection of the benefits in each category is given below. Tangible benefits

- Savings resulting from an old system no longer operating. These include savings in staff salaries, maintenance costs and consumables.

- Greater efficiency. A new system should process data more efficiently and reduce response times.

- Business benefits gained through improved management information e.g. reduced stock levels due to improved inventory control.

- Intangible benefits

- More informed decision making.

- Improved customer service, resulting in increased customer satisfaction.

Freedom from routine decisions and activities, resulting in more time being available for strategic planning and innovation.

Better understanding of customer needs through improved analysis of data.

Gaining competitive advantage. A fully integrated ordering and delivery system, for example, could reduce costs, generating the ability to price competitively.

5.4 Cost-benefit analysis

Once information on project costs and benefits is available it becomes possible to carry out a cost-benefit analysis. Results should be interpreted with care, however, as analysis is based on estimates of future cash flows, and on assumptions regarding likely costs and benefits. Two possible methods of performing such an analysis should be familiar to you from Intermediate level studies, namely Payback, and Net Present Value.

5.5 Payback

Payback calculates the time taken for project cash inflows to equal project cash outflows. The decision rule is to accept the project that pays back most quickly. Whilst projects that payback quickly may be inherently less risky, the overall return on a project is not considered, as cash flows occurring after payback are ignored.

Payback is often used as initial project selection tool, to exclude projects that payback too slowly to be acceptable. The remaining projects are then appraised using more sophisticated tools.

Payback example

	Project 1 (£100,000)	Project 2 (£100,000)
Cost	(£100,000)	(£100,000)
Net savings		
Year 1	£50,000	£30,000
2	£50,000	£38,000
3	£25,000	£45,000
4	£0	£37,000
5	£0	£29,000

Project 1 has paid back by the end of year two. Project 2, however, does not recover its investment until towards the end of Year 3. Using payback Project 1 would be selected, even though total return is greater for Project 2.

5.6 Net present value (NPV)

This method calculates the net present value of all the project cash flows. If NPV is equal to, or greater than, zero the project should be considered, as its return is at least equal to the discount rate used.

To perform an NPV calculation we do the following:

Step 1: Identify future incremental cash flows.

Step 2: Discount the cash flows so they are in today's terms (present values).

Step 3: The present values can be added up and netted off to give a net present value or NPV.

Step 4: If the NPV is positive, then it means that the cash inflows are worth more than the outflows and the project should be accepted.

Example

(uses cashflows from project 2 above, and a 10% discount rate):

Time	Cash flow £000	Discount factor @ 10%	Present Value £000
t = 0	(100)	1	(100)
t = 1	30	0.909	27.3
t = 2	38	0.826	31.4
t = 3	45	0.751	33.8
t = 4	37	0.683	25.3
t = 5	29	0.621	18.0
Net Present Value		35.8	

5.7 Standard costing and budgets

Standard costing enables the supervisor to control costs precisely. The principal items of cost under standard costing are those for direct labour and direct material. All other costs are typically controlled through the overhead budgets of departments. A standard labour cost is a pre-determined cost of using labour in the production of a product or the provision of a service, estimated as the cost that would be incurred if the product were manufactured or the service delivered under specified conditions. A standard material cost is an estimated cost based on the specification of materials, its expected price and an allowance for reasonable scrap and waste, for a stated period of time.

In many organisations there is a system of budgetary control under which targets are set by estimating fixed and variable expenses, sales, working capital and so forth for a specific future period in the light of past performance and present policy and strategy. The supervisor works to a budget and is required to control specific costs. The making and operation of budgets, like all forms of control, has an impact on subordinates and is affected by their behaviour. The supervisor needs to consider how the development and operation of a budget can be arranged to motivate his or her staff.

5.8 Cost estimation

Cost estimation invariably involves some judgement. For example, an estimation of labour time relies on the individuals in each section to give an opinion as to the time it would take to do a job. These estimates are more likely to be understated than overstated and the lack of consistency causes many problems. The costs of materials are easier to estimate because the purchasing department will provide the information, although increases in prices can change materials costs estimates over the budgeting period.

The supervisor can improve the accuracy of estimates by:

- learning from previous mistakes
- having sufficient design information
- obtaining a detailed specification, and
- breaking the project down into smaller jobs and detailing each constituent part.

There are different classifications to denote the accuracy of cost estimates:

- **Definitive estimates** aim to be accurate to within 5% and are produced after the design work is done.
- **Feasibility estimates** are accurate to within 10%. These are made in the early design stage.
- **Comparative estimates** are made when the project under review is similar to a previous one. The accuracy of this estimate depends on the similarity and the prevailing economic conditions.
- **Ball-park estimates** are a rough guide to the project costs and are often made before a project starts. They may be accurate to within 25%.

5.9   The supervisor's contribution to cost control

Cost control for a supervisor means that staff are working well and properly supervised and all work procedures are carried out as they should be. Good supervision ensures that costs are kept under control.

As a supervisor your role in cost control derives from your responsibility for resources – people, machines, materials, work in progress or whatever. You are in charge of activities that incur costs and have therefore a cost responsibility. You have the job of controlling costs within specified parameters or against clear cost standards. You may even be charged with reducing or eliminating costs.

The typical costs of an accounts department include the wages of permanent and temporary staff, the costs of equipment and software, stationery and overheads.

By your own application and diligence you can influence the behaviour of your subordinates in ways that will keep 'lost time' and 'non-productive time' at a minimum and thereby help to control labour costs. Similarly you can, for example by giving advice, control material cost and overhead cost by keeping scrap levels and the misuse or over-use of consumables down. However, you will only be able to control costs if you are given realistic standards to work to and reliable information about performance, especially about any variance or deviation that occurs. The standards should be derived from a thorough analysis of the job, the methods used and the efficiency of performance.

5.10 Cost reduction

Cost reduction means reducing the current or planned unit cost of goods or services without impairing their suitability for the use intended. The main areas that will be considered will be reducing staff levels, deferring expenditure on new equipment, changing operations to make them cheaper and using cheaper supplies.

Supervisors should check that they are contributing to cost reductions by considering the following questions:

- Do you use the wrong labour on jobs – highly skilled people on routine work?

- Do you use all of the talents of your staff?

- Do you try to minimise waiting time?

- Do you give your staff precise and clear instructions to help minimise unnecessary work or mistakes?

- Do you cut corners, sacrificing quality for quantity?

- Do you encourage your staff to be quality minded?

- Do you use the cheapest materials for the job (consistent with safety and specification)?

- Do you have a proper maintenance rota for equipment, saving on expensive repairs?

- Do you order materials, consumables etc in economic quantities and well in advance of need?

- Do you insist on good housekeeping at all times?

KAPLAN PUBLISHING

6 Performance management and appraisal

6.1 Performance management

Performance management is not just about the end-of-year performance rating; it is an ongoing process, the success of which depends on regular communication between the manager and the individual. The process involves periodic feedback and a year-end assessment, which includes a rating. The assessment should take into account both the performance indicators identified for the level of the job and the skills and competencies that contributed to these outputs.

6.2 Competence analysis

A competence is an observable skill or ability to complete a particular task. It also includes the ability to transfer skills and knowledge to a new situation.

Competences describe what job-holders must be able to do and the standard to which they must be able to do it. They are defined by means of competence (or capability, or functional) analysis. This process describes:

- the job's main tasks or key result areas
- the types and levels of knowledge and skill that these require · the acceptable standard of performance in each task or result area
- how performance is assessed.

Competence analysis is used in:

- recruitment (compare what the job holder should be able to do with what the candidate can do)
- performance management (compare what the job holder should be able to do with what he or she has done)
- training (compare what the job holder should be able to do with what he or she can actually do, thus identifying areas requiring personal development).

Installing a competence based system means:

- establishing the elements of competence – activity, skill or ability required by the job holder to perform the job
- establishing the criteria of performance of the skill or ability required and setting standards to measure it by

- measuring the actual performance against the standard

- taking corrective action where there is any deviation from the standard.

The control element of the system allows feedback to change the elements of competence or the criteria of measurement in the light of actions taken and feedback given by the job-holder.

6.3 Performance appraisal

The general purpose of any assessment or appraisal is to improve the efficiency of the organisation by ensuring that the individual employees are performing to the best of their ability and developing their potential for improvement.

Performance appraisal systems can be informal or formal.

- Informal performance appraisal is conducted on a day-to-day basis. The manager spontaneously mentions that a piece of work was done poorly or well. The subordinate then responds in an appropriate manner. It encourages desirable performance and discourages undesirable performance before it becomes ingrained.

- Formal appraisal occurs on a periodic basis. It is important that members of the organisation know exactly what is expected of them and the yardsticks by which their performance and results will be measured. The process usually entails:

    - clarifying a person's job

    - identifying criteria for assessment

    - assessing competence

    - interviewing the job holder

    - identifying and agreeing future goals and targets

    - agreeing action points e.g. training needs

    - giving regular feedback.

The benefits of performance appraisal include the following:

- It can help to reveal problems that may be restricting progress and causing inefficient work practices.

- It can motivate employees by setting challenging but achievable targets for performance and agreeing the value of incentives offered.

- It can develop a greater degree of consistency through regular feedback on performance and discussion about potential. This encourages better performance from staff.

There are other benefits associated with performance appraisal, for example:

- It can provide information for human resource planning, which will assist succession planning and also determine suitability for promotion and training.

- It can identify an individual's strengths and weaknesses and indicate how the strengths may best be utilised and the weaknesses overcome.

- It can improve communications by giving staff the opportunity to talk about their ideas and expectations, and discuss how well they are progressing.

- It can allow employees to solve any workplace problems and apply creative thinking to their jobs.

6.4 Methods of assessment

Appraisal systems can be used to measure attitudes, behaviour and performance. Measurement may be a combination of:

- quantitative measures using some form of rating scale e.g. (1) excellent, (2) good, (3) average, (4) below average, (5) unsatisfactory

- qualitative measures involving an unstructured, narrative report on specific factors and/or overall level of behaviour and work performance.

Employee ranking – employees are ranked on the basis of their overall performance. This method is particularly prone to bias and has hardly any feedback value. It does, however, have the advantage that it is simple to use.

Rating scales – graphic rating scales consist of general personal characteristics and personality traits such as quantity of work, initiative, co-operation and judgement. The rate describes the employee on a scale whose ratings vary, for example from low to high or from poor to excellent. It is called 'graphic' because the scale visually graphs performance from one extreme to the other.

Behaviourally anchored rating scales (BARS) – evaluate employees in terms of the extent to which they exhibit effective behaviour relevant to the specific demands of their jobs. Each item to be assessed is 'anchored' with specific examples of behaviour that correspond to good performance, average performance, poor performance and so on.

A simplified example is given below which relates to performance in communicating and co-operating with others in a production control environment.

Rating	Behaviour
Excellent	Reports, oral and written, are clear and well organised; speaks and writes clearly and precisely; all departments are continually informed; foresees conflict and handles with initiative.
Good	Conveys necessary information to other departments; does not check for misunderstandings, but willingly tries to correct errors.
Unacceptable	Does not co-operate with or inform other departments; refuses to improve on reports or to handle misunderstandings

Appraisers can then use the BARS as guidance against which to assess the expected behaviour of each person being rated. The number of categories in the rating scale will vary according to the particular nature of the job, but usually number between 5 and 9. There may also be a varying number of behavioural examples for each point on the scale.

Achieving objectives – another appraisal system is that of 'achieving objectives'. With this system, the manager discusses and sets objectives with members of staff at the beginning of the appraisal period. The appraisal is then based on the extent to which these stated objectives have been achieved. This method provides for participation by staff and also allows for at least some degree of self-appraisal.

Performance 'agreement' or 'contract' – is a variant of the 'meeting objectives' method. Based on the use of a performance 'agreement' or 'contract', members of staff create a succinct document, agreed with their superior, which sets out the individual's proposed contribution to the business plan of the organisation.

This document provides an agenda, which serves as the basis of the appraisal judgement. Instead of rating performance in terms of a traditional five-box scale (A, B, C, D or E), the question is simply 'Has the plan been met?' This approach turns the appraisal system into a dialogue. The extent to which the contract is met gives an indication of whether the business plan is realistic.

6.5 The appraisal process and employee development

The performance development process is the development of the employees' work related skills, knowledge and experience. It offers an opportunity to build on the employees' performance and to contribute to organisational goals. The questions that must be raised are:

- What are the new functions that the department will need to perform in the near term and over the next two to five years?

- What knowledge and skills will employees need to develop in order to perform these functions?

7 Training

7.1 Importance of training and development to the organisation and the individual

Few people would argue against the importance of training as a major influence on the success of an organisation. Training is necessary to ensure an adequate supply of staff who are technically and socially competent and capable of career advancement into specialist departments or management positions. It increases the level of individual and organisational competence and helps to reconcile the gap between what should happen and what is happening – between desired targets and actual levels of work performance. There is therefore a continual need for the process of staff development, and training fulfils an important part of this process.

7.2 Training model

The training model below takes account of all the major steps:

- **Stage 1** – Identification of training need: examining what skills and attributes are necessary for the job to be undertaken, the skills and attributes of the job-holder and the extent of the gap.

- **Stage 2** – Design, preparation and delivery of training.

- **Stage 3** – Discovering the trainee's attitude to training (reaction) and whether the training has been learnt (learning). Reaction involves the participant's feelings towards the training content, the trainer and the training methods used. Learning is the extent to which the trainee has actually absorbed the content of the learning event.

- **Stage 4** – Discovering whether the lessons learnt during training have been transferred to the job and are being used effectively in doing the job. After the training needs have been met, work activities could be rescheduled, for example to optimise the use and time of the available accounts department personnel.

- **Stage 5** – Evaluating the effects of the training on the organisation. This is the area in which there is perhaps most confusion, and subsequently little real action in the workplace.

- **Stage 6** – Reinforcement of positive behaviour. It is optimal that any positive outcomes are maintained for as long as possible. It is not a rare event for changes in behaviour to be temporary, with a gentle slide back to previous ways of working.

7.3 Roles and responsibilities of the training manager

The range of roles that can be played out by training staff is strongly influenced by the requirements of their jobs.

The trainer or training manager has four prime responsibilities:

1 Planning and organising training activities – this will involve establishing physical training facilities and equipment and also identifying human training resources (i.e. lecturers, course leaders, instructors); there may be a need to train the trainers.

2 Determining and managing training activities – this involves establishing a course structure, curriculum or syllabus, and establishing a manual or computer record system.

3 Directing training activities – the monitoring of standards and activities.

4 Consulting and advising – both on training matters and on technical matters.

The more senior the job, the wider the range of possible roles; a training manager's job would probably encompass all of the above-mentioned roles, with an emphasis on determining, managing, consultancy and advisory activities. By comparison, a job instructor would be mainly concerned with direct training or instructional activities and with some organising.

When performing their direct training roles, training specialists are involved in: · the identification or assessment of training needs · the design, content and methods of training to be employed · the evaluation of training.

7.4 Identifying training needs

Job training analysis is the 'process of identifying the purpose of a job and its component parts and specifying what must be learnt in order for there to be effective work performance'.

A training 'gap' or need is any shortfall in terms of employee knowledge, understanding, skill or attitudes against what is required by the job or the demands of organisational change.

All jobs make some demands on their job-holders:

* Simple jobs will require only a little knowledge with no need for any deeper understanding of what is involved; such jobs will also require little in the way of skill, but may demand more in terms of attitude i.e. attention to detail and acceptance of routine.

* Complex jobs will demand not only specialist knowledge, but also a real understanding of the basic principles or underlying concepts of the work involved. They will probably require a high level of specialist skill, and attitudes that foster an awareness of the importance of teamwork and the necessity for first-rate quality.

There are four main methods for determining the training needs of individuals.

(i) **Performance appraisal** – each employee's work is measured against the performance standards or objectives established for their job. Depending on the detail of the appraisal form, it can provide a substantial amount of relevant information about training and development needs. The current performance is assessed in terms of specific and measurable parts of the employee's job and potential performance is also considered. This allows training and development needs to be considered in terms of future job performance as well as in terms of improving current performance.

(ii) **Analysis of job requirements** – uses data concerning jobs and activities e.g. job descriptions, personnel specifications, on the one hand, and leadership and communication activities on the other. The skills and knowledge specified in the appropriate job description are examined. Those employees without the necessary skills or knowledge become candidates for training.

(iii) **Organisational analysis** – uses data about the organisation as a whole e.g. its structure, markets, products or services, human resources requirements, etc. The key success factors are identified and analysed into Human Resources (HR) activities.

The analysis involves asking such questions as:

- What knowledge and skills are required now and in the future?

- What is the shortfall between the capabilities of our staff at present and what we require of them?

- How much training is required to get to the position we wish to reach?

(iv) **Departments and/or individuals not performing up to standard will require additional training.**

Surveys of human resources use data about individuals e.g. appraisal records, personal training records, test results, notes made at counselling interviews and results of attitude surveys. Individuals are surveyed to establish any problems they are experiencing in their work and what actions they believe need to be taken to solve them. It involves asking such questions as:

- What is your present job?

- How effectively can you do it at present?

- What will be your job in the future?

- What training (if any) do you require to do the job as effectively as possible, to cope with changes in the job and to provide you with confidence and satisfaction?

The data obtained enables the training staff to draw a comprehensive picture of the areas of current and potential shortfall in requirements. One or more of the following methods is used for the collection of information for the training needs analysis:

- Analysing recorded data relating to the organisation, to jobs and to individuals.

- Analysing questionnaires and attitude surveys issued to employees.

- Interviewing managers and supervisors about their own or their subordinates' training and development needs.

- Observing the job performance of individuals.

- Monitoring the results of group discussions relating to current work problems etc.

- Analysing self-recorded diaries etc kept by managers, specialists and others.

The most popular of the above methods are the ones that use existing records, and those which involve interviewing managerial and supervisory staff.

KAPLAN PUBLISHING

7.5 Who gets trained?

This covers the whole spectrum of employees:

- New starters who require induction training. · Operatives who require skills training.

- Craft apprentices who require skills and knowledge appropriate to a specific craft or trade.

- Trainees accepted under a Government training scheme who require training in accordance with an agreed action plan.

- Supervisors who require supervisory training.

- Graduate trainees who require management training.

- Functional managers who require updating training.

Training may also relate to special activities such as safety training or to particular groups such as employees requiring preparation for retirement courses.

7.6 Training and development methods

Training and development methods vary tremendously depending on:

- the person

- the job

- the resources

- the organisation

- the economic environment.

They include: training courses, both external and in-house; on-the-job training; mentoring; coaching; computerised interactive learning; planned experiences; and self-managed learning. Other highly participative methods include discussions, business games, case studies, syndicates, outdoor training and the T-group system (establishing small unstructured training groups (T-groups) where the members all help each other).

Perhaps a majority of the required training and development will be implemented on an on-the-job basis, i.e. carried out in-house. This might involve such methods as:

- Induction training – is the means whereby a new employee is introduced to the organisation in as effective a way as possible.

- Structured coaching – is useful when there is a need to extend the depth and range of an employee's knowledge very quickly for reasons which may range from the introduction of new techniques to the need to train for a particular job, perhaps on the unexpected retirement of the present job holder.

- Professional training – companies will usually assist employees aiming for professional qualifications through the provision of study leave and payment of fees. Some provide in-house training as part of an industrial studentship.

- Computer based training (CBT) and computer assisted learning (CAL) – can be designed for use on computers. User-friendly systems enable trainees to work at their own pace, working on set programmes. Mentoring is used by organisations to show junior employees how things are done. The mentor (a senior experienced employee) is expected to guide the new recruit through a development programme and 'socialise' them into the culture of the enterprise.

Some of the required training and development may alternatively be carried out on an external basis, or bought-in. Some kinds of specialist managerial or professional training may only be available on this basis. It may also be considered that the trainee may benefit from the wider or broader view that may be taken by external agencies, particularly when it comes to managerial issues.

Nevertheless, the departmental manager must ensure that external training can successfully meet the department's training needs, and is appropriate to the achievement of its objectives.

7.7 How should training be evaluated?

The evaluation is part of the control process of training. To be useful, training needs to be evaluated both qualitatively and, if possible, in quantitative terms to establish:

- The cost/benefit relationship - the training should only go ahead if the likely benefits are expected to exceed the costs of designing then running the course. Costs will include the costs of the training establishment, training materials, the salaries of the staff training on or attending the course and travel expenses. Benefits might be measured in terms of quicker working – reducing overtime or staff numbers, greater accuracy of work or more extensive skills.

- Whether the objectives of the training have been achieved – validation means observing the results of the course and measuring whether the training objective has been achieved.

Like any other control process, training evaluation is firstly concerned with setting appropriate standards of training. These may take the form of policies, objectives, adherence to external standards, and standards of training and trainer qualifications. Clearly, the more precise the standards set, the easier it is to evaluate the success of training.

Evaluation methods aim to obtain feedback about the results or outputs of training, and to use this feedback to assess the value of the training, with a view to improvement where necessary.

- Training-centred evaluation aims to assess the inputs to training i.e. whether we are using the right tools for training.

- Reactions-centred evaluation, which is probably the most widely used method for evaluation, seeks to obtain and assess the reactions of trainees to the learning experiences they have been put through.

- Learning-centred evaluation seeks to measure the degree of learning that has been achieved. This is usually achieved by testing trainees following the training, as in a driving test.

- Job-related evaluation is aimed at assessing the degree of behaviour change, which has taken place on-the-job after returning from a period of training. It is, of course, a measure of learning, but learning which has been applied in the workplace. It is not an easy task to evaluate the degree to which learning has been applied, especially in cases where training in social skills, such as leadership, is concerned.

7.8 Safety awareness and training

There are many laws and regulations in the United Kingdom that affect safety. Such importance is placed on it that many organisations form safety committees whose job it is to ensure that safety practices are established and observed.

Even if the organisation does not set up a safety committee the provisions of the Health and Safety at Work Act 1974 will be enforced by factory inspectors appointed by the government's Health and Safety Executive. All inspectors have the right to enter the premises at any reasonable time to carry out an appropriate inspection.

The Health and Safety at Work Act imposes a duty on employers to provide training to ensure a healthy and safe workplace. As well as being a way to obtain compliance with health and safety regulations, safety training enhances employees' knowledge, understanding and commitment.

The purpose of safety training is generally the same as any other training programme. It improves job knowledge and skills and ensures optimum employee performance at a specified level. In health and safety training, specified performance standards include attention to safety rules and regulations regarding safe work behaviour.

The procedure is outlined in the diagram below:

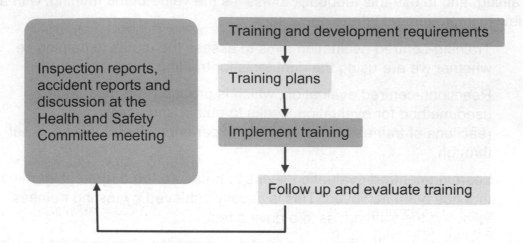

First, problems or training needs are identified by inspection, by accident reports and through discussion at the Health and Safety Committee meetings. Next, the planning, execution and evaluation of the training takes place.

The actual training is comparatively simple; the real difficulty is in ensuring that workers comply with the safety regulations once they have been trained. Follow up campaigns using posters, films, discussion groups and the like have been shown to have a limited effect only and need to be repeated at regular intervals.

8 Disciplinary procedures

8.1 Discipline

Maintaining discipline among employees is an integral part of the directing function of management and lack of discipline is certain to affect the efficiency of a section or department. An important part of any employee relations policy is to set out the broad standards of conduct that the organisation intends to follow in respect of unacceptable behaviour on the part of the employee.

The word discipline tends to be associated with authority, force, warnings, threats and/or punishment. However, discipline can also be used to maintain sensible conduct and orderliness. Most mature people accept the idea that following instructions and fair rules of conduct are normal responsibilities that are part of any job. They believe in performing their work properly, in following instructions, in coming to work on time and in refraining from fighting, drinking, stealing or taking drugs at work.

The types of disciplinary situations that require attention by the supervisor include:

- excessive absenteeism or lateness in arriving at work

- defective or inadequate work performance

- breaking safety rules and other violations of rules, regulations and procedures e.g. leaving work to go home early

- improper personal appearance

- sexual harassment

- being drunk

- open insubordination e.g. refusing to carry out a legitimate work assignment.

8.2 Disciplinary procedures

The aim of this type of procedure is to correct unsatisfactory behaviour, rather than punish it. A good disciplinary procedure should be clearly stated, in writing and should enable employees to feel assured of fairness and consistency of treatment if ever they should become subject to the procedure. It should specify as fully as possible what constitutes 'misconduct' and 'gross misconduct' and state what the most likely penalty is for each of these categories and how long an offence is kept on the records. In cases of proven gross misconduct, this is most likely to be immediate dismissal, or suspension followed by dismissal. There

should be a definition of who has the authority for dismissal. In cases of less serious misconduct, the most likely consequence is that a formal warning will be given. For repeated acts of misconduct, it is likely that the employee concerned will be dismissed.

Because of the serious implications of disciplinary action, only senior managers are normally permitted to carry out suspensions, demotions or dismissals. Other managers and supervisors are restricted to giving the various types of warnings.

You must be aware of the situations that are beyond your own authority and know who to refer serious disciplinary problems to.

Many organisations adopt a progressive discipline approach following a list of suggested steps:

(i) The informal talk – where the infraction is of a relatively minor nature and the employee's record has no previous marks of disciplinary action. The manager discusses with the employee his or her behaviour in relation to standards that prevail in the organisation.

(ii)   Oral warning or reprimand – emphasises the dissatisfaction with the subordinate's repeated violation, which could lead to serious disciplinary action.

(iii) Written or official warning – become a permanent part of the employee's record and may be used as evidence in the case of grievance procedures.

(iv)   Disciplinary layoff or suspension without pay – used when previous steps were of no avail.

(v)   Demotion – a form of constant punishment due to losing pay and status over an extended period of time.

(vi)   Discharge/dismissal – a drastic form of disciplinary action reserved for the most serious offences.

9 Appraising the working environment

9.1   The accounts department

When you are appraising the accommodation and equipment, you must remember that, as with all the procedures and processes, the aim of the appraisal is to highlight strengths or weaknesses. The aim is for a design that achieves the objectives of the department efficiently and effectively.

It is often the case that the reality of organisational structure is very different from that described in the organisation chart or operating manual. In particular, channels of communication are not always properly aligned to the authority structure, leading to waste and increased operating costs.

The central role of an accounts department and the service that it provides to all other functions would suggest that it should be sited as conveniently as possible to the areas it serves most. However, with the increasing availability of data-links, this aspect may not be so crucial.

Consideration must initially be given to the style of offices to be used by an accounts department. Amongst questions to be discussed would be the following.

*   Would one large open office be suitable?

*   Would all different sections of accounts be in the same room, or should there be different offices for financial and cost accounting staff and also for the wages section?

*   What criteria should be adopted in the allocation of individual offices to senior staff?

- What security arrangements for the confidentiality of information and also for the cashier's department are required?

- Where would the computers be sited and how can security be safeguarded?

9.2 The review of existing layouts

It is easier to design the style and layout of a new office than it is to modify an existing layout, which is proving unsatisfactory. A checklist of review guidelines is shown below:

- identify existing problem areas

- isolate causes of the problems

- prepare an up-to-date floor plan with a sensible scale

- indicate on the plan the location of such features as telephone points, network access points (for a wired network), electric sockets, light sockets, radiators and air vents if any

- prepare cut-outs and furniture, perhaps in different colours for different people or groups

- arrange the cut-outs in various formats until the one which aids the flow is obtained

- prepare a formal plan based on the results obtained in the exercise above.

An exercise such as the above, simple as it is, is often overlooked and yet over a long period this exercise has proved beneficial to many organisations.

9.3 Office styles

The layout of any office should endeavour to ensure that the following criteria are attained:

- space is used efficiently

- supervision is not hindered

- the work flow is enhanced by improving communication and avoiding unnecessary movement

- security, where necessary, is not neglected or impaired.

In recent years the traditional layout has been abandoned in many offices. Instead of the traditional approach where different sections occupy separate rooms, and desks are arranged in rows, two new popular systems have evolved as alternatives.

They are:

- **The open plan office** – here large numbers of employees, usually from different departments and sections, work alongside each other in a large room. There are advantages to having an open office – economy in floor space and occupancy costs, flexibility of layouts, better supervision and minimisation of movement of staff and documents. Economies in lighting and heating can be achieved. Although this style of office has the advantages of saving space and improving work flow, privacy can be lost and there is the constant distraction of the movements and actions of other occupants. This style is particularly suitable for related sections such as accounts receivable and accounts payable, or personnel and training.

- **The landscaped office** – this continues to use the principle of the open office but endeavours to enhance the appeal to the employees by spending extra money on creating an environment which is more aesthetically pleasing as well as more comfortable. This is achieved by using fitted carpets, air conditioning, curtains, screens and plants to form natural barriers between different sections. Landscaping often overcomes the problems of distraction in open plan offices. Desks are usually grouped at irregular intervals and equipment positioned so as to form natural barriers. Plants and screens are also used as barriers and to make a more pleasant atmosphere.

Apart from efficient and effective production, the advantages of good layout are to:

- achieve the optimal use of space

- allow for the most efficient flow of work

- facilitate effective control

- reduce materials handling to a minimum

- minimise waste

- promote employee satisfaction and motivation · allow for change and development, and

- maximise productivity.

9.4   Furniture and equipment

Having arranged the location of offices within a building it is necessary to arrange the layout of furniture and equipment within individual offices. Because it can aid efficient working and maintain staff morale, care must be taken when choosing the type and quality of office furniture. It is obviously important that furniture should be appropriate for its function, but it should also look attractive and appeal to the workers who must use it.

Consideration should also be given to its demands on floor space, its ease of movement, the correctness of the height for comfortable working and its fire risk.

Although circumstances may vary from one office to another, certain general principles should be adhered to. These principles include:

(a)   Free passage and movement of employees, with floor space kept free of obstructions to reduce the risk of accidents.

(b)   Many offices are concerned with the processing of information via the flow of documentation. If there are documentation flows within an office it may be sensible to endeavour to ensure that documents flow from the rear of an office to the front.

(c)   The office layout should be easy to clean.

(d)   All offices should be easy to evacuate quickly in case of accidents or hazards.

10   Checklist of tasks

At this stage in your studies you should be thinking about the system that you are considering for your project. The project is about improving the system and, therefore, you will want to outline what is wrong with the current system in terms of costs, location, resources and the skills of the staff.

To explain how you found out the system was not working as well as it might be you must identify the sources of this information and the methods you have used to identify the weaknesses. Having identified the problem, or problems, you must then continue by looking for alternative solutions and researching the constraints that will apply when you are evaluating these options.

11 Test your knowledge

Test your knowledge

1   What are the advantages of procedures for routine work?

2   How would you define 'culture'?

3   One of the ways to measure performance is productivity. What is it?

4   How would quality be managed in an accounts office?

5   What are the two main aspects of work study?

6   Describe a typical O&M investigation.

7   Why is it a good idea to eliminate waste?

8   What are the principles of form design?

9   If you had to reduce costs in your department or section what areas of spending would you tackle?

10 What is a job training analysis?

11 Outline the procedure for safety training.

12 If you were re-designing your office, list the conditions to achieve.

12 Summary

This chapter dealt with monitoring and improving the accounting system. One means of raising the efficiency of an accounts section is by work-study – finding ways of measuring work, analysing how things are done and how they can be done better.

Accounting departments should operate cost-effectively and the supervisor is likely to be involved in cost control and cost reduction methods.

Data can be collected in the form of charts, which can then be analysed to identify areas where improvements can be made.

Although the word discipline tends to be associated with authority, force, warnings, threats and/or punishment, it is generally used to maintain sensible conduct and orderliness. Disciplinary action is usually applied progressively from informal and formal warnings through suspension or layoff, demotion and finally dismissal.

Answers to chapter activities and 'test your knowledge' questions

 Activity 2

Data for an O&M study may be drawn from:

- organisation charts and manuals, job descriptions and specifications and procedure manuals

- observation of procedures, forms and control systems in action · discussions with managers, supervisors and employees · questionnaires.

 Activity 3

The management of quality involves four activities:

(i)   Establishing standards of quality for a product or service.

(ii)   Establishing procedures and methods which ought to ensure that the required standards are met in a suitably high proportion of cases.

(iii)   Monitoring actual quality.

(iv)   Taking control when actual quality falls below standard.

Activity 5

The principles of form design are as follows.

(a) Forms should be easy to read and to use, with clear and concise wording, adequate space for entries, and user-friendly layout (both for the person completing the form and the person who deals with it).

(b) Forms should not be too small and cramped (for use, and attractiveness), but size should take into account mailing and filing requirements.

(c) Paper and print quality should be considered in relation to the handling the form is likely to receive: for example the machines or writing implements that will be used, whether the form needs to last, or whether it will be read by somebody important.

(d) The number of operations involved in filling forms should be reduced as far as possible: document sets with selective carbon backing or the equivalent could be used instead of writing details in quadruplicate or photocopying. In this way, a single design and input of data can be adapted for many purposes.

(e) Colour coding of copies may be convenient in any set, and if copies of a master form act variously (for example as order, confirmation, goods received, invoice and so on) they should be clearly identified.

Test your knowledge

1   The advantages of procedures for routine work include the following:

- They indicate the most efficient way of getting a job done. · They eliminate discretion in routine tasks.

- They make jobs easier to do when staff are familiar with established procedures.

- They ensure that similar tasks will be done in the same way throughout the organisation even when a different person starts in a job or takes over from the previous holder.

- If staff are unsure how a job should be done, they can refer to written records in procedures manuals to learn quickly and easily.

- Disputes between departments about who should do what and when, should be avoided.

2   Culture can be defined as 'the way we do things around here'. The essence of a culture is that the values, attitudes and beliefs within the company are shared and accepted.

3   Productivity is the quantity of the product or service produced in relation to the resources put in, for example so many units produced per hour or per employee. It defines how efficiently resources are being used.

4   The management of quality involves four activities. Firstly, the standards of quality must be established. This could be a product or a service e.g. a cash budget or the number of times the phone rings before someone answers. The next step is to establish procedures/methods to ensure that the standards are met in the majority of cases. The quality must then be monitored and control action taken when the actual quality falls below standard.

5   The two main aspects of work study are method study, which is concerned with how work should be done, and work measurement, which is concerned with how long it should take.

6   A typical O&M investigation is likely to be concerned with getting a job done more efficiently, questioning whether work needs to be done at all, or whether it can be done more simply and with less effort and trying to establish whether better use can be made of existing idle time. This may be achieved by spreading employees' workloads more evenly over their working time.

7   Eliminating waste will increase productivity, reduce administrative costs and improve staff morale and satisfaction. It can bring about these benefits by cutting out unnecessary operations and streamlining remaining ones, using resources to the full and office space effectively.

8   Forms should be easy to read and to use, with clear and concise wording, adequate space for entries and user-friendly layout. The number of operations involved in filling in forms should be reduced as far as possible. Paper and print quality should be considered in relation to the handling the form is likely to receive and who is likely to use it.

9   You would concentrate on the high cost areas most likely to produce savings and areas of discretionary expenditure rather than costs that cannot be avoided, at least in the short term. The most obvious areas are reducing human resource levels, deferring expenditure on new equipment, using cheaper supplies or buying in bulk to obtain discounts and rationalisation measures to eliminate unnecessary duplication.

10   Job training analysis is the 'process of identifying the purpose of a job and its component parts and specifying what must be learnt in order for there to be effective work performance'.

11   Safety training begins by identifying problems or training needs by inspection, by accident reports and through discussion at the Health and Safety Committee meetings. Next, the planning, execution and evaluation of the training takes place.

12   The layout of any office should endeavour to ensure that space is used efficiently, supervision is not hindered, the work flow is enhanced by improving communication and avoiding unnecessary movement and security, where necessary, is not neglected or impaired.

WORKBOOK

QUESTIONS

Key techniques questions

3 The organisation

 Activity 1

Organisational structures I

An organisation can be structured in different ways.

Required:

(a) Explain the purpose of an organisation chart.

(b) Describe, with the aid of a diagram, two features of a functional structure.

(c) Describe, with the aid of a diagram, two features of a divisional structure.

 Activity 2

Organisational structures II

Recently a number of businesses have adopted a matrix structure.

Required:

(a) Describe, with the aid of a diagram, the matrix structure.

(b) Explain two benefits claimed of matrix structures.

(c) Explain two criticisms of matrix structures.

Activity 3

Authority

Describe how and explain why the management of an accounting and finance department may apply line, staff, and functional forms of authority within the organisation.

4 The organisation's environment

 Activity 4

Communication flows

Communication is vital in all organisations and the communication process may take many forms. It is important that managers and supervisors recognise the nature of information flows and use appropriate forms of communication. The direction of the three main information flows can be said to be downwards, upwards and lateral.

Required:

(a) Describe the purpose of these three main communication flows that might be found in an organisation.

(b) Explain three reasons why an organisation would use committees as part of the communication process.

Activity 5

Effective communication

Accurate communication is vital in any organisation and especially within the accounting environment. Communication within your organisation has been identified as poor. You have been asked to guide management on how to achieve effective communication.

Required:

(a) Describe the general guidelines that management might adopt to improve the effectiveness of communication in the organisation.

(b) When sending messages, what factors need to be taken into consideration to ensure that information will be received and understood?

5 Fraud in an accounting system

 Activity 6

Can you think of three ways that stock can be used to show a false increase in the value of the assets in the company?

6   Internal control

 Activity 7

Marshalls Ltd

Your firm is the long-standing auditors of Marshalls Ltd, a small one-off department store situated in a busy market town in Suffolk. The business was established more than 80 years ago by Arthur Marshall who built up the store from a stall in the local market.

The company is still largely family run. Arthur's son, George, is chairman. His grandson, Alec, is managing director and Alec's sister-in-law, Kate, is finance director. There are two other directors who have no connection with the family.

Despite having a good reputation in the area, the last few years have not been easy for the company. Three years ago a new out-of-town shopping centre opened about 20 miles away. Not surprisingly, the effect that this centre has had on Marshall Ltd's turnover and profits has been dramatic. In the last year, however, the store has been fighting back. Alec, the prime mover for change, has convinced his fellow directors to bring in some retail consultants to advise on marketing and organisation. This process began almost six months ago and since that time Marshall Ltd has entered into a dramatic programme of rationalisation, reorganisation and 'image update'. The company had adopted some sweeping changes and in terms of rationalisation the store has cut back from 11 departments to the core areas of ladies wear, menswear, children's wear, perfumes and household goods.

Early indications are that this exercise has been successful. Preliminary estimates for the current year show that turnover will be up by more than 15% on last year.

As senior in charge you have just completed the interim audit. The manager in charge of the job has reviewed your file and is particularly concerned about the changes that have been made to the store's purchasing procedures. From your work on this area you have discovered that the purchasing system now operates in the following way.

Each department has two buyers, i.e. a senior buyer and an assistant. It is the buyer's responsibility to liaise with suppliers, decide on quantity and negotiate the best price for the store. Once they have decided on a purchase, the buyers telephone through to the central purchasing department for it to place the order.

In the central purchasing department the purchasing clerk, Mr Weston, fills out a standard sequentially numbered three part order form. One copy is sent to the supplier, one copy is sent to goods inwards and the third is retained by Mr Weston, filed in number order.

When the ordered goods are received into the store Mr North, who is in charge of goods in, completes a two part goods inwards note (GIN). One copy he files with his copy of the purchase order, the other he sends to Mr Weston.

Mr Weston matches the GIN with the purchase order in his possession and files the two together awaiting the receipt of the supplier's invoice. He chases up orders which are outstanding for more than two weeks.

When the supplier's invoice is received, Mr Weston checks the prices, additions and extensions and enters the details from the invoice into the purchases day book and from there into the bought ledger. The invoice, together with the GIN and purchase order, is filed alphabetically by supplier.

On a weekly basis Mr Weston prepares a list of cheque payments to be made which is passed to the cashier, Mrs Easter, to raise the cheques. Mr Weston uses this list to write up the bought ledger. The cheques are signed by Mrs Southgate, who is Marshall Ltd's chief buyer and independent of any department.

Suppliers' statements are received by Mr Weston, reconciled to the purchase ledger and filed in alphabetical order.

Required:

Set out, in a manner suitable for inclusion in a management letter, the significant areas of weakness in the purchases system. For each weakness you should include a description of the specific weakness, the possible consequences of the weakness and a recommendation to remedy the weakness.

7   Information systems

Activity 8

(a) What are the purposes of computer system controls?

(b) What are the main controls over a computer system?

8   Improving the system

Activity 9

Cost-benefit analysis

A project feasibility study presented to senior management must always contain a detailed cost justification for any proposed computer system.

Categorise and give examples of the costs and benefits that would appear in such a report, including those that might indicate why a project showing a positive net present value is not necessarily of greatest benefit to the company.

KAPLAN PUBLISHING

Activity 10

Training and development plan

You have been asked by your manager to plan the training and development of your section for the next year.

Required:

Draft a report outlining the following:

- how you would identify the staff training and development needs

- what methods you would choose to satisfy the training and development needs

- the way in which you would evaluate whether the training and development had been effective.

 Activity 11

Disciplinary procedure

The accounts manager understands the need to motivate employees, but does not understand what is meant by discipline within the employment context. You have been asked to explain.

Required:

(a) Provide examples of situations where disciplinary action may be required.

(b) Describe the steps involved in a formal disciplinary procedure.

ANSWERS

Key techniques answers

3   The organisation

 Activity 1

Organisational structures I

(a) An organisation chart is a diagram that shows the formal structure of an organisation. Its purpose is to show:

- Each position in the organisation and the direct relationship between one position and those immediately above and below it.

- The formal chain of command. By studying an organisation chart, it is possible to establish the vertical chain of command and the vertical communication channels that are associated with it.

- The span of control. The number of subordinates each manager is responsible for can be seen by studying an organisation chart.

- The relationship between the various sub-groups that make up the organisation can be established e.g. teams and departments within the organisation.

(b) Functional structure

An example of a functional structure can be shown by the following diagram.

Two features of a functional structure are:

- The structure requires each department to be organised on the basis of specialisation of labour. The people in each department perform a narrow range of tasks that are not interchangeable with employees in other departments.

- The structure is divided into many layers. Each manager has a narrow span of control resulting in a tall pyramid shape.

(c) Divisional structure

An example of a divisional structure is as follows:

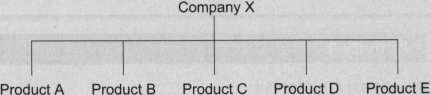

Company X

Product A   Product B   Product C   Product D   Product E

Two features of a divisional structure are:

- This structure requires the organisation to be divided into autonomous divisions that can operate as separate units. The managers and employees in each unit have a wider range of skills that are interchangeable.

- The shape of the organisation structure is fairly flat because the organisation has only a few levels of management and each manager's span of control is wide.

 Activity 2

Organisational structures II

(a) A matrix structure is a two-dimensional organisational structure. It is a flat structure that has no hierarchy. All members have equal status and have an equal say in the organisation's decision making.

The matrix structure can be illustrated as follows:

	Production	Marketing	Finance
Area A			
Area B			
Area C			

(b)   An organisation can obtain many benefits from using a matrix structure including:

- Direct communication between employees. A matrix structure does not use vertical communication channels, it uses horizontal channels in which each employee is free to communicate with all other employees without messages going through a third party. This removes many communication barriers found when other structures are used.

- This type of structure uses teamwork and empowerment. This allows employees to use their initiative, make their own decisions and do work their own way. Creative thinking is encouraged so new ideas are generated. Employees should be highly motivated and can produce a high quality of work.

(c)   The use of matrix structures also has many criticisms including:

- Loss of control

  When a matrix structure is used, people are allowed to do what they want. It is not possible to impose any system of central control over the organisation. As a result of this a lot of inefficiency will occur such as duplication of work.

- Sub-optimisation

  In an organisation using a matrix structure there is a high risk of sub-optimisation occurring. Sub-optimisation occurs when the objectives of one group of an organisation's members are placed before the whole organisation's objectives. When this occurs there is no co-ordination. An example of this is when expensive plant and equipment is purchased for a factory without finance being arranged beforehand.

Activity 3

Authority

Forms of authority

Line, staff and functional authority are concepts used in organisational structuring and refer to the formal relationships within an organisation.

Line authority

This refers to the relationship that exists between a manager and his staff, and occurs in most organisations. This line runs in an uninterrupted series of steps and is based on the 'scalar principle' of hierarchy in which there is a clear line of authority from the top of the organisation to the bottom. Essentially, the scalar chain is used to implement decision-making and the issue of instructions.

Individual line managers may not know or be able to encompass all the relevant specialised information that affects their departments, such as legal or accounting requirements. As a result the line manager may need the services of a staff specialist. However, line managers may be reluctant to take staff advice, as they are responsible for their department's actions.

Staff authority

This is an advisory form of authority, whose role is to research, investigate and give advice to line managers. Staff roles do not have authority to instruct, but rather to research, investigate and give advice to line managers.

Often staff roles provide recommendations to senior management on specific areas of the business. Examples would be operational research and personnel. They can provide creative or innovative recommendations with regard to future developments of policy and practices.

However, staff authority has a number of disadvantages. It can be difficult defining to what extent staff authority should be able to influence line management. Strong inter-personal skills are required in order that line managers do not see staff specialists as interfering and undermining their authority. In addition, as staff specialists do not take responsibility for the decision made and the implications of that decision, their advice can be seen as idealist and not in touch with the business implications and considerations.

Also line managers may receive conflicting information and advice from several different specialists, which can result in confusion and fragmented decision making.

Functional authority

Often there is a requirement for individuals with specialist knowledge in a particular area. Authority is delegated to an individual or department to influence activities undertaken by another function or department.

The line managers may have to give up a degree of their authority to the functional specialist, due to the knowledge they have which the line manager requires. An example would be management accounting. Usually functional authority is limited to control over obtaining information and data and monitoring procedures and standards.

The extent to which functional authority is effective will depend on how well the authority has been defined. If the role is not clarified confusion can exist, for example specialist staff who have line responsibility to their departmental manager, but functional responsibility to a specialist manager (see diagram below).

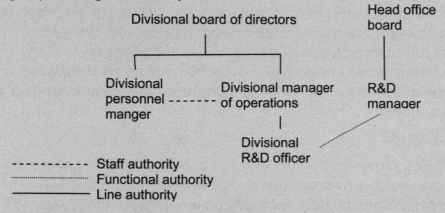

Some line managers will respond only to those functional directives which come from the functions which are perceived as powerful within the organisation.

Even though these problems exist, with the increasingly complex environments that organisations have to work in, the demand for functional specialists is increasing. The line manager does not have the time to gather information and data and analyse the implication of the external environmental influences on the enterprise.

It is normal practice to find the accounting and finance function responsible for the operation and management of the organisation's financial affairs. This function will have the authority to ensure that all line and staff managers comply with policies and procedures.

Often accountants will find themselves reporting to a line manager and a functional manager, which makes dual reporting inevitable. Therefore, it is important to be aware of and understand the scope and limitations of both types of authority and the issues of control, discretion, responsibility and definition.

4 The organisation's environment

 Activity 4

Communication flows

(a)   The purpose of the three communication flows found in organisations is:

Downwards

This communication flow is from top management down to the operational or bottom level. Through these downwards communication channels managers are able to communicate with people at lower levels. Messages can be communicated from higher to lower levels of management and employees. Many different types of message can be transmitted via downward communication channels e.g. plans, instruction, ideas, targets and standards.

Upwards

This communication flow is from the bottom level of operations upwards to top management. The upward communication channels can be used for many different types of message including reports, opinion, ideas, suggestions and feedback. Upwards communication channels enable lower level employees to communicate with managers at higher levels.

Lateral

This communication flow is horizontal and enables employees at the same level to communicate with each other. Lateral communication channels enable employees working at the same level to communicate with each other as well as employees in different departments. Lateral communication can be formal (e.g. meetings) or informal (e.g. chatting in the corridor). Lateral communication is essential for coordination and co-operation in an organisation.

(b) There are many reasons why an organisation should use committees as part of the communication process, including:

- **Pooling of knowledge**

  Committees allow people to get together and exchange ideas and knowledge. An example of this is when a committee comprising members with different skills, experience and knowledge can make a joint decision.

- **Removal of communication barriers**

  People meeting together as a committee are able to communicate freely with many communication barriers removed. An example of this is when members of a committee have equal status. Status barriers will not then exist. Another example is that a committee provides a direct communication channel with every member.

- **Joint decision making**

  Committees enable decisions to be made by managers jointly. This makes the decision more acceptable to people such as employees. Committees provide the means for all members to have the same information before the decision is made via the committee's communication system.

 Activity 5

Effective communication

(a) To improve the effectiveness of communication in the organisation the following can be adopted:

- Reviewing the existing communication system identifying any weaknesses that exist. The weaknesses will be in the form of communication barriers e.g. non delivery of messages and delays.

- Ensuring that the most appropriate method of communication is used for each message. Advantage should be taken of new methods such as email where appropriate.

- Avoiding information overload. This occurs when too many messages are being transmitted simultaneously. A communication system should not carry more traffic than it was designed to.

- Training managers and employees to improve their communication skills. This will make managers into more effective communicators.

- Use standardised elements in the communication system used throughout the organisation e.g. language. This will remove a source of misunderstanding.

(b) To ensure that information will be received and understood when sending messages, the following factors need to be taken into consideration:

- **Form**

  A message should be in a form that the recipient is able to use and understand e.g. messages sent by e-mail can be printed if the recipient requires.

- **Control**

  Measures should be taken to ensure that a communication system is properly controlled so that if a failure occurs it will be reported and corrected as quickly as possible.

- **The content of a message**

  A message must contain all the relevant information to enable a recipient to understand it. Information that is not relevant should not be included.

- **Timing**

  When a message is transmitted time must be allowed for it to be sent, translated and understood. This will be determined by the need for urgency and the recipient's needs and ability.

- **Quality**

  Information communicated from one person to another should be accurate and reliable so no mistakes are made.

5 Fraud in an accounting system

Activity 6

The ways of artificially inflating the value of stock include the following:

- Instead of being written off, obsolete or damaged stock may be shown at cost on the balance sheet.

- Records can be falsified at the stock count, i.e. generating stock that does not actually exist.

- Returns to suppliers may not be recorded or suppressed until after the year end stock count.

- Similarly with deliveries to customers – the reduction in stock may not be recorded or suppressed until after the year end stock count.

6 Internal control

Activity 7

Weakness	Possible consequences	Recommendation
(a) Buyers placing orders with the central purchasing department		
• Orders are placed with the purchasing department by telephone.	• Unauthorised orders may be placed on the same order by the two different buyers in each department.	• Orders should only be made in writing and authorised by the senior buyer in each department.

(b)	Placing orders with suppliers		
•	After receiving instructions to buy goods, purchase orders are placed without reference to the agreed price.	• Goods could be ordered for the wrong price.	• Written orders from buyers should detail the agreed price and the chief buyer should countersign all orders before they are sent to suppliers
(c)	**Purchase order documentation**		
•	No copy of the purchase order which is sent to suppliers is returned to the requisitioning department.	• The requisitioning department may not be aware that the goods it has requested have been ordered.	• An extra copy of the purchase order should be made and sent to the requisitioning department.
(d)	**Receipt of goods**		
•	Goods are not physically checked for quality or correct quantity on arrival at the store.	• The incorrect quantity of goods may be received. Also goods may be received which do not match the store's specifications or are sub-standard.	• All goods should be checked by Mr North for both quantity and quality on arrival at the store. Mr North should sign the GIN as evidence that this has been done.

(e) Payment of purchase invoices		
• Cheques are signed without the purchase invoice being made available to show what the cheque is actually paying.	• Cheques could be signed other than for legitimate purchases	• Suppliers' invoices and supporting documentation should be inspected by cheque signatories who should stamp the invoice 'paid' and initial it so that it cannot be paid twice.
(f) Suppliers' statements		
• Although suppliers' statements are reconciled to individual ledger accounts; there is no evidence that any differences found are investigated.	• The purchase ledger could incorrectly show old paid items or omit invoices that are a genuine liability of the company.	• Suppliers' statement reconciliations should be reviewed by the finance director on a regular basis to confirm that all discrepancies have been investigated.
(g) Control account		
• A purchase ledger control account is not prepared	• Any errors occurring in Individual purchase ledger accounts may go undetected.	• A purchase ledger control account should be prepared and reconciled monthly to total creditors as per the purchase ledger.

(h)	Management control		
	• The current level of management review in the purchasing department is not sufficient.	• Lack of management control could mean that errors or irregularities may be undetected.	• A director should be assigned to monitor the purchasing function on a regular basis.

7 Information systems

Activity 8

(a) The purpose of the controls is to ensure as far as possible that: the data being processed is complete

- it is authorised

- the results are accurate

- a complete audit trail of what was done is available.

(b) The areas in which we would expect controls to be assigned to provide protection to the system are concerned with input, file processing and output.

Input activities	File processing activities	Output activities
• Data collection and preparation • Data authorisation • Data conversion (if appropriate) • Data transmission • Data correction • Corrected data re-input	• Data validation and edit • Data manipulation, sorting/merging • Master file updating	• Output control and reconciliation with pre-determined data • Information distribution

Controls in these areas are vital and must deal with errors or problems as they arise instead of delaying their resolution to a later processing stage. Inaccurate data represents a waste of both computer time and human effort and may lead to further unforeseen errors occurring and misleading final results.

8 Improving the system

 Activity 9

Cost-benefit analysis

Note: The list of costs and benefits is straightforward. The need to mention factors that could distort the net present value is more complex: think about the problems of calculating NPVs for this type of project.

The costs and benefits associated with a proposed computer system can be divided into two main categories:

1 **Installation**

These are the costs and benefits involved in the changeover from the existing system to the new one, and will be incurred before the system begins to produce any operational benefit. Costs are likely to include:

- hardware purchase and installation

- software development or purchase

- personnel, including recruitment, training and redundancy

- file conversion

- the use of consultancy or bureau services during the changeover period.

The only benefit to arise at this stage would be the avoidance of renewal or major overhaul costs associated with existing equipment that is being replaced, and the disposal proceeds of any equipment being sold.

2   **Operation**

The costs and benefits associated with the operation of the new system will arise from year to year as the system is used. Costs will include:

- any equipment rental, maintenance and depreciation charges

- stationery and other consumables, including magnetic media

- overheads associated with office and computer room accommodation

- recurrent staff costs, such as salaries.

The benefits will consist partly of savings in these costs due to the greater efficiency of the new system, which will be taken into account in arriving at the net operation costs, and partly of the information improvement arising from a better system. This benefit is extremely difficult to quantify but without it any analysis is likely to be misleading because it is a major reason for changing processing methods.

The analysis of these costs and benefits using net present value calculations may give an inaccurate result for two main reasons:

- As can be seen from the categories of costs and benefits given above the major costs associated with the changeover are likely to be incurred at the start of the project, while the benefits will arise from the future operation of the system. This means that those benefits will only be experienced if the business has adequate resources to meet the initial costs. Any reduction caused by cash flow problems may make the new system uneconomical.

- The information benefits of the new system are usually very difficult to quantify, and any errors in their estimation may easily distort the results of the analysis, leading to an invalid decision.

Because of this, it is important that businesses should use a range of evaluation techniques and consider all the implications of proposed new systems.

Activity 10

Training and development plan

Report on the staff training and development plan for 20X2

For the attention of Accounts Manager

Prepared by A Student 12 October 20X1

1 Terms of reference

This report was requested to help plan the staff training and development in the accounts section next year. It covers the identification of the training and development needs, the methods available to satisfy those needs and the ways of evaluating whether the training and development has been effective.

2 Identifying the training and development needs

2.1 Organisational strategy

Training and development must be a part of the personnel or manpower strategy linked to the overall business strategy and, as part of this wider strategy, should promote organisational and individual learning. It is vital that the line manager has an understanding of the organisational strategy and departmental goals and objectives before he or she carries out the training needs analysis.

2.2 Training needs analysis

The training needs analysis (TNA) is an essential part of the process to determine the knowledge, skills and experience required to do a particular job. The results of the TNA will identify the training and development needs which will contribute to the business objectives outlined in the organisational strategy. By emphasising the 'needs' rather than the 'wants', the approach taken will be more cost effective in terms of financial resources.

2.3 Individual past performance

Identifying training needs and achieving departmental plans means the supervisor or line manager must have a knowledge of each individual in terms of their past experience, level of qualification and job performance. Some organisations have details of the training and development history of each employee on a computer database which can be accessed easily and used to determine the stage of development for each employee and also to identify whether they are ready to take on challenging roles and responsibilities.

2.4 The appraisal interview

Most line managers appraise their staff or carry out a performance review annually. If the management style is participative the appraisal will involve a discussion where the individual employee will be encouraged to assume ownership of the training and development plan. The aim of an appraisal will be:

- to review past performance and achievement of objectives

- to discuss individual aspirations, and

- to identify opportunities for training and development in the future.

This is the first stage of the TNA, where the present performance levels of the individual are matched and compared with the key competencies required in the future role to identify the 'learning gap'. This information will form the basis of the training and development plan.

2.5 Observation

Part of the job of the supervisor or line manager will be to observe individual performance levels. Although it is subjective, it still provides a valuable source of information for the identification of training and development needs.

KAPLAN PUBLISHING

3 Methods

3.1 Internal training and development

This can be a cost effective way of satisfying training and development needs, which has the advantage that the transferability of learning is immediate. The national vocational qualification (NVQ) is a means of gaining a qualification by demonstrating the skills learned in the workplace to the supervisor or line manager. Some organisations have their own training centre where customised training programmes can be developed.

3.2 External training and development courses

Another way of satisfying training and development needs is for the individual to attend a university or college to study for a professional or vocational qualification. This may require time away from the workplace e.g. day release or part of a day and evening. It is the traditional method used to gain professional management qualifications.

3.3 Distance learning

The obvious advantage of distance learning is that the individual remains at work although the cost of the course may be very high. It requires a high level of commitment from the individual as most of the studying is done outside working hours.

3.4 Computer-based learning

Sometimes called computer-based scanning, this is an ideal way of learning to use information technology. Learning packages are designed to offer flexibility to both the user and the organisation and are a useful method to update or learn new skills and knowledge.

3.5 Mentoring/coaching

Mentoring is a process where one person offers help, guidance, advice and support to facilitate the learning or development of another.

This method of satisfying training and development needs is most suitable for managers where the benefits include:

- opportunity to learn from the role model

- integration of work activities with learning and development

- quicker learning about the way the organisation works, and

- greater clarity of development goals.

4   Evaluation

To evaluate the effectiveness of training, an organisation needs information about training arrangements: content, objectives, assessments, etc, and criteria by which to evaluate the training. The trainer or manager should establish whether the trainees have learned anything and whether the learning can be applied back at the workplace. To do this the trainer can collect data, which can be used to see whether the learning has taken place and learning objectives have been met. This can be achieved with:

- End of course questionnaires - these are used to obtain immediate feedback on the perceived value of the training but may not be the best way of evaluating the effectiveness of the programme.

- Attainment tests – these are limited to the immediate knowledge and skills improvement and may not indicate whether the learning will be transferred to the workplace or job.

- Observation – the end results of the learning and development can be assessed by the observation of improvements in job performance levels.

- Interviews – the annual appraisal or performance review provides an opportunity to discuss the individual's progress during and after a training and development programme.

- Career development – the speed of promotion of an individual may be used as an indication of the effectiveness of the training and development and also the level of support given to the development plan by the organisation.

- Business/departmental results – the overall results of a business can often indicate the attention that the organisation pays to its training and development plan. The most successful organisations are those which associate the development of staff with the organisational strategy. At the departmental level the effective training and development of staff can mean the achievement of targets, goals and objectives.

KAPLAN PUBLISHING

Whatever evaluation method is used it should be done before, during and after the event.

- Before the event will clarify the existing skills, knowledge and attitudes to help the trainer plan the event and provide a yardstick to measure them by.

- During the event will determine the rate of learning, allowing the trainer to pace the learning to suit the trainee and offer remedial help where needed.

- After the event can be immediately after the training or over a long time.

 Activity 11

Disciplinary procedure

(a) Disciplinary action may be necessary in several situations at work including:

- *Poor attitude to work and the organisation*

  This would be when an employee refuses to co-operate with other employees and/or management.

- *Poor timekeeping*

  This would be when an employee is late on many occasions.

- *Poor performance at work*

  This would justify disciplinary action if an employee consistently did their job badly.

- *Breaking safety rules*

  An employer must take seriously any breach of safety rules committed by an employee.

- *Unauthorised absence*

  Employees who persistently are absent without a justified reason should be disciplined.

- *Drunkenness or drug abuse*

  Employees who are under the influence of alcohol or drugs at work should be disciplined.

(b) The stages in a formal disciplinary procedure are as follows:

1 *Documentation*

The first stage of a disciplinary procedure is to report the situation in writing. Disciplinary procedure is formal and should be subject to a strict code of practise. Each case should be fully documented.

2 *Investigation*

Research should be conducted to obtain the facts. Information should be obtained such as other parties interviewed and employment records checked.

3 *Representation*

Each employee who is subject to a disciplinary action should be given a fair hearing with a nominated representative

present. It is important that management should listen to an employee's story of events.

4 *Decision making*

Management should then make the final decision about what action to take. This will depend upon:

- The nature of the disciplinary offence and
- The facts surrounding the offence.

5 *Action*

Action decided upon should then be taken notifying the employee and recording it on the employee's file.

6 *Appeal*

Employees who have disciplinary action taken against them should be given the right of appeal.

SPECIMEN CASE STUDY

Specimen case study

BAYOU STORES LIMITED

This sample case study is intended to indicate the type of situation that candidates will be presented with, and as such should be considered as an abridged version of those that will actually be used for live assessments.

Bayou Stores Ltd. is a large wholesale warehouse supplying a range of groceries, cleaning materials, and other household goods to, small independent grocery stores. It was set up in 2008 by John Bayou, who having taken early retirement from his job as a fire fighter, used his pension and an inheritance to set up the business on the edge of Grantchester, a large industrial city. Besides the warehouse John, who is single, has only one hobby, which is golf. He usually spends all day Friday at the golf club – and other than this, he works very long hours for the other six days a week.

He employs 30 staff in the stores and three part-time staff in the small accounts department. You have just been employed to work as the senior accounts clerk and as the only full-time staff member, to supervise the running of the office. The store is open seven days a week, and operates from 7am until 10pm, Monday to Friday and from 10am to 6pm on Saturday and Sunday; whilst the accounts department only opens from 9am until 5pm Monday to Friday.

The accounts department's office is located on the first floor, over the warehouse store, which occupies the whole of the ground floor of the building. Access to the office is by stairs or an elevator from the ground floor – and this access is often used by the public – as the toilet facilities for staff and customers are also located on the first floor. Once on this floor access to the accounts office is gained through a keypad code; the code for which is UOYAB (Bayou read backwards). This code is relatively common knowledge throughout the company as it is also the alarm code for the building, and is used by the warehouse store supervisors and manager when they close up in the evenings .

Once inside the accounts office the working area is open plan, and anyone inside has full access to all the working areas.

The first job John has asked you to do is to review the accounting system and particularly the effectiveness of its internal controls. You are then asked to make any recommendations for improvement which you feel are necessary. (John knows there are many weaknesses – but is uncertain as to how these should be managed).

To help you in this he has asked the accounts clerks to prepare some brief information about themselves; an overview of the accounting system; and also a list of events that have occurred over the previous few months. This information can be found below.

The current staff in the accounting office are:

Jo Doyle (Wages Clerk)

Jo is 24 year old and has been working for the company for four months. She is employed as a wages clerk and prepares the wages and salaries for all staff, along with all the associated returns, on a two day a week basis on a Wednesday and Thursday each week. She has a young child, Harry who is three years old, and spends all her free time with him. Though she is willing to work some extra hours if needed she does not want to commit herself to any more permanent hours – as she would need to rearrange her child care. Jo gained her AAT NVQ level 2 in payroll four years ago – but has never progressed any further since due to the arrival of Harry.

Gary Idawo (Accounts Clerk)

Gary is eighteen years old and has been working for Bayou Stores for just a year since he left the local 6th form college, with three GCSE Advanced 'A' levels, including one in accounting. His main responsibilities are as the accounts receivable (sales ledger) clerk and his duties include running all the trade credit accounts for the company. He works four days a week – and has chosen not to work on a Friday. This is because his main hobby is music, and he plays in a band every weekend – and Friday is his rehearsal day. He has had no formal accounting training, but was trained on-the-job by the previous accounts receivable clerk before she left the company. He has, however, expressed an interest in learning, and wants to increase his accounting skills – but is uncertain how to go about this.

Marion Smith (Accounts Clerk)

Marion is 57 years old and she has been employed at Bayou Stores for eight months. She has recently been widowed and decided she needed to return to work to supplement her income. Her main role is that of accounts payable (purchase ledger) clerk. She is employed on a part-time basis of five half days per week, and she often likes to work these together to save on her bus fares to work. So for the past few months she has been working all day Tuesday and Wednesday and a half- day on Thursday morning. She has several years experience in operating accounting systems, but has not worked in this area for over ten years, since she left her last role to care for her sick husband.

The current accounting office practices and systems are outlined below.

Information technology systems

There are three computers in the office, as John has provided one for every member of the accounts team. These are all run on a stand-alone basis, though they are all linked to the same printer. Because John had some knowledge of Microsoft Office Excel spreadsheets whilst he was in the fire brigade (as they use this as their stock control system) – he has based the stock system for Bayou Stores on this same method; and because of this the wider accounting system is also being run using Excel.

Two computers were purchased new when the company was established and are running on Windows Vista operating system; they are also loaded with Microsoft Office 2007 version (with a three user licence). Six months ago a further new computer was also purchased and loaded with Sage Payroll software to enable the payroll to be run in-house.

When the computer system was set-up a password was installed to protect the work. This is also UOYAB, as John uses the same security code for everything throughout the company because he feels this makes life easier.

Wages and salaries

Until six months ago the payroll was completed by the company accountants, Pearl & Johnson. However, this was beginning to become very costly, as the individual hours worked each week by staff are so variable that the payroll run was different every week, and the accountants charged for the time taken to complete this. John made the decision that the wages and salaries could be run in-house. For the first two months he used a temping agency (but again this was an expensive option) to operate this – until four months ago when Jo started working for the company.

All store staff are paid weekly, in cash, and pay packets are available from the store manager from 8am on a Friday morning. The office staff and store manager are paid monthly, by cheque, on the last working day of each month.

Store staff are paid a basic rate of £7 per hour for the first 40 hours worked and time and a half for any hours over this from Monday to Saturday. Any hours worked on a Sunday are paid at double time. The store supervisors, of whom there are four, are also paid the same overtime premiums but based on a basic rate of £9 an hour.

The supervisors are responsible for preparing staff rotas for their own departments to ensure that there is adequate staff coverage for all of the opening hours. Most of the warehouse staff are willing to work overtime-so this does not usually create any problems. Once the week has finished, the completed rotas are given to Jo who uses them to calculate the amount of hours that the individual store staff have worked.

Jo prepares the payslips from this information on a Wednesday, calculating manually any overtime payments due, and any Sunday working. From this, she calculates how much cash needs to be drawn from the bank and uses the company cheque book (which is kept locked in Marion's desk) to prepare a cheque ready for John's signature. On a Thursday she then prepares the pay packets, which are stored in the office safe for the store manager to collect, (though often it is the supervisors who actually do this), and to hand out to the staff the following day. Any pay packets not given out are returned to the office safe and remain there until collected by the relevant member of staff.

Only Statutory Sick Pay (SSP) is paid to the warehouse store staff, but the office staff are salaried and are allowed four weeks contractual sick pay per year.

John has always trusted his workforce completely and there is no requirement, or system in place, for either store or office employees to sign in when they arrive or leave work.

Accounts payable (purchase ledger)

All inventory (stock) is purchased on credit terms from a very wide range of suppliers. This is John's main role and he does enjoy spending time researching new stock lines, and also meeting the sales staff from different suppliers. He has a favourite group of suppliers he tends to use, mainly because the sales staff from these treat him to an occasional game of golf.

All inventory (stock) levels are maintained on the Excel spreadsheets. These have been set up to show suppliers; cost prices; selling prices; profit margins; and re-order levels and quantities. Marion has worked on Excel previously, but this was over ten years ago – and whilst she is competent at inputting data - she sometimes struggles with anything beyond this.

Suppliers are paid at the end of the month that their invoice is received, as long as funds are available. However, due to the current credit crunch some suppliers are now beginning to request payment earlier, within thirty days of the date of invoice, and this is beginning to cause John some concern.

All suppliers are paid by cheque. These are completed by Marion, and the only authorised signatory is John. The cheque book is stored in a locked drawer in Marion's desk in the accounts office.

Accounts receivable (sales ledger)

Gary is responsible for the running of this function. Whilst many customers do pay cash for their goods, over fifty per cent take extended credit terms. When Gary first started at Bayou Stores, anyone who applied for a credit account was accepted. However, he realised that this was not good practice and he now uses a credit reference agency to ensure that potential new credit customers have no history of poor payments. Other than this check any new customer who applied is automatically granted an unlimited line of credit.

All new credit accounts are set up on the first day of the month – and Gary often works extra hours on this day to ensure this task is completed. All sales orders are received by the warehouse store staff for processing and after completion are passed to the accounts department the next morning, so that Gary can prepare the invoices and enter these in the accounts. Gary has designed a form in Microsoft Office Word which he uses as a pro forma for invoicing.

Bayou Stores offers sixty days credit to all their customers, and Gary is responsible for ensuring payment occurs. The policy on this is that once payment is seven days overdue Gary will telephone the customer. If payment is not received within seven days of the telephone call, then a 'stop' will be placed on the account and that customer is then not allowed any more goods or credit until payment has been made for any invoices more than sixty days old. Gary allows two half days per month for the task of telephoning customers who are late in paying; drawing the information from an aged debtors control listing which has been set up on the Excel system to indicate customers whose accounts are outstanding for more than sixty days.

Cash and banking

Gary opens the mail every morning and sorts through it. Any cash or cheques received from customers are entered manually into a day book to record the receipt, which is then used to update the accounts. The cheques and cash are then placed in the office safe until a banking day.

At the end of every day, all cash and cheques are removed from the tills, leaving a float of £100 cash in each till for the start of the next day. The principle is that the till should be balanced to ensure that the cash content is correct – but during the week this does not happen as the store closes at 10pm – and the supervisors feel that they should not be asked to do an extra job at this time of evening. Therefore common practice is that all cash (except for the till floats) and cheques are removed and bagged as takings from individual tills before being stored in the safe in the accounts office.

Banking is carried out on a Monday and Thursday, and this is normally Gary's job which he does during his lunch break. The Thursday banking of cash is often lower as John has now started to reduce the cheques drawn for wages by the amount of cash available in the office safe on a Thursday morning. His idea is that any cash available can be used to supplement the making up of the wages to reduce the amount of cash needed to be drawn from the bank.

There is no petty cash system as such. If cash is needed for any incidental expenses, this is taken from the till floats and a note put in the till to cover this.

DIARY OF EVENTS FOR THE LAST THREE MONTHS

October 2009

One Tuesday, David Singh, a worker from the warehouse store, who has been off ill for five days, came into the office to collect his wages for the previous week, which he had not received due to his illness. His supervisor sent him upstairs to the accounts office, but even after a thorough search of the office safe, and then the office itself, the pay packet could not be found.

David was naturally annoyed at this and Gary tried to help. As Jo was not at work that day, and no-one else could operate the Sage payroll system it was not known how much David was owed. Gary decided that the rota said David was due to work 45 hours that week and so calculated his pay accordingly as:

$35 \times £7$ plus $5 \times £14$ (Sunday working) plus $5 \times £10.50$ for overtime. Therefore he thought David was due £367.50 – so he gave him this amount of cash from the safe.

Later in the month Gary caught flu and was off work ill for two weeks. He therefore did no credit control work during this time. Marion worked one day extra a week to cover his work – but could not manipulate the data, or access the pivot table on the Excel spreadsheet that Gary uses to highlight outstanding payments.

In an unheard of incident John has taken the last five days of the month off to attend a golfing tournament he has been invited to by a supplier. However, this was a last minute invitation – and he only informed the accounts staff by telephone as he was on his way to the airport. He knew that he would need to pay suppliers during this time, and also staff wages – so he went to the office at 6am and signed a cheque book full of blank cheques to cover this. He had taken his spare keys with him, so was surprised when he discovered Marion's desk drawers unlocked.

On the last Friday of the month, Marion called into the office to pick up her salary cheque. As no one was about, and she knew that Jo had prepared these earlier in the week, she helped herself to this from Jo's desk drawer.

November 2009

John told the accounts staff that after a telephone conversation with the bank manager he was very concerned over the size of the company overdraft and he had been informed that this must be reduced over the next four months.

He sat down with Gary to review he amounts owed by customers and was surprised to discover that more than twenty small retailers, who all are very good customers, owed more than £75,000 each. It became clear that they all take advantage of the full sixty day credit terms given by Bayou Stores and only make the minimum payment due, at the very end of this period. During this meeting Gary asked John about undertaking some accounts training, and John says he was very happy for him to do this, and would be willing to pay for it, if Gary could locate a suitable course.

On the first Monday in the month an irate supplier again telephoned the accounts office regarding late payments, and threatening to withdraw Bayou Stores credit facility. As Marion was not at work, Gary took the call and promised the supplier that the cheque would be in the mail that evening. He knew where the cheque book was kept, and that the drawer was often left unlocked; he thought he could complete the cheque and ask John to sign it and send it to the supplier immediately. However, he discovered that there was still a blank cheque which had already been signed by John during his golfing break, so he completed this and mailed it to the supplier to ensure they are satisfied. He was subsequently busy that week and so forgot to inform Marion of his actions – and as each accounts staff member only normally works on their own computer, he did not update the accounts payable system.

On the second Friday in the month the telephone in the accounts department was ringing incessantly. At lunch time Stevan Teery, a warehouse store supervisor, went into the accounts office to answer it - only to hear from a credit controller in a supplier company, who was chasing up an invoice that had not been paid within their thirty day terms. Stevan could only try and placate the supplier, and take a message for the accounts office staff.

The following week, five warehouse staff complained to Jo that their wages were wrong. They had been asked to work extra hours to cover staff sickness, but this had not been marked on the rota sheets, and therefore they had been underpaid for the extra hours they worked. Equally it meant that the two staff who were off ill, had been overpaid for these hours (but they have not reported this to the accounts department).

December 2009

Jo had booked two weeks holiday over Christmas, as she wanted to spend this time with Harry. As she knew that she is the only member of staff who can operate the Sage payroll system she decided to complete three weeks pay packets on the same date – all based on the hours worked in the current week. She completed the pay packets and placed them in the safe, informing the supervisors that Gary will give them out on the correct Friday –and that any over or under payments will be adjusted during the following week after she has returned to work.

On the last Monday in the month a warehouse store worker, Matthew Perkins, came into the office to complain. Unbeknown to the other warehouse store staff he was having matrimonial problems, had recently left his wife to live with his girlfriend, and had taken a few days holiday last week for this move. His wife was aware that he was on holiday and had turned up at Bayou Stores and asked the supervisor for his pay packet saying that he was too busy to call in for it. As the supervisor knew his wife, (he had met her with Matthew at the staff Christmas party last year) he had handed her Matthew's pay packet without question – leaving Matthew with no money for the week.

TASKS

Complete a business report to John Bayou. This should be approximately 3500 - 4000 words long, and should cover the following tasks:

Task one

Complete a review of the accounting system

This can be of the complete system or of one or more of the accounting functions, depending on your findings – but must specifically cover the following areas:-

1   Record keeping systems - the purpose of financial reports, and the suitability of the organisation's current reports to meet organisational needs. (EAS 1.2 & PIC1.2)

2   Internal systems of control – identify how internal control supports the accounting system and the types of internal control in place, and any controls that are missing. (PIC2.4, PIC3.2 & EAS 1.4)

3   Fraud - causes of fraud, common types of fraud, methods used to detect fraud and potential areas for fraud within the organisation (EAS 1.4, PIC2.2 & PIC2.3, PIC 3.1)

4   Working methods/practices – including the use of appropriate computer software, and the operating methods in terms of reliability, speed and cost effectiveness (PIC 3.4 & EAS 1.5)

5   Training (PIC 3.3) – Identify how training is or can be used to support staff.

The review should cover all aspects of the assessment criteria, as mapped above, when it can naturally be introduced into the report. If it cannot be covered in the report then a can be covered within a written explanation included in the appendix.

Whilst a SWOT analysis may be a good starting place, this should not be placed in the body of the report

Task two

Identify weaknesses and make recommendations for improvement

- Once the review of the system has been completed the weaknesses that have been identified should be clearly explained along with their impact upon the organisation. (EAS 1.3 & PIC 3.1).

- For every weakness that has been identified there should be a recommendation made to attempt to improve the situation. (EAS 2.1 & PIC 2.4 & PIC 3.2)

The recommendations should concentrate on the effect that the changes would have both on the organisation, and on individual members of staff. (EAS 2.2 & PIC 1.5). They may also highlight training needs or aids to improve staff performance . (EAS 2.3 & PIC 3.3).

Task three

Prepare a Cost Benefit Analysis

- At least one of the recommendations made should be subject to a cost benefit analysis. Whilst not all benefits are quantifiable all costs are – and students should make any necessary assumptions or 'guesstimates' to allocate costs to such items as time, unknown salaries, or any other unknown expense involved in the recommended changes.

- All benefits should be identified, included those which cannot be allocated a financial figure. This can include such things as improved customer relationships, improved documentation systems or staff morale (though this could be allocated a financial benefit as improving staff turnover cuts recruitment costs). (EAS2.4)

Note on Appendices

Any charts and diagrams or supporting evidence should be included here and cross -referenced within the text. Any appendices included should be referred to in the main body of the report – or in the case of supporting statements to cover missing assessment criteria, mapped and cross - referenced to a copy of the unit standards.

Specimen case study – Guidance notes

Guidance to preparing the report based on the Bayou Stores Ltd Case Study.

The below gives you a guide as to how you should answer this Case Study.

The Learning Outcomes you need to satisfy include:

Principles of internal control

- Demonstrate an understanding of the role of accounting in an organisation.

- Understand the importance and use of internal control systems.

- Be able to identify and use appropriate accounting systems to meet specific organisational requirements.

Evaluate an accounting system

- Evaluate the accounting system and identify areas for improvement.

- Make recommendations to improve the accounting system.

Preparing the Report

The report needs to begin with the following three elements:

- **Terms of Reference**

  This shows the reasons behind the report and includes: (1) Cover the requirements of the Internal Control and Accounting Systems Unit at the Technician Stage of the AAT Qualification. (2) A review of the accounting systems at Bayou Stores Ltd to assess the internal controls and identify areas for improvement and their potential effect on the organisation

- **Executive Summary**

  This gives a general overview of the whole report and includes the background of the report, the purpose of the report, the scope of the investigation and a summary of findings and recommendations.

- **Methodology**

  This shows how you planned and prepared the report and should include an overview of any research method you have used.

(1) Introduction

You need to write a brief overview of the business its structure and purpose. Outline the structure of its accounting function and identify what reports of both a financial and management accounting nature you would expect the management to receive on a periodic and timely basis.

(2) Internal control systems

Considering the following functions at Bayou Stores

- Sales Ledger and Credit Control.

- Purchase Ledger and Accounts Payable

- Inventory Control.

- Wages and Salaries

- Cash and Banking;

prepare a detailed schedule of the internal control that you would expect to see working effectively in each function and identify the ones you consider are currently absent from the functions.

Internal controls

An internal control system is defined as: It comprises the control environment and control procedures. It includes all policies and procedures (internal controls) adopted by the owner managers of the entity to assist in achieving their objective of ensuring, as far as practicable, the orderly and efficient conduct of its business, including adherence to internal policies, the safeguarding of assets, and the prevention and detection of fraud and error, the accuracy and completeness of the accounting records, and the timely preparation of reliable financial information.

Specific control procedures include the following.

Supervision: There should be adequate supervision of work to ensure controls are being complied with.

Organisation: Enterprises should have a formal, documented organisation structure with clear lines of responsibility.

Arithmetic and accounting: The Company should ensure that there are adequate controls to ensure the completeness and accuracy of its financial records, such as reconciliations of key control accounts.

Physical: There should be adequate physical control to ensure the security and safe keeping of the company's assets such as stock and cash.

Management: There should be good controls in place to ensure management can effectively run the business, for example using budgets and implementing internal audit procedures.

Authorisation: All transactions should be authorised.

Personnel: Employees should be appropriately qualified and experienced to perform their required tasks.

Segregation of duties: There should be an appropriate division of responsibility to reduce the opportunity for fraud and manipulation.

The following example sets out the control objectives and internal controls that should be embedded in the Wages and Salaries procedures.

We firstly need to consider an overview of the payroll cycle.

- Clock cards submitted and input.
- Gross pay, deductions and net pay calculated
- Other amendments input
- Payroll calculated and payslips produced
- Payments to employees
- Payments to HMRC
- Payroll costs and payment entered into Wages and Salaries Control, Wages and Salaries Account, PAYE/NI creditor and the cash book.

Controls:

The main control objectives and types of control include:

Clock cards: to ensure that only bona fide employees can be paid for work which they have done.

- Control on the issue of clock cards.
- Authorisation of clock cards by supervisor before processing.
- Comparison of returned clock cards against employee lists.

Calculation: to ensure that calculations for gross and net pay and all deductions are accurate.

- Comparison of total gross, net and deductions with previous amounts.
- Review of week's starters and leavers.
- Check that each amendment in the week is correctly reflected on an individual and total basis.

Other amendments: to ensure that any amendments to standing data (starters, leavers, pay rises, bonuses) are valid and authorised. Otherwise invalid changes could occur, leading to the creation of fictitious employees, keeping past employees on the payroll and paying unauthorised rises to existing employees.

- Standardised pre-numbered amendment forms.

- Authorised management signature on all amendments before acceptance for input.

- Supporting documentation for starters, leavers and pay rises to be attached to amendments form.

Payslips: to ensure accuracy of payroll report.

- Review of the payroll to ensure totals seem reasonable. Review to be signed.

- Check individual payslips against an employee list to ensure completeness.

- Check total deductions figure and maintain deductions control account. All deductions for PAYE and NI should be accurately recorded, if errors occur the company may incur penalties.

Payments: to prevent payments being made that are not the net pay to which the employees are entitled.

- Use a credit transfer facility to avoid the need for cash controls.

- Authorisation and documentation of changes to employees' bank details.

- Comparison of the total net pay for the period against the total funds transferred from the company's bank account.

Recording: to ensure that payroll details for each period are posted correctly to the wages and salaries account, the wages and salaries control and the deductions control account in the general ledger.

- Entry on the main ledger account code beside the relevant figure as posting occurs.

- Use of wages and salaries control which should carry a nil balance at the end of each pay period.

- Review of deductions control account to verify the amount due to HMRC.

Summary: Now that we have identified the desired controls you need to check which are currently in operation at Bayou Stores Ltd.

For example:

Clock cards: we list three controls none of which are currently present as it states in the scenario that "John has always trusted his workforce completely and there is no requirement or system in place, for either store or office employees to sign in when they arrive or sign out when they leave work"

If you review the controls we have identified as desirable then comment as to whether Bayou Stores Ltd maintain such controls in their Wages and Salaries procedure (see the example above)

(3) **Fraud in accounting systems**

Outline the potential areas and causes of fraud and its possible implications on the business. Focus your examples on the specific functions outlined in (2) above.

Fraud may involve:

- Falsification or alteration of accounting records or documents misappropriation of assets or theft.

- Suppression or omission of the effects of transactions from records or documents.

- Recording of transactions without substance.

- Intentional misapplication of accounting policies and;

- Wilful misrepresentation of transactions or the entity's state of affairs.

Example

Referring again to the Wages and Salaries procedures there are a number of areas that would be open to fraudulent activity.

AREA	PROBALITY, (Risk)	IMPACT
Wages and salaries		
Clock Cards	High	There is no recording of times. Hours worked are simply taken. Supervisor's rotas and these may be inaccurate. (Employees may be paid for work not done.) Adverse effect upon cashflow.
Calculation of Pay	Medium	No segregation of duties, danger of dummy employees on payroll.

You need to examine all the functions in the Accounting procedures and identify possible areas of fraud (see example above)

(4) Working methods/ practices

Prepare a review of the computer software and operating methods currently in use in each of the accounting functions.

(5) Training

Prepare a skills audit on each member of staff and identify clearly their training and development needs and how in the short term these can be met.

Model: For each employee we need to identify the training need by examining what skills and attributes are necessary for the job role, the skills and attributes of the job holder and the skills gap.

Example

Name	Competence	Training reqiuirement	Date
Marion Smith	Working knowledge of EXCEL spreadsheets. Assisting with Inventory Control spreadsheets.	Course in Basic and Advanced Excel spreadsheets.	ASAP

You need to consider the training needs of all the key staff.

(6) **Weaknesses in internal control and recommendations for improvement**

Prepare a detailed schedule to show:

Function	Area of weakness	Recommendation for improvement
Sales ledger	Example: Credit terms 60 days – far too long, adverse effect upon cashflow.	Immediate review to standardise terms to 30 days as part of a review of the Credit Control policy.
Purchase ledger		
Inventory control		
Wages and salaries		
Cash and banking		
Office/IT systems		

(7) **Cost benefit analysis**

Consider each function and the recommendations you have made and prepare an analysis of the costs and potential benefits.

It is possible to quantify the costs but the benefits may be more difficult to quantify. Those benefits that cannot be quantified in financial terms should also be included.

There will be a number of areas where there will be costs and benefits to quantify.

For example:

On a recent review of the aged debtors list it seems there are 20 customers currently owing in excess of £75,000 each and are taking advantage of the 60 days credit terms.

There is therefore working capital of £1.5m tied up by this lax credit control policy.

Assuming that the company is heavily in overdraft any shortening of the debtor days will yield benefit.

If it was possible to reduce this to 30 days and assuming bank overdraft interest to be say 10% this would be a saving on bank interest of 10% (30/365 × £1.5m) £12,328 and the costs associated with this would be the administrative time spent on negotiations with customers.

(8) **Summary**

Please note the report should be written in third person. It should be in the form of a report to management and each section and paragraphs should be separately numbered. This referencing is necessary as you will be required to cross reference your report to the learning outcomes.

INDEX

KAPLAN PUBLISHING